ly:

Towards a   nse
Understanding of Relational Becomings

Speaking, Actually:

Towards a New 'Fluid' Common-Sense Understanding of Relational Becomings

John Shotter

First published 2016 by
Everything is Connected Press
9-11 Main Street, Farnhill, UK, BD20 9BJ

British Library Cataloguing in Publication Data
A.C.I.P. for this book is available from the British Library

ISBN 978-0-9930723-4-5 (pbk)
ISBN 978-0-9930723-5-2 (ebk)

Speaking, Actually: Towards a New 'Fluid' Common-Sense
Understanding of Relational Becomings by John Shotter
Produced by Gail Simon for Everything is Connected Press
Cover image based on a photograph from www.nasa.gov
Layout by Andrew Hinkinson, www.copydevil.co.uk

www.eicpress.com

Dedications

Cherrie: my beautiful wife.
My children: Mark, Laura, Emily, & Joachim.
Cherrie's children: Kern & Frank.
Andy Lock.
Marley, our dog.

Acknowledgements

To those who have been for so long academic, practitioner, and personal friends of mine: Ken and Mary Gergen, Rom Harre, Sheila McNamee & Jack Lannamann, Harlene Anderson, Ann Cunliffe; and those whom I worked alongside in many, many workshops giving practical voice to the ideas expressed in this book: Jim Wilson, Jaakko Seikkula, Justine van Lawick, Peter Rober, and Mick Billig, along with Hari Tsoukas, Marcelo Pakman and Arlene Katz.

To all these, I must add an especial acknowledgement of Gail Simon, without whose energy and enterprise in beginning the *Everything is Connected Press*, this book would never have seen the light of day.

Contents

"The actually performed act — not from the aspect of its content, but in its very performance — somehow knows, somehow possess the unitary and once-occurrent being of life; it orients itself within that being, and it does so, moreover, in its entirety — both in its content-aspect and in its actual, unique factuality".

(Bakhtin, 1993, p.28)

"Certainly ordinary language has no claim to be the last word, if there is such a thing. It embodies, indeed, something better than the metaphysics of the Stone Age, namely, ... the inherited experience and acumen of many generations of men. But then, that acumen has been concentrated primarily upon the practical business of life. If a distinction works well for practical purposes in ordinary life (no mean feat, for even ordinary life is full of hard cases), then there is sure to be something in it, it will not mark nothing: yet this is likely enough to be not the best way of arranging things *if our interests are more extensive or intellectual than the ordinary*. And again, that experience has been derived only from the sources available to ordinary men throughout most of civilised history: it has not been fed from the resources of the microscope and its successors. And it must be added too, that superstition and error and fantasy of all kinds do become incorporated in ordinary language and even sometimes stand up to the survival test (only, when they do, why should we not detect it?). Certainly, then, ordinary language is not the last word: in principle it can everywhere be supplemented and improved upon and superseded. Only remember, it *is* the *first* word".

(Austin, 1970, p.185, my italics)

"There is ... either in the man who listens or reads, or in the one who speaks or writes, a *thought in speech* the existence of which is unsuspected by intellectualism".

(Merleau-Ponty, 1962, p.179)

"An entire mythology is stored within our language".

(Wittgenstein, 1993a, p.133)

"When we study, discuss, analyze a reality, we analyze it as it appears in our mind, in our memory. We know reality only in the past tense. We do not know it as it is in the present, in the moment when it's happening, when it is. The present moment is unlike the memory of it. Remembering is not the negative of forgetting. Remembering is a form of forgetting.... The present — the concreteness of the present — as a phenomenon to consider, as a structure, is for us an unknown planet; so we can neither hold on to it in our memory nor reconstruct it through imagination. We die without knowing what we have lived".

(Kundera, 1996, pp.128-129)

"Intellectualism in the vicious sense began when Socrates and Plato taught that what a thing really is, is told us by its *definition*. Ever since Socrates we have been taught that reality consists of essences, not of appearances, and that the essences of things are known whenever we know their definitions. So first we identify the thing with a concept and then we identify the concept with a definition, and only then, inasmuch as the thing *is* whatever the definition expresses, are we sure of apprehending the real essence of it or the full truth about it."

(James, 1909/1996, p.218)

Prologue

Turning things back-to-front, and inside out

"Since... the course of action in life must consider the importance of single events and their circumstances, it may happen that many of these circumstances are trivial, some of them bad, some even contrary to one's goal. It is therefore impossible to assess human affairs by the inflexible standard of abstract right; we must rather gauge them by the pliant Lesbic rule[1], which does not conform bodies to itself, but adjusts itself to their contours."

(Vico, 1990, p.34)

"If I had to say what is the main mistake made by philosophers of the present generation ... I would say that it is that when language is looked at, what is looked at is a form of words and not the *use* made of the form of words."

(Wittgenstein, 1966, p.2, my italics)

There is something deeply wrong with the current *rationalistic* or *intellectualistic* ways of thinking we employ in those inquiries in which we try to discover what to do for the best in particular problematic situations in our everyday lives — ways of thinking based in *theoretical* and *conceptual* formulations that we take as *corresponding* in an *ideal* fashion with reality. For, as we will see, such ways of thinking work to separate their focal topics from each other, so that, sooner or later, we then need to seek ways of re-relating them back into a *holistic* reality again. While these ways of thinking have worked (and are still working) spectacularly well in the *physical* and *natural* sciences, it is when we turn to difficulties in our relations to each other (and to ourselves) that we find them inappropriate.

In fact, as we will also soon see, although our ordinary, everyday, spontaneous *ways of speaking* have in fact been disparaged as vague, as full of contradictions and ambiguities, they are, in fact, crucial to our intelligible acting in the world, in that they 'work' to *orient* or to *relate*

---

[1] Clearly, here, Vico is remembering Aristotle (1955), who, in commenting upon the fact that everything cannot be regulated by law, notes that it is "because there are some cases that no law can be framed to cover, so that they require a special ordinance. An irregular object has a rule of irregular shape, like the leaden rule of Lesbian architecture [used by stone masons to fashion a shape to 'fit into' one already existing]: just as this rule is not rigid but is adapted to the shape of the stone, so the ordinance is framed to fit the circumstances" (1137b30-32, p.200).

us to events occurring in our surroundings in ways shared by all the others around us. In the very uttering of our words[2], we can arouse shaping and directive tendencies or anticipations both in our listeners, and in ourselves — as Austin (1962) pointed out, we can *do things* with words. But more than this, as living beings, we will find all our bodily movements are *expressive,* in that they can arouse expectations in those observing us as to *where* next and *what* next we might do in our activities — where we 'show'[3] the directive shaping and differencing tendencies at work, 'in the moment', in the course of activities as they unfold.

But it is not just how we can 'do things with words' by speaking that I want to explore in this book. In the *process view* I want to adopt here, I also want to explore why it is that the 'things' that in the past we have *called* or *named* as 'beliefs', ideas', 'knowledge', 'judgement', 'thoughts', or 'wisdom', and such like, and tried to study as already existing things (with their own implied agential powers) hidden inside the heads of individuals, are better talked of as *emerging* within the material *intra-actions* (Barad, 2007) occurring within the world at large — material intra-actions within which we ourselves are wholly immersed as "participant parts" *of* the world.

Thus, rather than as external agents wholly in control of the unfolding processes of importance to us, we need to see ourselves as being internally related to a still-in-process world of flowing streams of intermingling activities, each with their own agential powers. As such, rather than being in a monological, one-way causal relation to our surroundings, we are essentially always living within two-way, *dialogically-structured* (Bakhtin 1986; Gadamer, 2000) relations with them.

This means that, *instead of discovering pre-existing things in our inquiries, we continually bring such 'things' into existence.* So,

---

2 Socrates remarks, when Thaetetus asks him how he describes *thinking* that: "Thinking is that the mind is simply carrying on a conversation: it asks itself questions and answers them, saying yes or no. And when it reaches a conclusion... stops being divided and starts to affirm something, we call this its belief" (Plato, 1987, pp.96-97).

3 Wittgenstein's basic philosophical aim, is to bring us to a recognition that the way in which we inhabit a languaged-world, the way that we are always already in the midst of it and cannot ever get outside of it, means that we can never give it a foundation in truths. For truths are *arrived at* after a great deal of practical activity, done in agreed ways. Thus, as Wittgenstein (1953) points out: "What people accept as a justification — is shown by how they think and live" (no.325)./ "We expect this, and are surprised at that. But the chain of reasons has an end" (no.326) — and its 'end' is to be found what I am trying to 'elucidate' in this book: What I am calling an already instituted, thick, prospective, *before-the-fact*, holistic common-sense that provides all the participants within it, with a shared *sense of the circumstances* they are currently occupying, prior to their more deliberate undertakings.

although we may talk of our (actionable or performative) understandings as coming into existence as a result of our "thoughts," "ideas," or "actionable knowledge," i.e., as the result of a nameable causal process, the fact is, such processes can *only* be seen as *having been at work* in people's performances *after* they have been completed. Indeed, we argue that this is the case with many our *named topics of study* in philosophy, in the social sciences (and indeed in the physical sciences): what can be seen as an *outcome* of a person's actions can only be seen as such, *after* those actions have been performed.

Moreover, as nameable 'things' we often feel that we can *foreshadow* them, so to speak, in the very *way* in which, prior to the conduct of our investigations, we commit ourselves to a particular way or ways of looking into, and talking of, the phenomena before us, i.e., what happens in our lives as a result of our *use* of words. But, as Wittgenstein (1953) points out, there is a danger in this, he expresses it thus:

"How does the philosophical problem about mental processes and states and about behaviourism arise? — *The first step is the one that altogether escapes notice. We talk of processes and states and leave their nature undecided.* Sometime perhaps we shall know more about them — we think. *But that is just what commits us to a particular way of looking at the matter.* For we have a definite concept of what it means to learn to know a process better. (The decisive movement in the conjuring trick has been made, and it was the very one that we thought quite innocent.) — And now the analogy which was to make us understand our thoughts falls to pieces. So we have to deny the yet uncomprehended process in the yet unexplored medium. And now it looks as if we had denied mental processes. And naturally we don't want to deny them" (no.308, my italics).

Indeed, as we will see, there is much at work in our everyday surroundings that, on the one hand, continually (mis)leads us into believing that when we *intend to do* something, the process begins with an event in our heads, whereas — strange though it may be to say it — following Wittgenstein, I will be saying that it begins from within the midst of our ongoing, unfolding involvements with what is going on around us. The process begins, not in our heads, but *in* the dynamics of the *dialogically-structured* relations within which we are inescapably immersed — the dynamics of our everyday lives together that affect us much more than we can affect them, but *from within* which everything we do, must initially, be drawn.

As Wittgenstein (1953) puts it, in pondering on the pre-existing nature of a thought *before its expression*: "But didn't I already intend the whole construction of the sentence (for example) at its beginning? So surely it already existed in my mind before I said it out loud! ... But here we are constructing a misleading picture of 'intending', that is, of the use of this word. An intention is embedded in its situation, in human customs and institutions. If the technique of the game of chess did not exist, I could not intend to play a game of chess. In so far as I do intend the construction of a sentence in advance, that is made possible by the fact that I can speak the language in question" (no.337) — for as children, in learning language, we did not simply learn 'words stand for things', but that words 'work' to determine the *'whatness'* of events and circumstances for us, in ways shared by our fellows.

In other words, and this is the most important point in this book: *'Something else' altogether is guiding people in the performance of their actions than the nameable things whose nature we seek to discover in our inquiries.* Our everyday lives, reality, are not only much more complicated and detailed than can ever be captured in any *idealizations* in theory-based inquires, they are also *not rational* — the actions of everyday actors are shaped, as we shall see, only very partially by their 'plans', 'desires', or 'intentions'. Their often unnoticed embedding in a particular situation is also influential. So although our task in this book is to explore how people might develop what in our everyday talk we might call an intuitive "expertise," or "professionalism," or simply "common-sense," it is the nature of that 'something else' — to do with their 'in-touchness-with-reality', and how it can be publicly studied — that I will be concerned with below.

Instead of the "the way of theory" — another mode of inquiry

Currently, however, as professional inquirers, our task *is* function in a *rational* manner. Consequently, we quite often find ourselves working as thinkers, as arguers and debaters, concerned only to criticize the theoretical *idealizations* of others and to replace them with our own. One way of expressing what is wrong with this way of proceeding, is that we arrive on the scene *too late*, and then look in the *wrong direction*, with the *wrong attitude*:

too late, because we take the 'basic elements' in terms of which we must work and conduct our arguments to be already fixed, already determined for us by an elite group of academically approved predecessors;
in the wrong direction, because we look backward toward supposed already existing actualities, rather than forward toward possibilities;
and *with the wrong attitude*, because we seek a static picture, a theoretical representation, of a phenomenon, rather than a living sense of it as an active agency in our lives.

Or, to put it another way, this kind of critical concern with *theoretical entities*, is that it is both "beside the point" and "after the fact."

It is (i) *beside the point*, for in orienting us toward regularities, toward already existing forms, it diverts our attention away from those fleeting moments in which we have the chance of noting new reactions in ourselves, previously unnoticed responses that might provide the new beginnings we seek. It is also (ii) *after the fact*, for our aim is to understand the not-as-yet-happened, the as-yet-non-existent activities involved in approaching nature differently, and that cannot be done simply by proving a theory true:

i) The "way of theory" is *beside the point* in the sense that it is aimed, ultimately, at justifying or legitimating a proposed action by providing it with an already agreed grounding or basis. Whereas, what we require in our daily affairs, is not so much legitimation in terms of an already agreed status quo, as *clear guidance in how to act in unique and novel circumstances*: we wish to know in an unconfused, incontestable sense, in this or that particular, never-before-occurring situation, what is the right thing to do. (The practitioner's problem — and they make us only too well aware that they find our theories of little help in their daily practices.)

ii) The "way of theory" is thus *after the fact* in the sense of that its focus is retrospective: from within it, we look back on successfully completed events with the aim of finding an order or pattern in them that can be instituted mechanically, unthinkingly, according to rules or recipes. Whereas, in our daily affairs, we need to focus, not on their final outcome, but on the particular, moment-by-moment unfolding, constructive details of our practical activities. We need to come to a grasp of all the influences that might be at work in any one moment as we make our way toward such outcomes. To represent this loose-textured, temporal, disorderly process - in which many possibilities are considered but few are chosen — as an already orderly and coherent process is to hide from ourselves the character of the social negotiations, navigations, and struggles productive of its order.

As I noted above, our everyday lives are not only much more complicated and detailed than can ever be captured in any *idealizations* in theory-based inquires, the actions of everyday actors are shaped by their often unnoticed embedding in the details of a particular, unique situation.

Understanding the 'precise part played' by our wordings in all realms in our daily lives

To orient ourselves intellectually in relation to such complicated phenomena, to the events that happen as a result of our *trying to use* words in the context of all our other expressive activities, we require another mode of inquiry altogether: One that on the one hand, takes the *wordings* of our expressions as the *subject matter* our inquiries. While on the other, it is *in* the very way we *word* our expressions — in their punctuation, their emphases, their intonings, their pausings, their unfolding time-shapes, and so on, to do with the distinctive *movements of feeling* we can arouse in our listeners — that we can find the *tools* or *methods* we need in conducting our investigations.

But where might we begin our explorations, if we cannot begin them from assumptions and suppositions? We can only begin with our *noticings*, with events that make a difference in our lives, and especially with events that happen contrary to our expectations, or events which, whilst seeming to matter to us, we cannot make any sense of them at first at all.

In other words, as Wittgenstein (1980a) puts it: "Actually I should like to say that ... the *words* you utter or what you think as you utter them are not what matters, so much as the difference they make at various points in your life ... *Practice* gives words their sense" (p.85). While elsewhere (Wittgenstein, 1953), he says:

"It would never have occurred to us to think that we *felt the influence* of the letters on us when reading, if we had not compared the case of letters with that of arbitrary marks. And here we are indeed noticing a *difference*. And we interpret it as the difference between being influenced and not being influenced./ In particular, this interpretation appeals to us especially when we make a point of reading slowly — perhaps in order to see what does happen when we read. When we, so to speak, quite intentionally let ourselves be *guided* by the letters. But this 'letting myself be guided' in turn only consists in my looking carefully at the letters — and perhaps excluding certain other thoughts./ We imagine that a feeling enables us to perceive as it were a connecting mechanism between the look of the word and the sound that we utter. For when I speak of the experiences of being influenced, of causal connection, of being guided, that is really meant to imply that I as it were feel the movement of the lever which connects seeing the letters with speaking" (no.170).

Just as I took it above, that in (1) one context we take "language" to be our *topic* of study — set or established by how we *word* (or *do* 'wordings' ~ as a verb) our experiences — while in (2) another context — set by an appropriate *structuring of the dynamic unfolding of our expressions* — we take it as providing the *tools* or *methods* we will need in our investigations, so here, we need to conduct a similar, back-and-forth, *topic-tool* oscillation in our sense-making activities. By the subtle sequencing, of my choice of words, and appropriate punctuation, I hope that *you*, my readers, can find yourselves *guided* by those letterings on the page to such an extent, that you can find them arousing distinctive movements of feeling within you working to connect *your* seeing the letters on the page with *my* speakings.

For my aim here, as in all that follows, is the Wittgensteinian (1953) aim of coming to "*a clear view* of our use of words" (no.122), where his aim (and mine) is not that of fitting what we experience into an already existing theoretical-scheme, framework, or perspective scheme in order to *explain* it, but that of grasping how, in our everyday contexts of *the use of language*, we can negotiate or navigate between us the collaborative construction of extremely subtle outcomes, sensitive to the particular *details* of the particular situation in question.

This is why Wittgenstein is continually asking us to consider particular cases, for he wants to draw our attention to our *actual use of words* — a use which is complicated and woven into the deeds and actions of our everyday lives. For it is when we place our expressions back into their everyday context, that we can get a clear picture of their actual use, and we are not tempted to postulate hidden, hypothetical mental processes. The process involved is always of a collaborative, distributed nature, spread out amongst all the participants within the communicative process. This becomes very clear when it comes cases in which a participant (or participants) lack a wide range of expressive possibilities available to them. Let me introduce an example.

Overcoming the practicalities facing those with great difficulty in communicating clearly:

A brain-damaged person

Rob, a successful New York lawyer, at 60 yrs old in 1979, suffered a massive stroke in the left hemisphere of his brain. Indeed, the stroke was so massive that Rob, who had made his living through his ability to use language, was, after intensive speech therapy, left with only three words: *Yes*, *No*, and *And*. The tape for the article, Goodwin (1995), that I am going to quote from, was made in 1992, 13 years after the stroke, when Rob was 73 years old.

The major point here is that, with the three words at his disposal, and with the help of his family members, they managed to create between them a collaborative process for the co-construction of meaning; this was achieved (1) by him attending to the sequential placement of his talk, and (2) by him using the full expressive powers of his body (intonation, gesture, affective displays of his face and body). By these means, Rob was able to build abroad range of subtly differentiated expressive-actions, each one fitting in fine detail into the contingencies of a local organization in which it could be placed.

Indeed, luckily for Rob (and, in fact, for very young children, as we will have to emphasize over and over again), understandings are not encoded *in* the self-contained sentences of isolated speakers, but instead are constituted within collaborative structures distributed amongst the expressive actions and utterances of all those participating within a particular *dialogically-structured* intra-action. Thus, the fact that Rob's severe deficits in the production of words are *not* accompanied by equal restrictions on his ability to recognize, and actively participate in, the pragmatic organization of talk-in-interaction, is crucial. Rob is able to make himself understood, and to constitute himself as a meaningful actor, by his visible *participation* in the activity of the moment.

For instance, a Nurse is trying to pull on a sock over Rob's leg. She has just moved her hands to work on the upper part of the sock.

Rob: Nyuh nuh. ((points toward sock)) (1.3 sec.) ((Nurse looks to Rob and then back to sock))
Nurse: Up more?
Rob: Yes.(1.8 sec.) ((Nurse pulls lower part of sock))
Rob: Yes.

In line 3 the nurse states a guess about what Rob is trying to bring to her attention. As a question, her utterance builds a context that shapes the interpretation of whatever will be said as a reply to it. In order to make himself understood, Rob both relies upon, and helps structure the sequential organization of the talk within which he is embedded. Thus his subtle sensitivity to sequential organization is crucial. But notice too, his 'Nyuh nuh'; it is not just a 'flat **No**', but a 'hesitant No', a 'No' that means that there is 'more to come'.

Similarly, when the nurse is at the refrigerator asking Rob what he wants for breakfast, there is a similar negotiated, rather straight forward exchange (toast/yes-no/one spread/jelly/no/butter/yes/just butter):

31 Nurse: English muffin?
32 (3.4 sec.)
33 Husband: Yes.
34 (0.4)
35 Nurse: And what would you like on it?
36 Wife: Just one.
37 (0.8)
38 Nurse: Jelly?

39 (1.0)
40 Husband: No
41 (0.8)
42 Wife: Butter?
43 Nurse: Butter?
44 (0.3)
45 Husband: Yes.
46 (0.6)
47 Nurse: Okay.

Rob's talk does not stand alone as a self-contained entity, but emerges from, and is situated within the talk of others, to which it is inextricably linked. Later, we will meet what Bakhtin (1993) calls the "emotional-volitional tone" of people's utterances: Although what a person is *stating* in their utterances matters, it is what they are *trying to do* in making such a statement that is crucial; we need to get a sense of an expression's 'point' and 'purpose', a sense of speaker's degree of commitment to it, and why they are motivated in such an aim, and so on.

My aim in my writing here — precision in meaning

"What we find out in philosophy is trivial; it does not teach us new facts, only science does that. But the proper synopsis of these trivialities is enormously difficult, and has immense importance. Philosophy is in fact the synopsis of trivialities".

(Wittgenstein, 1980c, p.26)

"The contexts of sentence are best portrayed in a play. Therefore the best example for a sentence with a particular meaning is a quotation from a play. And whoever asks a person in a play what he's experiencing when he's speaking?"

(Wittgenstein, 1990, vol.1, no.38)

"In language there are only beginnings and beginnings and beginnings."

(Gertrude Stein)

In all of this, then, 'the devil is in the detail': To say that "context helps communication," is to state an abstract *after-the-fact* generality. Whereas, Rob's family, and Rob himself, in developing the special style of collaborative communicating — in which, with his three words, Rob could convey, eventually, quite *precise* linguistic meanings — needed to explore intonation-patterns and gestures, different presuppositions and forms of turn-taking, and so on. And it is in these preliminary, *before-*

the-fact details that we can find, for Rob and his family, what for them is the significant meaning of the word "context," and the way in which they all drew on those details as a *resource* in coming to final, agreed meaning for Rob's initially very vague expressions.

I emphasize this need for the attention to *details* because, the aim of my writing here is not topic-based or subject-oriented — I am not concerned with the *results* of any inquiries into the workings of *meanings* or *gestures* in general; nor with any *causal explanations* — instead, I will often be trying to craft short *vignettes* or *dramatic portrayals* or *synoptic condensations*, where my point or purpose is to try to convey *precisely* what Rob was *trying to do* in expressing himself as he did. My task in these vignettes, portrayals, synoptic condensations provided, is not to *explain* or *define* any thing, but to arouse in readers a distinctive *from-to movement of feeling*, a *pointing* towards a next place to go in one's current activities. In other words, my concern is not to provide *you* with the *completed ends* of *my* investigations, but with *possible beginnings* for *yours* (Shotter, 2007, 2012).

The influence of details comes to light when actions are displayed in 'slow motion'

So, in my own writing, let me point out some of the *tools* or *devices* or *structurings* that I have already been *self-consciously using* in my writing above in an effort to arouse in you such distinctive *from-to movements of feeling*, particular feelings or sensings that *point* towards *openings* for a new, next step forward. One, that I am most aware of, is that of bringing attention particular words by the use of *italics*[4]. Another, is bringing attention to *differences* by means of *comparisons* between *open* and *closed* constructions: So I say, for instance: "This means that, *instead of discovering pre-existing things in our inquiries, we continually bring such 'things' into existence*" — in other words, we move from a phrase in which *nouns* are focal, to one in which *verbs* are, for again, what is *in movement*, not what is *static*, is central.

Of course, my copious use of punctuation is there, to slow things down somewhat so that — even if I do not say 'in other words' — you are given time, as a reader, to consider the possibility of other descriptions. Thus such phrases as 'as it were', 'so the speak', 'in a manner of speaking', point up the fact that I want to leave what I am trying to describe partially *vague*, or better, "*specifically vague*"[5]; in other words, while

---

4 Usually considered a matter of bad style, in that their use will be *distracting* — where that is, of course, my purpose here, to slow things down — while another consideration is that their over-use will lead to them being ignored — I will just have risk that *that* (sic) is not the case here.

5 Garfinkel (1967) notes that in ordinary, everyday conversations: "The events that were

being partially specified or determined, I want still to leave an event or situation open to further inner specification or determination (as in fact we do in our ordinary, everyday conversations). It may seem crazy to say this, for after all we hope when we read philosophy or any intellectual inquiry to gain a clear inner mental understanding of the landscape of possibilities open to us for making a deliberate choice, a deliberate decision, of how next to act.

But this is not my aim. Instead of expecting our *thinking* to turn *inwards* to tell us what next *to do*, we must turn *outwards* to 'see' what is before us afresh[6], with the hope that a new way forward can be opened up, and a blocked way left behind.

My aim, then, in my writing is to *hear* it, or to *read* it, not as offering the *end* or *outcome* of a philosophical deliberation, or as an *explanation* that we can put to use instrumentally, but instead — by reading it in accord with its hesitation-producing punctuation (aimed at undermining its seeming fact-claiming nature) — the writing will be read as the *beginning* of a philosophical investigation, and will invite further investigation our circumstances out in the world around us.

But without the punctuation to slow us down, it is unlikely that we will pause to consider the specific vagueness, ambiguity, and multiplicity of meanings available, not only in my writing here (and also in Wittgenstein's remarks), but also in our everyday lives — which we nonetheless cope in an unproblematic way, as we will see, due to their setting within a particular context. And it is by drawing our attentions to particular cases in particular settings, that Wittgenstein draws our attention to how we actually do this by our use of words. For, it is when we place our everyday expressions back into our everyday activities in our everyday lives, that we can get a clear sense of *what* we are using our words *for* — their particular point and purpose within those activities — and we are not tempted to suggest that they have issued from hypothetical mental processes solely within our heads of a general kind.

---

talked about were *specifically vague*. Not only do they not frame a clearly restricted set of possible determinations but the depicted events include as their essentially intended and sanctioned features an accompanying 'fringe' of determinations that are open with respect to internal relationships, relationships to other events, and relationships to retrospective and prospective possibilities" (pp.40-41, my italics).

[6] Wittgenstein (1953), in confronting us with the fact that there is not something in common to what we call 'games', remarks: "For if you look at them you will not see something that is common to *all*, but similarities, relationships, and a whole series of them at that. To repeat: don't think, but look!" (no.66).

If our 'words stand for things' then they work to 'picture' states of affairs— but in fact words have countless uses

The trouble is, if we do lapse back into thinking that our 'words stand for things' — as it is quite easy to do in our more deliberate intellectual inquiries in philosophy or the social sciences than in our everyday circumstances — then, rather than a movement of feeling, we find ourselves experiencing a 'picture' (a representation) of a state of affairs. Wittgenstein (1953) provides the following example: As philosopher or psychologist, we might say to ourselves of someone to whom we were speaking:

"While I was speaking to him I did not know *what was going on in his head*" (no.427, my italics).

We might go so far as to say: "I wish I could have seen the nature of the *brain processes* taking place, for soon, when we learn how to de-code them, they will allow us to read his thoughts." Whereas, in our everyday lives, from a more *practical* point of view, we would say:

"While I was speaking to him I did not know what was going on in his head. In saying this, one is not thinking of *brain processes*, but of *thought-processes*. The picture should be taken seriously. We should really like to see into his head. And yet we only mean what elsewhere we should mean by saying: *we should like to know what he is thinking*. I want to say: *We have this vivid picture* — and that use, *apparently contradicting the picture, which expresses the psychical*" (no.427, my italics).

The "vivid picture" to which Wittgenstein is here referring, is that of the *inner* character *we feel compelled to ascribe to mental items* when we regard them as being *in the mind*. Yet, from early on in his work, Wittgenstein noted that our notion of the *inner* seemed to separate the contents of the mind from the public world in which we live and act (see my account of Cartesianism below). As a consequence, we tend to picture the mind as a kind of *nonphysical inner space* whose hidden contents are phenomenological or psychological as opposed to physical or neurological. Indeed, he remarks with respect to the process of remembering something: "But you surely cannot deny that, for example, in remembering, an inner process takes place." — What gives the impression that we want to deny anything?," he asks, and he goes on to reply: "What we deny is that the picture of the inner process gives us the correct idea of the use of the word to remember'. We say that this picture with its ramifications *stands in the way of our seeing the use of the word as it is*" (no.305, my italics).

Indeed, in *standing in the way* of our seeing what in fact is actually happening, such 'pictures' are misleading illusions — we seek to inquire into *brain processes* rather than noting noticing that we can observe *what* a person is thinking from 'it shows up' in their activities. This is why Wittgenstein is so concerned to 'spell out' the *detailed influences* at work in particular cases. As he sees it: "The work of the philosopher consists in assembling reminders for a particular purpose" (no.127). In "assembling reminders," Wittgenstein takes himself to be "putting before us" what "lies open to view" (no.126), "always before one's eyes" (no.129); and in the midst of an assembly of such reminders, we are expected to "see connections" (no.122), to produce for ourselves "a perspicuous representation" (no.122) — an overall view of a *landscape of possibilities* that will cure us of our disorientation, of our *not knowing our* "way about" (no.123).

Thus discovery and proof in philosophy is not deduction from pre-existing premises, but the hermeneutical fitting of an expression into its precise context so as to get a true sense, not of what a person's expressions mean in themselves, but of what *precisely* he or she meant in expressing them.

1 Our current 'Newtonian-Cartesian' common-sense

Speaking matters. Our words in their speaking matter. We can *shape* both ourselves and our world in our speakings. And, indeed, as John Austin (1970) makes clear, once we have 'grown up into' a particular languaged social group, and begin to make *use of* the ordinary, everyday ways of speaking already at work within our surroundings, we find ourselves saying and doing various 'things' spontaneously, in an effortless way, with the others around us *responding* to us as we *expect* them to respond. Thus, as Austin (1970) notes: "Certainly, then, ordinary language is not the last word: in principle it can everywhere be supplemented and improved upon and superseded. Only remember, it *is* the *first* word" (p.185, my italics). Thus *speaking, actually* — speaking in all its variations — in speaking a language in common with all the others around me, I am assuming in the context of this book, that this is the primal *human* activity.

Everything of importance that happens in our lives, happens *within* our face-to-face encounters with our fellow human beings. In short, although I will expand a great deal on this theme later — to the extent that we live in a still developing, somewhat *undifferentiated*, only partially determined, 'fluid' world, within which many turbulent strands of formative activity[7] intra[8]-twine — as active participants within some regions of these 'flowing' activities, we can *make a difference* within them. We can act to make a difference to the structure of the world that would not have occurred if we had not acted.

In fact, in our efforts to communicate with the others around us, if we are to tell the others around us of our experiences, it must always be our *first word* because, for having grown into the *communal ways* of making sense of events happening around us, we must, initially at least, express ourselves in ways that enable them to *relate themselves* to our experiences as we ourselves initially relate to them. If we do not initially draw on this realm of *shared background understandings*, then we are

---

7 And, as I put it in Shotter (1984): "Such formative processes are clearly always open to further specification ... but only (and this is most important) of an already specified kind. In other words, at each point in the process, what has been specified so far is known in terms of its already specified further specifiability" (p.187). What is so important about such *difference making*, developmental processes, is that they also work to constitute within an otherwise undifferentiated 'flux' of activity, organized unities of many particular kinds, within which each *particular differencing* also produces a *particular relating*.

8 I write 'intra-' here, rather than 'inter-', because, as we will see, we will need to assume a world, a cosmos, in which nothing, no-'thing', exists *in separation from* any thing else; 'things' exist only *in relation to* what is around them (see endnote 2).

liable simply to confuse and bewilder our fellows.

So what is this background 'it' that we can, in an untroubled fashion, turn to in beginning to tell our fellow human beings of something that is currently mattering to us?

Well, the fact is, we are never not immersed within a continuous flow of intra-mingling activities which, here and there, at this moment or at another, create unfolding, moving, *particular* dynamic stabilities — time-shaped events that we can notice and 'point out' to each other, effortlessly.

Wittgenstein (1953) gives the following example: "I see a landscape; suddenly a rabbit runs past. I exclaim "A rabbit!"/ Both things, both the report and the exclamation, are expressions of perception and of visual experience. But the exclamation is so in a different sense from the report: *it is forced from us.* — It is related to the experience as a cry is to pain ... The very expression which is also a report of what is seen, is here a cry of recognition" (pp.197-198, my italics).

Our utterances, our expressions, are 'called out' from us by our circumstances. Initially, we do not first deliberate and then decide that this is how best to express ourselves, we just act, spontaneously, and as we shall see, it is very important that we do so.

For us to be able to respond to the background 'it' differentially as we do, what must be the nature of the 'flowing stuff' that we are immersed in? What, actually, *is* our experience like *initially*, such that we seem able to draw on a 'common world' in our efforts at communicating our experiences linguistically to the others around us; what is the nature of the 'cosmos" — as a readily available objective order and determinateness, a world that is transindividual, general, and valid for all — that we seem able, initially, to draw on in our practical, communicative activities? And what is going on when we are concerned, in principle, to ensure that, as Austin (1962) puts it, "it can everywhere be supplemented and improved upon and superseded"?

Because, overall, our *common world* seems to be an unfinished, still evolving, not fully differentiated world, such that every 'thing' exists within it, initially, only within a partially ordered, *intra-mingling movement*, with each region of that movement dynamically unfolding with its own distinctive, *orchestrated* or *concrescent*[9] time-shape —

---

9 As we will see, although *concrescence* is the name Whitehead (1985) gave to the process in which a "concrete unities of feeling" are gradually formed as we experienced many different fragments of a complex whole; later, we shall find it more enlightening to liken the process to the *hermeneutical* process, in which a *particular meaningful whole* emerges from our fragmented but nonetheless intra-connected experiences.

thus, as such, presenting us at any one moment with a number of possible next directions of movement.

This is where our spontaneous *linguistic expressions* become so important to us; for just as the dynamic event of a rabbit running by 'calls out' a *cry of recognition* from us, so it can also 'call out' a similar such spontaneous response from all the others around us. As a consequence, the event becomes an "objective" event, a "witnessable recognizability or recognition" (Garfinkel, 2002, p. 68), a 'thisness' or a 'thatness' of a distinctive kind that one can not only 'point out' to others, but also tell those others of its possible *meanings*, i.e., what it could lead to; for the different words we use will arouse in our listeners different "structures of anticipation" (Bakhtin, 1986) as to what might happen next, as the rabbit runs by.

But what is shared here is our immersion in a distinctive *movement*, a movement that initially is undifferentiated as to whether it is occurring out in the world *as an objective physical movement*, a movement that, in fact, owes its formation to the larger context of intra-mingling flowing activities within which it occurs, or whether it is occurring within ourselves *as a subjective movement of feeling*, or both. Thus, given 'its' essential *non-locatability*, along with its *unbounded* nature — and given our irritable impatience with ill-defined states of affairs, along with the current preference for 'scientific' ways of thinking and observing — we are easily tempted to 'see' it *as* simply a *spatial* shape (pattern or form) that we can *match*, or make *correspond to*, or *represent by*, a similar spatial shape within a bounded formal (logical or theoretical) system of our own devising.

From a thin, after-the-fact objectivity to a thick, before-the- fact objectivity

Here, then, is the concern of this book: I want to suggest that our notion of *objectivity* needs revising. For too long, in awe of the remarkable success of the sciences, we have taken as central to all our attempts at thinking and speaking rationally, what I will call a retrospective, *after-the-fact*, achieved version of a thin, itemized objectivity. As an *achieved* version of objectivity, it does not, like the *common-sense* enacted in our spontaneous uses of our everyday ways of talking, pre-exist as an already shared, taken-for-granted, designation of the facts of the matter. It is an objectivity that needs to be established in a particular local circumstance *as required* for a particular purpose. Indeed, we have accepted that if, in the 'workings' of our thinking, we can justify each step we take by reference to the facts of the matter, then that is also sufficient for us to feel justified in our arriving at our final step, our conclusion.

But this — our being able to justify to each other the steps we take within the process of coming to a conclusion — is, I think, a precisely wrong view of what *objectivity* actually "is" for us: For it leaves unquestioned and unexamined in the background the fact that in our growing up into a community of language users, we acquire shared *ways of being-in-the-world*, along with shared *ways of talking*, both embedded in the richer objectivity of an already shared "cosmos."

In establishing a local objectivity, we not only ignore this fact, but we can also very easily act in contradiction to the already existing, taken-for-granted, common-sense, shared *certainties* that make it possible for us to use language and to act in many practical situations in an untroubled way, without the need for prior thought. As Cassirer (2000) puts it, we encounter the idea of "cosmos," of a thoroughgoing, pre-established of order 'things':

"wherever a determinate unified structural law becomes apparent within multiplicity and diversity. The rule of such a structural law: this is the most general expression of what we denote, in the largest sense of the term, by 'objectivity'. In order to render this fully clear for us, we need only refer to the essential meaning of the concept of *cosmos,* which ancient thought had already established. A 'cosmos', an objective order and determinateness, is readily available wherever different subjects relate to a 'common world' and consciously participate in it ... What we grasp as the 'meaning' of the world we encounter everywhere is that, instead of enclosing ourselves in our own image of the world [*Vorstellungswelt*][10], we turn toward a world that is transindividual, general, and valid for all" (p.13).

In other words, prior to all our *after-the-fact* forms of itemized objectivity, we in fact live within one or another version of a thick, prospective, *before-the-fact*, already instituted, intra-woven form of objectivity, a holistic common-sense that provides to all the participants within it, a shared *sense of the circumstances* they are currently occupying — a sense that, as we will see, although already partially specified, is still open to further specification, as the *boundaries of the circumstances* they occupy, still remain to be agreed upon by all in the group.

Thus, while spatial 'things' have 'boundaries' and can exhibit a *self-contained* existence, temporal 'things' are always 'unbounded', 'unfinished', 'incomplete', and thus open to further development. But we can place temporary, temporal boundaries around them, for the moment. These temporary boundaries allow temporal things and events

---

[10] Which is, essentially, what we have done in situating ourselves within a Cartesian worldview — see below.

to have, for practical purposes, a unique wholeness to them, momentarily: Someone *replies* to a person's utterance only when they *feel* that it has 'come to an end', when they *sense* that the speaker has 'completed' what they *wanted* to say; they then go on in their 'reply' to it, to develop its *meaning* further; and so on — where the *meaning* of a person's expression is experienced, not as an *objective representation* that has to be *thought about*, but as a *subjective movement of feeling* providing a structure of anticipations as to one's possible next moves.

This is why, as Bakhtin (1993) puts it: "What underlies the unity of an answerable consciousness is not a principle as a starting point, but the fact of an actual *acknowledgment* of one's own participation in unitary Being-as-event, and this fact cannot be adequately expressed in theoretical terms, but can only be described and participatively experienced" (p.40). If we try to start our inquiries as thinkers, by trying to posit formal, theoretical schematisms, principles, rules, or laws prior to our inquiries (as we will see in more detail below), we will find, not only that we *immobilize* what was in movement, but also in *selecting* certain features as essential to our schematisms, we *exclude* others, crucially the *specific tendencies* to change and development present in almost all our human activities.

This is why, alternatively, I want to suggest that, in our inquiries, we focus on the back-and-forth, turn-taking nature of people's performances within their *actual*, everyday performances of their languaged activities. For it is in their dialogically-structured engagements with each other, as they move 'this way' and 'that way' in their possibly unending 'explorations' of the situations of their concern, that what we might call the different "discursive realities" they experience themselves as acting within, begin to come into existence between them. In other words, rather than fixing, finalizing, and excluding features from consideration, they can potentially open themselves up to arriving at, as Wittgenstein (1953) puts it: "just that understanding which consists in 'seeing connections'" (no.122).

A new, thick, richer "common-sense"

So why do these considerations lead me to suggest that we need to establish a new 'common-sense' amongst us? Why should we need to focus on the practicalities of our currently *actual* ways of speaking in our everyday lives? Because, for at least the last 300 years or so, we have been living within a very largely taken-for-granted, unquestioned, 'common-sense' [*sensus communis*], structured primarily by Descartes' notorious 'Mind-Body dichotomy', along with a whole set of other sharp, binary distinctions: those between *res cogitans* and *res extensa*, between subjectivity and objectivity, between the *freedom of thought and decision* and *causal necessities*, between *Culture* and *Nature*, and many others. All of this — especially when anchored in his infamous *Cogito*: "I think therefore I am" — has diverted our attention away from the fact that *we have* in fact enclosed ourselves within an image of the world of our own devising, from the fact that, as users of a common language, *we must already be living in a world shared in common with all the others around us*, or else the forming of specialist social groups oriented towards common tasks (as well as academic disciplines) would be impossible.

Now it is not that many others have not already noted the crucial importance of our immersion in an already existing, shared background of understandings as to the nature of the world we share in common with those around us. Merleau-Ponty (1962), for instance, notes: "There is ... either in the man who listens or reads, or in the one who speaks or writes, a *thought in speech* the existence of which is unsuspected by intellectualism" (p.179). In other words, in our 'growing up', our bodies 'grow into' *ways* of spontaneously responding and reacting to *events* happening within our surrounding circumstances that arouse within us *movements of feeling*, whose 'time-shapes' we are immersed in along with the others around us within our immediate circumstances. Thus, "what we have said earlier about the 'representation of movement'," says Merleau-Ponty (1962), "must be repeated concerning the verbal image: I do not need to visualize external space and my own body in order to move one within the other. It is enough that they exist for me, and that they form a certain field of action around me. In the same way I do not need to visualize the word in order to know and to pronounce it ... I reach back for the word as my hand reaches towards the part of the body which is being pricked; the word has a certain location in my linguistic world, and is a part of my equipment" (p.180).

Vico (1988), in his *On the most ancient wisdom of the Italians*, Vico (1710/1988), suggested long ago that we can gain a sense of the embodied influences spontaneously at work in shaping people's everyday dealings with each other, and the world around them, from their *unconsidered ways of talking*. He thus undertook to "treat in this first book those locutions that provide a basis for conjectures regarding the opinions that those early sages of Italy held on the first truth, on God and on the human mind" (p.43). In other words, Vico is here assuming that in their everyday talk, people were talking with a pre-existing shaped inner sense guiding, not just their talk, but how they were applying their talk to the conduct of their affairs out in the world around them.

More recently, Wittgenstein (1953) also makes a similar suggestion: "When philosophers use a word — 'knowledge', 'being', 'object', 'I', 'proposition', 'name' — and try to grasp the essence of the thing, one must always ask oneself: is the word ever actually used in this way in the language-game which is its original home? — What we do is to bring words back from their metaphysical to their everyday use" (no.116). And what we do, when we bring our words back from their decontextualized, generalized use in technical and professional circles, is to bring to our attention to the fact that, primarily, in our everyday activities — because we are always immersed within an ongoing, temporally unfolding, still largely undifferentiated flux of activity — is to *use* our words to *determine*, or to *bring attention to*, features or aspects[11] of the flux to which we can, as needs be, respond.

In refusing to *determine* the nature of 'things' and events *actually occurring out in the world at large* by seeking within them pre-established, theoretical *forms*, common to all the 'things' we tend to 'name' in the same way, Wittgenstein (1953) offers us an alternative: Instead, he suggests that we desist from exclaiming that "'There *must* be something common, or they would not [for example] be called "games"' — but *look and see* whether there is anything common to all. — For if you look at them you will not see something that is common to *all*, but similarities, relationships, and a whole series of them at that" (no.66).

Indeed, our seeing of similarities (and differences) seems to be a very basic human capacity, so that rather than seeking a perfect *formal correspondence* between a thing or establish out in the world, and a symbol in a theoretical schematism (in the service of Cartesian dreams of achieving *certainty*[12]), Wittgenstein suggests instead the *making of comparisons* — where the purpose is not that of seeing an 'object' *as* an object, but that of seeing it within a larger context of intra-mingling flowing activities within which it has a *meaning*. As Wittgenstein (1953) puts it: "What I perceive in the dawning of an aspect is not a property of the object, but an internal relation between it and other objects" (p.212). Indeed, by linguistically describing it in *this way* rather than *that way*, we can arouse in ourselves (and others) particular *anticipations* as to how next to act towards a happening 'thing' or event.

Thus Wittgenstein's (1953) whole aim, then, in his method of comparisons, is to motivate us, deliberately, to imagine likenesses that might enable us to see the significance of things *beyond their merely logical sense*. Thus rather than wanting to perform a logical analysis of a situation, with the aim of *explaining* how, causally, it might have come about, his aim is to have an *effect on us*. As he remarks, in relation

---

11 An *aspect* is not some frozen 'thing' like an unchanging object, but is a *recognizable* 'thisness' or a 'thatness' within a flowing stream of activity, within the unfolding process of a person's actions that can be *witnessed by others*.

12 A linguistically depicted model or picture is presented "as an object of comparison — as, so to speak, a measuring-rod; not as a preconceived idea to which reality *must* correspond" (Wittgenstein, 1953, no.131).

to an example, in which a picture of a "cube" *fits*, or *fails to fit*, what we know a cube to be: "What was the effect of my argument? It called our attention to (reminded us of) the fact that there are other processes, besides the one we originally thought of, which we should sometimes be prepared to call 'applying the picture of a cube'" (no.140).

In other words, Wittgenstein wants us to work on our *before-the fact* ways of making sense of our experiences, to avoid the fixings, the finalizings, the selections and exclusions that our *thin* forms of achieved objectivity impose on us currently in our inquiries, so that by placing our problematic circumstance within a *certain field of comparisons*, thus to see it within a much *thicker*, rich in possibilities, objectivity, shared with all the others around us[13].

From coordinating our activities in a Cartesian world according to laws, to coordinating our activities in terms of anticipated consequences.

"In order to put all these new truths in a less crude light and to be able to say more freely what I think about them, without being obliged to accept or to refute what are accepted opinions among philosophers and theologians, I resolved to leave all these people to their disputes, and to speak only of what would happen in a new world, if God were to create, somewhere in imaginary space, enough matter to compose it, and if he were to agitate diversely and confusedly the different parts of this matter, so that he created a chaos as disordered as the poets could ever imagine, and afterwards did no more than to lend his usual preserving action to nature, and to let her act according to his established laws" (Descartes, 1968, p.62).

We in fact live in a much larger, richer world than Descartes' simple world of particles of matter in motion according to pre-established laws. Indeed, as living beings, we exist within our continually changing surroundings as a much more richly structured, and structuring, entities than as mere *subjectivities*, encased in simple world of *objective* things.

Living immersed in a flowing flux of activity that influences us much more than we can influence it, our expressions work, not by arousing finished 'representations' (pictures) of events or states of affairs in myself and/or others, but by bringing us into contact with "a speaking subject, with a certain *style* of being and with the 'world' at which he

---

[13] "I wanted to put that picture before him, and his *acceptance* of the picture consists in his now being inclined to regard a given case differently: that is, to compare it with *this* rather than *that* set of pictures. I have changed his *way of looking at things*" (Wittgenstein, 1953, no.144).

directs his aim" (Merleau-Ponty, 1962, p.183) — where in their unfolding, the expressions of a speaking subject exhibit a step-by-step, back-and-forth process (a developmental trajectory), in which in their exploratory moves in *this* and/or *that* direction, speakers show or exhibit the 'world' they are intent on bringing into being.

Descartes' pre-established ontology, his (and consequently our) assumption that *what* beings *are* for us is achieved by our objectification of them — that is, by our being able to *represent* them in such a way that we can, by essentially mathematical (geometrical) methods, be sure, and that means certain, of their *ways* of being in the world — has highjacked almost all of the imaginative spaces available to us for our further explorations of what is possible for us in our seeking new ways of being human beings.

Indeed, all this has not only (mis)led us into assuming that a *systematic thought process* (sometimes occurring within us *unconsciously*) *must precede all our actions*, but also has (mis)led us into 'measuring up' the outcomes of our processes of deliberate, systematic thinking 'from the outside', in relation to judgmental criteria, i.e., theoretical ideals and/or idealizations, of our own devising. Thus, instead of valuing the efficacy of practical action, of being prepared to *arrive at* collaboratively-shared outcomes within a socially-shared exploratory process, we have come to value the *evidence-based truth* of theoretical statements more — truths evaluated solely in terms of perfect, like-for-like, formal (pictorial) correspondences.

The assumed primacy of thought has also led us to ignore the fact that *from within* our everyday activities we need continually to 'measure up' the steps we take in their performance, not only in relation to our own inner, *anticipatory intentions* (as well as those of the others around us), but also in relation to the already existing *felt forms of expression* enabling us all within our socio-linguistic group to *account* for our actions to each other — so that we all can 'see' our otherwise indeterminate activities *as* we all intend them to be 'seen', to see them in a determinate sense as 'our' actions, and not as imposed on us by outside others.

Without our *linguistic accountability* to others, we would not be able either to sustain our social institutions in existence, or to continually update them to fit them to the new contexts we continually create from within them (Shotter, 1984). As C.W. Mills (1940) put it long ago: "The postulate underlying modern study of language is the simple one that we must approach linguistic behaviour, not by referring it to private states in individuals, but by observing its social function of co-ordinating diverse actions. Rather than expressing something which is prior and in the person, language is taken by other persons as an indicator of future actions" (p.904). Indeed, Mills goes so far as to claim that:

"There is no need to invoke 'psychological' terms like 'desire' or 'wish' as explanatory, since they themselves must be explained socially. Anticipation is a subvocal or overt naming of terminal phases and/or social consequences of conduct. When an individual names consequences, he elicits the behaviours for which the name is a redintegrative cue" (p.906) — for, as he sees it, our *naming*[14] of an action gives us a sense of its "*anticipated consequences*" (p.907).

Treating our thought as primary, (mis)leads us into ignoring the agreements, the shared anticipations, the shared judgments, embodied in our common-sense, everyday practices that make the social function of language in co-ordinating many diverse actions amongst us possible; we far too easily forget how amazing it is that so many diverse activities can come to be *intra*-related to each other in such a way that we feel justified in saying that they all are *expressions* of a common or unitary culture — even when we cannot specify a set of objective features common to 'things' and 'events' that will *characterize them* as 'belonging' to the culture.

Oscillating between 'fluidity' and 'fixity' in our practical affairs

"Scientific thinking, a thinking which looks on from above, and thinks of the object-in-general, must return to the 'there is' which underlies it; to the site, *the soil of the sensible* and opened world such as it is in our life and for our body — not that possible body which we may legitimately think of as an information machine but that actual body I call mine, this sentinel standing quietly at the command of my words and my acts" (Merleau-Ponty, 1962, pp.160-161, my italics).

But why a new 'fluid' common-sense? Because central to the new realm of inquiry that I want to introduce is the assumption that, as living beings, instead of the classical Newtonian-Cartesian world of separate particles in motion according to laws, we live immersed within an oceanic world of ceaseless, intra-mingling currents of activity — many quite invisible — which, to repeat, influence us as much, if not more, than we can influence them. We are thus not like machines with already

---

[14] We shall have good reason to question the efficacy of the mere 'naming' of an event; as Wittgenstein (1953) remarks: "... one forgets that a great deal of stage-setting in the language is presupposed if the mere act of naming is to make sense" (no257); for Mills, clearly, it is the relationally-responsive (Bakhtin, 1986) function of a name-word, its *use*, that is important, rather than its *referential-representational* (picturing) function as a name.

well-defined inputs, leading to equally well-defined outputs, unresponsive to the larger contexts in which we operate. We are more like plants growing from seeds, existing *within* a special confluence of different flowing streams of energy and materials that our bodies are continually working to *organize* in sustaining us as viable human beings. Buffeted by the wind and waves of the social weather around us, we inhabit circumstances in which almost everything seems to merge into everything else; we do not and cannot observe this larger flow of activity *as if* from the outside. Indeed, it is too intimately interwoven in with all that we are and can do from within it for it to be lifted out and examined scientifically, as an object, from the outside.

After all, whenever and wherever we move, we will still find ourselves within one or another region of it. We are too immersed in it to be aware of its every aspect. We are thus continually uncertain as to *what* the situation *is* that faces us, and *how* we might act for the best within it — it is thus up to us to *determine* what are essentially, open and still *indeterminate* circumstances according to our *interests* (Habermas, 1972), as well as, of course, in terms of what is socially legitimate within them. Luckily, we are never wholly 'at sea' within utterly featureless surroundings. There is something very special — of a pre-cognitive, a pre-conceptual, and thus of a pre-intellectual nature — that seems to be at work within us in the course of our growing up as a member of a particular culture, with its own particular history, and with its own particular, linguistically-structured forms of thought and social institutions and activities that allows us to feel, mostly, *oriented*, i.e., that we know *where* and *who* we are.

Indeed, as living beings, functioning continually in a dynamic, back-and-forth, dialogical-hermeneutical relation both to the others and othernesses in our surroundings, more than simply living in an undifferentiated, flowing, holistic *environment*, we find ourselves living in world made shareable by the fact that we share in *a whole structure of anticipations* (Mills, 1940) with our fellows, in relation to events happening around us.

In failing to attend to what we already share with all those around us — in particular, our spontaneously responsive *uses* of language — we ignore our direct 'in-touch-ness' with our circumstances, and as a consequence, rather than acting in direct relation to what we *sense* 'as required by' our circumstances, we act instead as 'we think fit', in accord with a whole set of *theoretical frameworks* of our own devising, aimed at satisfying our *wants* and *desires*, rather than our *real needs* (see the work of Samuel Todes, 2001, discussed later). And in so doing, we have no idea, no sense, of whether, overall, we are acting for the best in sustaining and developing further our human ways of being human. As Aristotle (1955) puts it, the task of the *prudent* person is "to be able to deliberate rightly... not in particular respects e.g. what is good for health or physical strength, but what is conducive to the good life generally" (p.209). In other words, more than the mere solving of immediate problems, one after another, is needed if we are to act within the particular practical situations confronting us in our everyday lives, *prudently*, with *practical wisdom*, with a *sense* of what, overall, it is best for us to do.

This is the point and purpose of the writing in this book. For Aristotle's account of what is involved in achieving *practical wisdom* is quite different from what is involved in achieving *knowledge*, in our *becoming a more well-informed* person. As he points out, practical wisdom *cannot be taught in the classroom;* it cannot be captured in *rules* or *principles* or *generalities* of any kind; practical wisdom is concerned 'to grasp' the particular facts involved in a particular case; it thus requires both experience of life and a special virtue, a strong sense of ethical 'standards', of treating others as one would like to be treated oneself. However, this does not make it a merely subjective enterprise, as there is 'a truthful expression' of the matter in question to be arrived at, a 'truthful expression' that cannot be 'proved' by argumentative talk alone; for those who 'see it' differently, usually 'experience it' differently, i.e., *account* for it differently, linguistically. But I believe that, although it cannot be taught, it can be *learned*; we can, I believe, begin to identify what we might call 'instructive experiences' conducive to the acquisition of practical wisdom; and it is to the identification of such experiences that the main body of this book will be devoted.

Re-orienting ourselves: from being 'masters' to being merely 'participants'

All this means that we need to *orient* ourselves quite differently from how we orient ourselves currently, in what we are pleased to call our *research* inquiries in the social sciences. Among a large number of other re-orientations, it requires, I shall argue, our becoming sensitive, not so much to *positive* happenings in which we feel people's lives being enhanced by those around them — although these events are clearly heartening, and can be sustaining in depressing times — but our becoming sensitive to *negative* happenings, events in which we can feel, see, or hear 'out loud', so to speak, the *lack* of 'a something' that is needed for the event to 'have worked out well' for those involved within it (I will call this sense, a sense of 'disquiets'[15]).

---

[15] As Merleau-Ponty (1964) puts it, in our everyday talk of the circumstances in which we need to act: "Expression is a matter of reorganizing things-said, affecting them with a new index of curvature, and bending them to a certain enhancement of meaning. There is that which is to be said, and which is as yet no more than a precise uneasiness in the world of things-said... I would never take a step if my faraway view of the goal did not find in my

Elsewhere (Shotter, 2011, Chap.7), I have set out the more prominent features of the Cartesian common-sense that 'goes without saying' in spontaneous everyday thought and talk with each other, so I will not repeat that account in detail here. But there is one prominent feature that is crucial. Amongst the many pre-suppositions of especial importance to us within our current Cartesian common-sense, is the one that arose out of Descartes' resolve "to leave all these people [current theologians and philosophers] to their disputes" — that is, all the others in his surroundings at the time of his thinkings — and *to start afresh with his own deliberate thinkings*, thus to ignore what he already shared with them, i.e., to ignore the language he already shared with them making him, not only accountable to them, but able in fact to argue intelligibly with them.

The idea of a "tabula rasa" or "clean slate" has been with us for some two thousand years. It was first proposed by Aristotle, and later expanded upon by John Locke in his 1689 *Essay Concerning Human Understanding*. The idea is that we are born completely blank and we are free to shape our own individuality however we want; but it is Descartes' espousal of this notion, and its subsequent 'cementing' into our modernistic, and now neo-liberal, common-sense, that I need to question here.

We can easily see how he came to espouse it. As is well-known, while beginning his search for a foundational certainty from which to begin his thinking, he resolved "to pretend that nothing which had ever entered my mind was any more true than the illusions of my dreams" (p.53). But then he went on to realize that:

"... while I decided thus to think everything was false, it followed necessarily that I who thought thus must be something; and observing that this truth: *I think therefore I am*, was so certain and so evident that all the most extravagant suppositions of the sceptics were not capable of shaking it, I judged that I could accept it without scruple as the first principle of the philosophy I was seeking" (pp.53-54).

Thus it is that we end up with the pre-supposition, currently enshrined in the so-called "cognitive psychology" movement of the present day, that rather than our being primarily living beings, more like plants living in spontaneously responsive relations to our surroundings — in which we develop more as creatures of our environments than wholly as makers of them — we are primarily mechanistic bodies *animated by* our thinking minds. As he put it: "I have a clear and distinct idea of myself in so far as I am only a thinking and unextended thing, and

---

body a natural art of transforming it into an approaching view" (p.19) — my utterances always presuppose a larger context, an emergent shared setting, within which they *will be* understood.

because, on the other hand I have a distinct idea of the body in so far as it is only an extended thing but which does not think, it is certain that I, that is to say my mind, by which I am what I am, is entirely and truly distinct from my body, and may exist without it" (p.156).

I emphasize this, as this mistaken assumption lives on within us as the assumption that all innovative action begins, and must begin, with our thinkings, with our reflections, with our new 'good ideas' or 'theorizing', rather than with our deeds out in the world at large, rather than with any of our actually performed 'responses' to events happening to us[16]. This is because we assume that our deliberate thinkings are primary — and we are still following two major aspects of Descartes' (1968) deliberate thinking: (1) His fundamental belief that the world is essentially structured in a *mathematical* or *geometrical* fashion, thus rendering it amenable to being perfectly *representable* or *picturable* within a well-ordered, formal system of representative symbols; and (2) his instrumental, manipulatives aim in our following of his "methods," of "thereby mak[ing] ourselves, as it were, masters and possessors of nature" (p.78).

Starting our inquiries 'from within the midst' of our lives — participative or withness thinking

"My participative and demanding consciousness can see that the world of modern philosophy, the theoretical and theoreticized world of culture, is in a certain sense actual, that it possesses validity. But what it can see also is that this world is not the once-occurrent world in which I live and in which I answerably perform my deeds" (Bakhtin, 1993, p.20).

My major point in this writing, then, is that we cannot start our inquiries with theories, models, or principles, with reflections on the ways in which we *already* make sense of 'things'. Like Heidegger (1962, 1977), I want to distinguish between 'big B' *Being* and 'little b' *beings*, and to point out that we continually ignore the original openness and unfinishedness of world processes in general, and continually act as if all 'things' have already been determined and are simply awaiting our discovery of them.

Instead, I want to suggest, we must start with where we are now, immersed in 'big B' Being, with our usually, unnoticed, taken-for-granted, background ways of thinking and talking, and the *ways* in which they pick out for notice certain *dynamic stabilities* in the overall

---

[16] "The origin and primitive form of the language game is a reaction; only from this can more complicated forms develop. Language – I want to say – is a refinement, 'in the beginning was the deed'[Goethe]" (Wittgenstein, 1980a, p.31).

flow of activities within which we are immersed and have our being. It is really strange to say it, but our spontaneous, unconsidered ways of talking are much more basic than we have ever thought. Aristotle said it, Heraclitus said it (listen to the *Logos*), Vico said it, Heidegger said it, Gadamer says it, Merleau-Ponty says it, Wittgenstein says it.

But we far too often think that we can just think afresh, and lead everyone else to think in the new ways that we, as individual intellectuals, think is best, while being unaware that we are in fact 'working' to replace all the relations *already in existence* amongst us and everything else in our surroundings — what arrogance! Especially when there is no need to seek for an alternative, when we can, in fact, 'get in touch' with 'big B' Being *from within* the ongoing, unfolding dynamics of the *dialogically-structured* relations within which we are inescapably immersed in our everyday lives together — the 'background' from which our sense of all the 'little b' beings we come to be aware of can be drawn.

If getting in touch with 'big B' Being is not, to repeat, a task of reflection? What kind of task is it? It is a writing-task: Heidegger (1977), in his *Letter on Humanism*, puts it like this: "Language is the house of ['big B'] Being. In its home man dwells," he says, "Those who think and those who create with words are the guardians of this home. Their guardianship accomplishes the manifestation of ['big B'] Being insofar as they bring this manifestation to language and preserve it in language *through their saying*" (p.193, my italics).

I have emphasized that it is only *through their saying*, i.e., 'in' the unfolding dynamics of them *coming to say something* — not in the *content* of what they have *said* — that Heidegger feels that those writers who are to be the guardians of our 'at homeness' in 'big B Being', of our 'rootedness' in the actualities of our everyday lives, can arouse in us those particular 'movements of feeling' that can orient us towards it the precise ways needed to 'bring home' its nature to us.

Rather than in an illusory 'reality' of our own constructing, our task, then, is to seek to understand what we experience and perceive only in terms of what we experience and perceive, to understand 'it' in its own terms, rather than in terms of another, external, eternal, perfect, hidden world, in fact, of our own creation — to explain what is real for us only by what is real for us; the situated and time-bound only by the situated and time-bound; and our speaking only in terms of our speakings (not in terms of what is *said*).

That is, we must talk *from within* our actual lives as we are living them, rather than from *illusory* places outside them.

Switching to this new starting point in the *Logos*, in our everyday, spontaneously responsive *ways of speaking* and of *accounting* for ourselves to each other (Shotter, 1984) — *ways* of spontaneously responding learnt in the course of growing up into *this, that,* or *some other* linguistic culture — thus works to shift the whole 'centre of gravity' of social inquiry away from the general and eternal, to the particular and practical, to the situated and timely, away from a 'thin' practicality of satisfying an immediate *want* or *desire* to the 'thicker' practicality of 'doing justice' in one's actions to the 'requirements' of one's circumstances[17], with the need, always, to consider the overall human cost of our human attempts to better ourselves.

Instead of enclosing ourselves within our own preferred images of the world, our task now is to turn toward the actual world, the rich, before-the-fact, objective 'cosmos' that is shared in an embodied fashion by all within our languaged social group; it is, we might say, a crucial aspect of our *language-structured* or *discursive consciousness*[18].

Involved in doing this requires us to engage in what has been called "*participative thinking*" by Levy-Bruhl (1926) and Bakhtin (1993), and what elsewhere (Shotter, 2005b&c; Shotter 2011) I have called *withness*-thinking — the *relationally-responsive* kind of thinking and speaking we do spontaneously in our everyday conversations, in contrast to the kind of *aboutness*-thinking we do in *referential-representational* thought when talking philosophically or theoretically. Persons who can think "participatively," according to Bakhtin (1993), "know how not to detach their performed act from its product, but rather how to relate both of them to the unitary and unique context of life and seek to determine them in that context as an indivisible unity" (footnote p.19).

---

[17] As Steiner (1989) puts it, rather than merely offering an accurate, external, descriptive account of the observed 'properties' of a thing or circumstance, our task is that of being *answerable* to the thing or circumstance in question: "The authentic experience of understanding, when we are spoken to by another human being or by a poem, is one of responding responsibly. We are answerable to the text, to the work of art, to the musical offering, in a very specific sense, at once moral, spiritual and psychological" (p.8).

[18] Giddens (1984) distinguishes between what he calls discursive consciousness and practical consciousness: Discursive consciousness denotes the capacity of agents to 'give reasons' and to 'rationalize' their conduct, whereas practical consciousness refers to agents' 'stocks of unarticulated knowledge' that they use implicitly to orient themselves to situations and to interpret the acts of others.

In other words, it is a kind of thinking *from within* a particular flowing circumstance in which we open ourselves up to being 'moved' by that flow. Thus, an engaged encounter of this kind is not simply a matter of 'seeing' of objects, for what is sensed is in fact invisible; nor is it an interpretation (a representation), for it arises directly and immediately in the course of one's living encounter with an other's expressions; neither is it merely a feeling, for carries with it as it unfolds a bodily sense of the possibilities for responsive action in relation to one's momentary placement, position, or orientation in the present interaction.

In short, we can be spontaneously 'moved' toward specific possibilities for action in such a way of being. And this where another person's *words in their saying* can be helpful — in entering into our inner dialogues, they can help to orient us, help us to be responsive to what we might otherwise ignore: "Look at this, notice that, think about it this way..., and so on!"

In trying to come to a rich sense of the *before-the-fact*, already instituted, intra-woven form of objectivity, a holistic common-sense that provides to all the participants within it, a shared *sense of the circumstances* they are currently occupying, we can turn to Levy-Bruhl's (1926) account of *participative thinking*.

As he sees it, although primitive peoples live and act as we do, in an environment of beings and objects, besides the properties we also recognize them as possessing they are also imbued with *mystic* attributes. Their before-the-fact objective reality is mingled in with another reality: People feel themselves surrounded by countless other imperceptible entities of an awe inspiring nature that are invisible to sight. Levy-Buhl (1926) describes their nature of their experience thus:

"But the collective representations of primitives are not, like our concepts, the result of intellectual processes properly so called. They contain, as integral parts, affective and motor elements, and above all they imply, in the place of our conceptual inclusions or exclusions, participations which are more or less clearly defined, but, as a general rule, very vividly sensed. Why, for example, should a picture or portrait be to the primitive mind something quite different to what it is to ours? Whence comes that attributing of mystic properties to it, of whence we have just had an instance? Evidently from the fact that every picture, every reproduction 'participates' in the nature, properties, life of that of which it is the image" (p.79).

We shall examine the radical nature of *participative* or *withness* thinking, and its role in our more thick, already instituted, before-the-fact forms of everyday objectivity, more fully in the next chapter.

What is common to us all before we turn to 'the sciences' — the problem of fragmentation

2

"Since the days of Romanticism, the science of history, classical philology, and archaeology, the sciences of language, literature and art, comparative mythology, and the science of religion ... have conceived their task ever more precisely and have developed their specific instruments of thought and research with increasing finesse. But all these triumphs that knowledge was able to achieve within the course of a single century faced a serious lack and an internal defect. If research in each of these particular fields was able to progress inexorably, their inner unity had become all the more problematic. Philosophy was unable to maintain this unity and was unable to put a stop to the growing fragmentation." (Cassirer, 2000, pp.34-35).

"A philosophical problem has the form: 'I don't know my way about.'" (Wittgenstein, 1953, no.123).

"Since everything lies open to view there is nothing to explain. For what is hidden, for example, is of no interest to us./ One might also give the name 'philosophy' to what is possible *before* all new discoveries and inventions." (Wittgenstein, 1953, no.126).

Above, I tried to make the case for the existence of a unified, before-the-fact common-sense within which we are all immersed, that provides us with, as Austin (1970) put it, our *first words* in making a *shared sense* of events occurring to us. In drawing on such a shared sense, as Wittgenstein (1969) remarks: "*My life shows* that *I know or am certain* that there is a chair over there, or a door, and so on. — I tell a friend e.g. 'Take that chair over there', 'Shut the door', etc. etc." (no.7, my italics).

Indeed, in our everyday, spontaneous, unconsidered actions and utterances, such a shared, before-the-fact common-sense, allows us simply to *show in our lives* what some 'thing' *is* for us in our surroundings. Yet, although *I know, or am certain* that there a well-known *thisness* that stands before me, and that others will see it *as such* also, I also know that I can run into trouble in expressing my recognition of *what it means* for me, for the anticipatory tendencies aroused in my listeners by the words I use might very well go against their expected next steps. As Wittgenstein (1953) puts it: "If I need a

justification for using a word, it must also be one for someone else"
(no.378).

This means, of course, as well as being simply wrong in how I describe
'it', I can also find myself caught up in a *value*-controversy, i.e., a
controversy as to whether the particular *thisness* in question *qualifies* to
be described in the words *I* choose: For instance, although I 'see' what I
take to be a "chair" before me, my friend, a fashion conscious woman
whose 'taste' I respect answers me: "Call that a 'chair', it looks more like
a ramshackle assemblage of sticks and string to me!" In other words,
the fact is that *what* we see before us does not present itself to us with a
verbal name-tag already around its neck; the different ways in which we
word our descriptions of what we 'see', can *shape* both ours, and
other's subsequent actions and utterances, both ethically and politically
(as well as in a merely practical fashion), in relation to *what* we take our
experience to be.

So, although, as we shall see, our circumstances are always open to
being further articulated or specified in countlessly many differently
worded ways, they are not open to just any old further specifications,
for, as we will see when we turn to Saussure's (1911/1959) account of
language as a *system of similar differences* (without *positive* terms),
they can *only* be further specified in already specified terms[19].

This is where the tendency to *fragment* our holistic grasp on what
Cassirer (2000) calls our "cosmos" — the "objective order and
determinateness, [that] is readily available wherever different subjects
relate to a 'common world' and consciously participate in it" (p.13) —
begins. For, instead of *readying* ourselves to face the risky task
(ethically and politically) of moving around in an exploratory fashion
within the *particular* circumstance that is, initially, bewildering us, thus
to arrive at a *distinctively felt sense* of its 'thisness' (and not 'thatness'),
we find it all too easy to formulate for ourselves, ahead of time, a
rational schematism, a unambigous theoretical single order of
connectedness, that seems to us to *correspond with* crucial, objective
features out in the world before us. A move that enables us to avoid
stepping out into the still 'wild', 'open', and 'fluid' world, full of
unforeseeable, unclassifiable happenings, unfolding in time — a world
that is not yet an aspect of our cosmos, a world of *dynamic stabilities*
that we do not yet feel 'at home' in.

---

[19] With respect to making "distinctive differences" within the speech flow, Jakobson, R.,
Fant, G. and Halle, M. (1952) show how our skill at manipulating possibilities within our
vocal tract — such as touching the roof our mouth with our tongue, making our larynx
buzz, or pursing our lips, and so on — we can with a very limited number of such binary
features (between 8 & 15 differences) produce an uncountable number of speech
sequences.

As I remarked above, we feel we can 'tame' the always 'wild', 'unbounded', 'unfinished', 'incomplete', and 'still developing' existence of temporal events, by placing temporary boundaries around them, boundaries that allow temporal things and events to have, momentarily, for practical purposes, a unique, classifiable, i.e., nameable, wholeness to them. And the *practical value* of such a move is undeniable. Yet it is also undeniable that our urge for effective practical outcomes in our professional practices is leading to the fragmentation of our cosmos.

To appreciate this, we only have to consider the fact that there are now countless *social scientific disciplines* — listed either as *the science of ...X...*or as an *-ology* of one kind or another — each with their own precise forms of inquiry, and each with their own internal controversies as to *what* are their "proper objects of their study." And this profusion of separate sciences has emerged, and is still emerging, tainted by the classical Cartesian-Newtonian assumption of a mechanistic world, constituted of separate entities in motion according to pre-established laws or principles. Thus we still seem to assume — given the remarkable success of the natural sciences in enlarging the whole sphere of our practical activities — that we can begin our inquiries simply by reflecting on the world around us, by our *thinking* of possible ways in which it might be constituted, and by allowing our proposed conceptualizations to guide our actions in our inquiries (Shotter, 2015a).

But as Cassirer (2000) points out, although "research in each of these particular fields was able to progress inexorably, their inner unity had become [and is still becoming] all the more problematic. Philosophy was [and still is] unable to maintain this unity and was unable to put a stop to the growing fragmentation" (pp.34-35) — where a major consequence of this fragmentation is that, as I noted above, we ignore to our cost that fact that many of the events occurring around us are already *internally related*, both to each other, and to ourselves, and not just *externally related*, in terms of our own devising.

We thus end up by tying ourselves in knots of our own making, trying to *solve problems* that we ourselves have created in our attempts at *solving other problems* in our lives. We also end up producing professional groups of experts who, because of the *bounded* nature of their expertise and its associated well-defined vocabulary, find it difficult by the use of their words to arouse in lay listeners, or listeners from other professions, shared *structures of anticipation* as to how next to act in a particular current circumstance; we thus reach a situation in which people become separated from, and thus unfamiliar and distrustful of each other.

From thin idealizations to the emergence of thick bounded traditions

Kuhn (1970) gives an account of the preliminary symbolic work required prior to the establishment of a research tradition as follows: "Effective scientific research scarcely begins," he says, "before a scientific community thinks it has acquired firm answers to questions like the following: What are the fundamental entities of which the universe is composed? How do these interact with each other and with the senses? What questions may legitimately be asked about such entities and what techniques employed in seeking solutions?... Normal science,... is predicated on the assumption that the scientific community knows what the world *is like*" (pp.4-5, my italics). Only then can various sections of the scientific community move on from working with mere *similarities* (and *differences*), to more precise definitions and conceptual idealizations in their testing of specific theories.

But it would be a mistake to think that once a scientific community has achieved a more precise account of what it is that they are researching into, that they leave behind the vague background knowing from out of which their more precise accounts have emerged. For, in still specifying *what* the bounded field of 'entities' that we need to inquire into should *be like*, as Kuhn (1970) makes clear, different groups adopt different paradigms[20]. Thus, like the duck/rabbit illustration which we can see in two very different ways, we can also see indeterminate physical circumstances in a number of different ways. As Wittgenstein (1953) puts it with regard to such illustrations: Just as "we can also *see* the illustration now as one thing now as another. — So we interpret [notice an aspect of], and *see* it as we *interpret* it" (p.193, my addition), so we can also see events embedded in the larger 'flow of things' as open to different *interpretations* — thus as coming into existence as the result of a *synthetic* hermeneutical process, rather than of an abstract, *analytic* process.

Indeed, the still existing nature of larger background context became crucial in the circumstance in which Fleck (1979) — in seeking a solution to "the problem of how a 'true' finding can arise from false assumptions, from vague first experiments, and from many errors and detours?" — suggests, yet again, that it can, perhaps, "be clarified *by a comparison*" (p.79, my italics)[21].

---

[20] Leading to the arguments I mentioned above, as to *what is* the "proper object of their study."

[21] To repeat, *making comparisons* in coming to an understandings of otherwise an indeterminate circumstance, involves a hermeneutical, synthetic process quite different from an analytic one — it is not a matter to do with the properties of objects, but to do with their internal relations with other objects.

The comparison Fleck (1979) offers is with the rain falling here and there on the land, running into rivulets and streams, and then into rivers, so that in the end he asks: "How does it come about that all rivers finally reach the sea, in spite of perhaps initial flowing in a wrong direction, taking roundabout ways, and generally meandering? There is no such thing as *the sea as such*. The area at the lowest level, the area where the waters actually collect, is merely *called* the sea! *Provided enough water flows in the river and a field of gravity exists, all rivers must finally end up at the sea*. The field of gravity corresponds to the dominant and directing disposition, and water to the work of the entire thought collective. The momentary direction of each drop is not at all decisive. The [emergent] result derives from the general direction of gravity" (pp.78-79).

And he goes on to suggest that "the genesis and development of the Wassermann reaction [the overall topic of his book] can be understood in a similar way. Historically it too appears as the only possible junction of the various trains of thought. The old idea about the blood and the new idea of complement fixation merge, in a convergent development with chemical ideas and with the habits they induce to create a fixed point. This in turn is the starting point for new lines everywhere developing and again joining up with ethers. Nor do the old lines remain unchanged. New junctions are produced time and again and old ones displace one another. This network in continuous fluctuation is called reality or truth" (p.79).

These are most illuminating remarks: They suggest that, at the heart of a still developing practice — based in a hermeneutically-structured background that is coming to be embodied by all those within the "thought collective" that is in the course of developing a "tradition" — is a *shared way of working*. To repeat, as Fleck puts it: "The field of gravity corresponds to *the dominant and directing disposition*, and *water to the work* of the entire thought collective" (p.79, my italics). In other words, something very like a *gravitational field* provides practitioners with a 'felt meaning', a 'shaped and vectored sense' of how to move around within the field of their inquiries as they work within it, orienting them towards the attainment of their overall "interest" (Habermas, 1972) within it, or towards their "end in view" (Dewey, 1928, p.12, and Wittgenstein,1953, no.132).

In Bakhtin's (1986) terms, such 'works' or 'workings' give rise to unfinalized (and in fact, unfinalizable) *relationally-responsive, dialogicaly-structured understandings* (Shotter, 2010), not to an understanding of 'things' as self-contained objects, but to them as having particular *meanings*, as 'pointing beyond themselves' to other 'things within their surroundings', as having a specific function or use in relation to all else around them. Elsewhere (Shotter, 2005b&c; Shotter

2011), I have called the kind of *guided*-thinking in the face of indeterminacy to which such understandings can give rise, *withness-thinking*.

The creation of novelties, discontinuities, the unpredictable, and unforeseen

> "An utterance is never just a reflection or an expression of something already existing and outside it that is given and final. It always creates something that never existed before, something absolutely new and unrepeatable, and, moreover, it always has some relation to value ... What is given is completely transformed in what is created"
> (Bakhtin, 1986, pp.119-120, my italics)

> Hamlet: "There's a special providence in the fall of a sparrow. If it be now, 'tis not to come. If it be not to come, it will be now. If it be not now, yet it will come — the readiness is all"
> (Shakespeare, Hamlet, Act 5, Scene 2)

Thus, to the extent that all our everyday understandings, along with the 'works' to which they give rise, are produced in our dialogically-structured engagements with each other, their outcomes are not only unfinalized, and still open to further articulation, but are *novel* in the sense of having never existed before. This means that, although we may now feel that we have little use for "objective or calculated truths," for "fixed and finalized, thin truths," or for what we have in the past, we have been pleased simply to call "The Truth," the fact is, we now have *a major use* for the *still-in-evolution* realm of unfinalized, indeterminate, still open, shared, thick, Prospective Truths.

For, despite the fact that the events *emerging* in this realm of reality cannot be easily 'classified', 'categorized' or 'named' — because more often than not, they are of an utterly unforeseeable, and unforeseen, kind — 'truths' of this situated, 'before-the-fact' kind, can serve a shared *action guiding* function, enabling individuals within a group of inquirers, all to investigate a range of different possibilities within their field of studies, while still all, at the same time, intra-relating their activities to each other. For, as *emerging and emergent hermeneutical unities*, such before-the-fact Prospective Truths exists neither simply 'in the thoughts' of any of the individuals, nor as precisely defined 'objective things' out in their shared world. They exist amongst all the members as invisible "Real Presences" (Steiner, 1989, p.), as "felt meaning[s]" (p.9), or as action guiding "feelings of tendency" (James, 1890) which are at work in influencing the unfolding structure of all our intelligible actions as individual members of a "thought collective"

(Fleck, 1989).

As such, the particular hermeneutical unities we constitute here are not at all like the abstract generalities, defined in terms of a few distinctive features common to many instances; they are particular, holistic unities constituted from a collection of unmerged particularities, unities within which the particularities are internally-related to each other, or intra-linked, without losing their particularity.

A crucial implication of the fact that most of our everyday 'works' *emerge* from within our dialogically-structured activities, is that what we all too easily think of as a continuous, cause-and-effect, quantitative process of development, is nothing of the sort — instead, the process is marked by gaps, by discontinuous, quite unpredictable *qualitative* changes.

Vygotsky provides us with two good examples: (1) The child learning to write transforms speech utterly, in a way which seemingly 'disconnects' it from its origins: "In written speech, we are obliged to create the situation, to represent it to ourselves. This demands detachment from the actual situation" (Vygotsky, 1986, p.182) — we also exhibit this de-contextualizing or detachment from actual situations in our 'academic' or 'intellectual' forms of *speech*. (2) Another example is as a consequence of the child being explicitly taught *grammar* in school: "[The child] may not acquire new grammatical or syntactic forms in school but, thanks to instruction in grammar and writing, he does become aware of what he is doing and learns to use his skills consciously. Just as the child realizes for the first time in learning to write that the word *Moscow* consists of the sounds *m-o-s-k-ow* and learns to pronounce each one separately, he also learns to construct sentences, to do consciously what he has been doing unconsciously in speaking" (Vygotsky, 1986, p.184).

The point here is: No amount of investigation in biological or naturalistic terms will uncover the nature of our current linguistic abilities to talk in such a detached manner. But the point is also, that such discontinuities are, in fact, only apparent; they are functional. At each stage, what is transformed is the *imagined*, or the intra-linguistic context in terms of which we represent ourselves to ourselves. The fact is, the thick, before-the-fact, publicly shared, everyday objectivity remains 'on hand' in the background ready to be drawn upon if so required — and, as Wittgenstein (1953) puts it: "What *we* do is to bring words back from their metaphysical to their everyday use" (no.116).

In other words, to repeat, while objective truths are what we might call 'thin truths', consisting solely in a set of selected features, thought of as common to all the 'entities' described under a concept, what we could call *Prospective Truths*, 'thick truths' are very different. They consist in a whole set of *inexhaustible aspects* present in an unbounded region of a person's inner mental 'landscape', a region that can only be identified in terms of its placement *in relation to* that landscape as a whole. But, to the extent that such 'truths' are expressed in people's 'works' within a particular circumstance, they are organized into a unique structure of expressions that work to arouse in those to whom they are addressed, particular feelings of expectation which can guide them also in their talk and action in relation to that particular circumstance. And, as we get near to the overall ends such 'truths' aim at, we come to sense the possibility of a 'yet more', their ultimate unfinalizability.

I will return to this most important issue towards the end of this book: For it is all too easy to adopt an approach that stands in the way of our realizing that completely new acts and qualities can, and do, appear in the course of organic and human evolution; and that these qualities appear unpredictably, and can never be regarded as merely gradual developments of a previous state.

In other words, it is not that our usual methods of rational inquiry — beginning in our reflections on the nature of our current, after-the-fact, already 'realized' reality — leads us into offering a false and inadequate 'explanation' of them, but that it leaves us blind to such untoward and unexpected *happenings*; we simply do not know at all *how to see* them. And why this is of the utmost importance is because the *fragmentation* it produces in the *ways* in which we understand ourselves, leaves us 'out of touch' (see Chapter Seven) with *Eros*[22], with the life-giving, form-creating tendencies at work within our flowing-world at large — influences which, clearly, if we could recognize them for what they are, we would also recognize that we cannot explain or derive them from any pre-existing circumstances. They are *emergents*, and as such come into existence *unexpectedly*, *discontinuously*, and *unpredictably*. It is our blindness to, our unpreparedness for the occurrence of the unforeseeable, that we need to wake up to — what is its *meaning* for us?

Beginning to overcome the fragmentation — first steps

Beginning our inquiries in the retrospective, reflective manner required of us in our 'doing science', means, as we have already seen above, that we miss the fact that 'something else' altogether — *situation specific* movements of feeling related to situation-specific details — are actually

---

[22] Eros, the God of Love: Far too easily assimilated to what is *erotic* and *sexual*. However, here, I will be much more concerned with what Frankfurt (1998) calls "volitional necessities," ultimate values that we find ourselves to have adopted as a *part of ourselves*, that we cannot give up or betray without ceasing to be who we take ourselves to be.

guiding us in the performance of our actions. Due to their selective and exclusionary nature, our concepts and conceptualizations cannot offer *positive* guidance in relation to possible steps forward. They can, nonetheless, play a crucial role in our everyday activities: We can make use of our conceptualizations, from time to time, *negatively*, in *monitoring* or to *assessing* whether our actions are in fact, *in accord with*, what we know to be the legitimate *standards* of the day.

Such standards, clearly, are of great importance, but due to their *general*, abstract, after-the-fact and beside-the-point nature, they cannot function as a major shaping and guiding influence on our actual actions in *particular* circumstances. We need instead *before-the-fact*, hermeneutically-structured[23] inquiries that can 'set out' before us, the rich inner 'landscapes of possibilities' to think-with, and to provide action-guiding structures of anticipation, that can become available to us, *prior to* the more scientifically organized efforts we may make later in attempting to achieve socially desirable outcomes in particular socially shared situations.

As Wittgenstein (1953) notes in the epigraph quote above, the special kind of philosophical activity we require, needs to be conducted *before* we can turn towards any new discoveries or inventions. We need a grasp of the particular cosmos — of what Wittgenstein (1969) calls our *World-Picture* or *Weltbild* — that provides each of us, not with an unambiguous system of logically inter-connected, separately existing symbols representing states of affairs *in general*, within which one can 'calculate' outcomes, in terms of their *external* relations to one another. Instead, a *Weltbild* provides us with a particular, detailed inner sense of the *landscape of the livable lives* we can share with the others around us.

William James (1897/1956) describes very nicely, I think, what he calls "the three great continua in which for each of us reason's ideal is actually reached" (p.264) — the continua of memory or personal consciousness, with space and time being the other two. As he puts it: "In the realm of every ideal, we can begin anywhere and roam over the field, each term passing us to its neighbor, each member calling for the next, and our reason rejoicing in its glad activity. Where the parts of a conception seem thus to belong to each other by inward kinship, where the whole is defined in a way congruous with our powers of reaction, to see is to approve and understand ... In these great matrices [of space, time, and personal memory], we are absolutely at home. The things we meet are many, and yet are one; each is itself, and yet all belong

---

[23] See footnote 2 — in a *hermeneutical* process, we find a *particular meaningful whole* emerges from a set of particular fragmentary but nonetheless intra-connected experiences.

together; continuity reigns, yet individuality is not lost" (pp.264-265). These *great matrices*, *Weltbilden*, or *cosmoses*, sit in the background to all our spontaneously performed, taken-for-granted, practical activities; they provide, as Wittgenstein (1969) puts it, "the substratum of all my enquiring and asserting. The propositions describing it are not all equally subject to testing" (no.162) — indeed, the starting points for our inquiries are not, as we will see, hypotheses, but what I have already called above 'disquiets', events which call the matter-of-course, usually unmentioned foundation for our inquiries, into question.

Rather than problem-solving, then, our task is that of achieving a *resolution*, of bringing a particular determination to an otherwise, particular indeterminate situation, without losing its particularity. To do that, instead of immediately trying to analyse it into a set of smaller, more well-known[24] 'parts' or 'elements', we need to treat the *other* or *otherness* as a *being* that is still radically unknown to us; to come to 'know' it as the unique, unclassifiable being it is, we need to 'open' ourselves to being spontaneously 'moved' by it, to 'entering into' a living, dialogically-structured relationship with it.

In doing this, in becoming involved or engaged in an active, back and forth relationship with it — a relationship in which, if we go slowly, and allow time for the imaginative work that each response can occasion within us to take place — we can begin to gain a sense of the 'invisible landscape of possibilities' from within which the unique *other* confronting us, is drawing from in shaping their actions and utterances.

The process involved goes, I think, something like this: (1) We enter a new situation; (2) we are confused, bewildered, we don't know our way about; (3) however, as we 'dwell in' it, as we 'move around' within the confusion, a 'something', an 'it' begins to emerge;(4) it emerges in the 'time contours' or 'time shapes' that become apparent to us in the dynamic relations we can sense between our outgoing activities and their incoming results; (5) a *comparison* image or picture of what 'it' *is like* comes to us, we find that we can express this 'something' in terms of an image; (6) but not so fast, for we can find another, and another image, and yet another — Wittgenstein uses a city, a toolbox, the

---

24 Analysing a circumstance into a set of smaller, well-known, nameable 'parts' or 'elements' (expressible in symbols) makes the *data* relevant to a problem *known* prior to its solution — albeit, in the selective and reduced terms we take to be central to it being the situation it is for us. Whereas, in our task of *resolving* on a line of action to take in an at-first bewildering, particular circumstance, no *data* as such are available to us; but the fact is, as we come to find ourselves responding spontaneously to aspects of the situation in *this way* (but not *that*), do we begin to find that the circumstance itself, so to speak, is 'teaching' us how to 'see' it *as itself*, in all its particular, uncategorizable detail. As such, it is precisely unique, and can only be seen *as like* some 'thing' already well-known to us, but never as identical to such a 'thing' — see Shotter (2005c, 2010, & 2011) for an account of 'withness'-thinking as opposed to 'aboutness'-thinking.

controls in the driving cab of a train, and many different types of games, all as metaphors for different aspects of our experiences of the use of language.

The overall outcome of this step-by-step process of imaginative exploration is the achievement of what Wittgenstein (1953) calls "a perspicuous representation," where what is important is that instead of telling us of the *properties* of the 'parts' constituting the situation in question, it "produces just that understanding which consists in 'seeing connections'" (no.122) — in other words, it is a process aimed at bringing to light the always already existing *internal relations* at work within the contexts of our everyday practical activities — in Heidegger's (1962, 1977) terms, its aim is to put us in touch with 'big B' Being.

Merleau-Ponty (1968) expresses the special nature of this 'in touchness' with 'big B' Being as follows: A person does not just *live in* the world, "... he who sees cannot possess the visible unless he is possessed by it, unless he *is of it*, unless, by principle, according to what is required by the look of things, he is one of the visibles, capable of a singular reversal, of seeing them — he who is one of them" (pp.134-135). In other words, we too are both participants in, and partakers of, the world's differential becoming, and as such, not only are we creating *facts*, we are often also giving a determinate material form to what prior to our acting lacked any such determination — while, of course, what we determine acts back on us to shape in new ways our further actions.

Reversibility (that I will explore at length in Chapter Ten), is at the heart of what Merleau-Ponty (1968) wants to call his "endo-ontology" (p.226), i.e., our reciprocal, back-and-forth *way-of-being-in-the-world*, always on the way to somewhere else from where we are *now*. Moving on from a phenomenology of consciousness (of mere experiences) to a phenomenology of bodily-doings, he begins to realize that what is needed is to draw attention, not simply to *what is* experienced, but to the *experiencing* of what is experienced — for we need to describe the distinctive qualities that makes it 'nameable' as something distinct and *justifies* people's claims as to its nameable distinctness. It is precisely in virtue of my body being something touchable that I can touch another — and so on[25] — it is in the *reversibility* of our relations to our surroundings (in that we are *of* them, not just *in* them), that gives our body its special status in the world — that we can *know* it and *live* it *from within*.

---

[25] "The chiasm, reversibility, is the idea that every perception is doubled with a counter-perception (Kant's real opposition), is an act with two faces, one no longer knows who speaks and who listens. Speaking-listening, seeing-being seen, perceiving-being perceived circularity (it is because of it that it seems to us that perception forms itself *in the things themselves*) – Activity = passivity" (Merleau-Ponty, 1968, pp.264-265).

Our task is thus to avoid transgressing the *internal relations* already in place, by providing an instructive description of the larger, holistic, still flowing and developing context, within which our activities and utterances are to take place, and consequently, to take on a linguistic-value, a meaning, in relation to everything else in their surroundings.

In other words, to repeat, Wittgenstein (1953) wants us *to avoid* the fixings, the finalizings, the selections and exclusions that our *thin* forms of achieved objectivity impose on us currently in our inquiries, by placing our problematic circumstances within a *certain field of comparisons*, thus to see them within a much *thicker* form of objectivity, rich in possibilities, shared with all the others around us[26] — a crucial aspect of our possession of a *language-structured* or *discursive consciousness*. By working on the task of giving a linguistic expression to our *before-the fact* ways of making sense of our experiences, he wants to bring to light what our immediate urge to *explain* scientifically (mis)leads us into leaving in the dark, unmentioned, the *evidence* that we in fact make use of in that process, because of its unclassifiable[27] nature.

Next steps — from the allure of generalized conceptualizations in academic psychology to the acceptance of situated hermeneutical unities

> "And it is not enough that we have them before us as mere raw material. We must have penetrated their meaning; we must understand what they have to say to us. This understanding possesses its own method of interpretation: an independent and highly difficult and complex 'hermeneutics'... Generally considered it consists in determining the 'what' of each individual form of culture, the 'essence' of language, religion, and art. What 'is' and what does each of them mean, and what function do they fulfill? And how are language, myth, art, and religion related to one another? What distinguishes them and what joins them to each other?"
>
> (Cassirer, 2000, p.97)

---

[26] "I wanted to put that picture before him, and his *acceptance* of the picture consists in his now being inclined to regard a given case differently: that is, to compare it with *this* rather than *that* set of pictures. I have changed his *way of looking at things*" (Wittgenstein, 1953, no.144).

[27] He call such unclassifiable evidence, "imponderable evidence" (p.228). It includes, he says, "subtleties of glance, of gesture, of tone" (p.228), that clearly, we experience in our meetings with others, and make use of in determining how we will relate ourselves to them — whether we will be friendly or hostile, helpful or critical, etc.. But in each case, we must remember that we are in a *unique*, never-before-happening situation, thus as such, the sense we make of such *evidence* still requires our making use of comparisons.

Given the current organization, say, of academic psychology — in terms of a set of independently existing, chapter-heading, text-book topics to which we give such *names* as 'attention', 'perception', 'cognition', 'motivation', 'personality', developmental psychology', 'abnormal psychology', and so on — with each one defined and/or conceptualized precisely in terms of *sequences of written words*, there is no doubt that we are being asked to see such 'topics' as existing quite separately and independently of each other. There is, however, a difficulty: We can find that many of the crucial words used in defining or conceptualizing the topic in question are also used as specialized nouns or nominalizations, i.e., as *names* 'standing for' (or representing) pre-existing 'things', that play a crucial part in constituting *what*, essentially, overall, the topic in question *is* (see Billig, 2013)[28]; and the question we now face is whether the *meaning* of *these* words, should be understood in their flexible, everyday, contextualized sense, *or whether also they need a special, precise, context-free definition?*

Given this lack of clarity, and the potential oscillation between their flexible, everyday and their pre-established technical meanings, it is somewhat obvious that sooner or later, such definitions and conceptualizations are going to be found wanting in our efforts at trying to satisfy our everyday needs in terms of such 'thin', un-situated understandings.

For instance, among the terms used to describe 'perception' *theoretically*, we find a number of other words, such as 'recognition', 'interpretation', 'sensory information', 'environment', 'interaction', 'meaningful', and so on, which, in providing us with a sense of the particular *theory of perception* in question, are all internally-intra-related within the boundaries of the proposed relevant conceptual scheme. As academic investigators, we thus cannot just go on to use the word 'perception' anymore, in the way that we might use it as a lay person in our everyday talk. Indeed, until we have come to a sense of what the written statements composed of word-sequences *mean as a whole*, we cannot say precisely what the word 'perception' means in itself (i.e., 'stands for' or represents) in the proposed theory — for strangely, within the boundaries of a conceptual scheme, as we shall

---

[28] As Billig (2013) shows, "the big concepts which many social scientists are [currently] using — the 'ifications' and the 'izations' — are poorly equipped for describing what people do. By rolling out the big nouns, social scientists can avoid describing people and their actions. They can then write in highly unpopulated ways, creating fictional worlds in which their theoretical things, rather than actual people, appear as the major actors. The problem is that, as linguists have shown, using nouns and passive sentences is a way to convey less, not more, information about human actions" (p.7) — indeed, we can also add that the *common-sense* background needed for determinate meanings to be given to our use of everyday words has also been eradicated.

see[29], each word does not have a meaning in itself, but most importantly, it has its meaning only in terms of the differences it makes in relation to all the other words of significance within the conceptual scheme.

We thus cannot, in academic psychology, first learn what 'perception' *is*, and then go on to discover empirically its relations to what we call 'recognition' or 'sensory information', as if we already know precisely *what* 'recognition' and 'sensory information', as explicit 'things' in themselves, *are* — although in our conceptualizations of perception it is, of course, assumed that we already know the many different *meanings* of these terms in our everyday *uses* of them. Instead, it would seem, if we are to persist with a theory-driven approach in the cultural sciences, the meaning of all three terms must first be learned together as 'parts' of a whole new way of orienting or relating ourselves to that aspect of a person's behaviour that we call perception — a point that is unfortunately obscured by our failure to fully recognize the degree to which we make use of what elsewhere (Shotter, 2011) I have called our everyday *relationally-responsive* usage of words in later *formalizing* our special *representational-referential* use of them in our theorizing.

In other words, in constituting within ourselves a sense of *what is* the subject matter of our inquiries, we must first undertake, essentially, the kind of imaginative hermeneutical exploration described above — an undertaking that could be, but is not yet, institutionalized as a recognized aspect of all our professional practices.

What currently stops this from happening? The present structure of our discursive consciousness, and the currently amazing success of science and technology at providing many seeming 'solutions' to our everyday, practical problems.

But, to repeat, in our not being *discursively aware* — aware of the *performative* function of our everyday, taken-for-granted talk, and how it can in fact shape our actions by creating illusory anticipations of our own devising as to what *should* follow from it — we enclose ourselves within boundaries of our own making. As a result, in thinking that our talk (by providing *representations*, by our words simply *standing for*

---

29 At issue here, as we will see, is what later I will explore under the heading of particular 'hermeneutical unities'. Such particular, holistic, hermeneutical unities emerge, for instance, in our reading, say, of a good novel. As it unfolds, each fragment of text begins to inter-link with previous already read fragments to arouse within us, not only a sense of 'what has happened so far', but also a 'structure of anticipations' as to what might be coming next — such that, if none are satisfied, and something else altogether happens, we are somewhat surprised. And further, once we come to its end, we can not only answer questions as to what, overall, the novel was 'about', but countless particular questions relating to the characters and times and places depicted, but also their relations to each other, and so on.

things) just tells us 'the way things are', we ourselves create artificial problem-situations, by ignoring all pre-existing internal relations. We can then make things even worse by then turning to trying to solve these artificial problems, when in fact, no such problems existed prior to our abstract, *aboutness*-talk as what we *thought* were the properties of the elements constituting the initial 'problematic' situation we faced.

As I made clear, I hope, above, rather than problem-solving, our task is that of achieving a *resolution*, of bringing a particular determination to an otherwise, particular indeterminate situation, without losing its particularity. To do that, we need to 'open' ourselves to being spontaneously 'moved' by it, to 'entering into' a living, dialogically-structured relationship with it. And this is what is needed, if we are ever to come to get a grasp of what actually it is to be a human being, to being a human person, to be a human *bio-social becoming* (Ingold & Palsson, 2013).

What actually is it to be a human being?

In turning now to our task of trying to arrive at an organized sense of *what it is to be* a fully human person in relation to all the other human persons around us, we can begin by drawing upon the knowledge we have already come to possess from our myriad involvements with them in the course of our everyday lives so far. We need to construct an account of our personal being in the ordinary sense of the term account[30], as simply a narration of a circumstance or a state of affairs which, in its telling 'moves' us this way and that over or through the current 'terrain' of personhood, so to speak, sufficiently for us to gain an 'inner sense' of it as a whole, even though we lack a vantage point from which to view it — it is a view or a sense 'from the inside', much as we get to know the street-plan of a city, by living and moving about within it, rather than from seeing it all at once from an external, 'up-in-the air' standpoint[31]. It is a grasp which allows us to 'see', or at least to 'sense',

---

[30] As I put it in Shotter (1984): "Accounts can be distinguished from theories in that an account is an aid to perception, functioning to constitute an otherwise indeterminate flow of activity as a sequence of recognizable events, i.e. events of a kind already well-known within a society's ways of making sense of things. While theories, on the other hand, are not concerned with activities and events as they *are*, but are cognitive devices in terms of which we can reshape and reproduce events, which already make one kind of sense to us, and act and talk of them in terms quite different from what ordinarily they seem to be. Further, while theories are of use to third-person outsiders, to those unconcerned with the personal situation of first and second persons, and thus may be (to an extent) context-free and impersonal, and couched in terms of generalities; accounts are addressed to second persons involved in a situation with first persons, and thus need to be both context-dependent and personal, and couched in terms of particularities of relevance in the situation" (p.4).

[31] See William James' (1897/1956) account above of what such a holistic grasp of a hermeneutical unity can be like: "We can begin anywhere and roam over the field, each

all the different aspects of what it is to be a person amongst others, as if all arrayed out in relation to each another, within an 'inner landscape' in which no single standpoint is central to any other.

Achieving such a comprehensive sense, as Gadamer (2000) puts it, is a *hermeneutical* achievement: "... the subject matter appears truly significant only when it is properly portrayed for us. Thus we are certainly interested in the subject matter, but it acquires its life only from the light in which it is presented to us. We accept the fact that the subject presents different aspects of itself at different times or from different standpoints. We accept the fact that these aspects do not simply cancel one another out as research proceeds, but are like mutually exclusive conditions that exist by themselves and combine only in us" (p.284). For, as Gadamer sees it, the hermeneutical process involved here is not just one of the possible, deliberate mental 'doings' of a subject — as when we read a text, say, with a particular aim in mind — but is our very mode of being-in-our-everyday-world as we move about within it in a responsive manner[32], spontaneously 'shaping' our movements to 'fit into' what we sense as the 'demands' or 'requirements' of our circumstances.

It is, we might say, a kind of thinking that just comes to happen within us spontaneously — and as such, provides the basis for the more deliberate thinking that we, as individuals, can do[33] — a kind of thinking that is spontaneously 'done' by all those within a social group who have all come to share in learning a common language. As such, the basic hermeneutical unities they constitute amongst themselves here are not at all like the abstract generalities, defined in terms of a few distinctive features common to many instances, that certain members of such group might later formulate for their own particular purposes within the group. Nor are they at all like mechanical, or logical forms of order, consisting in a single, systematic order of connectedness, or objective

---

term passing us to its neighbor, each member calling for the next ... Where the parts of a conception seem thus to belong to each other by inward kinship, where the whole is defined in a way congruous with our powers of reaction" (pp.264-265).

[32] "Heidegger's temporal analytics of Dasein has, I think, shown convincingly that understanding is not just one of the various possible behaviors of the subject but the mode of being of Dasein itself. It is in this sense that the term hermeneutics' has been used here. It denotes the basic being-in-motion of Dasein that constitutes its finitude and historicity, and hence embraces the whole of its experience of the world" (Gadamer, 2000, p.xxx).

[33] As Merleau-Ponty (1962) comments: "Every perception takes place in an atmosphere of generality and is presented to us anonymously. I cannot say that *I* see the blue of the sky in the sense in which I say that I understand a book or again in which I decide to devote my life to mathematics. My perception, even when seen from the inside, expresses a given situation: I can see blue because I am *sensitive* to colours, whereas personal acts create a situation: I am a mathematician because I have decided to be one. So, if I wanted to render precisely the perceptual experience, I ought to say *one* perceives in me, and not that I perceive..." (p.215).

frameworks. They are particular unities constituted from collections of unmerged particularities, unities within which the particularities are intra-linked with each other, or internally-related to each other, without losing their particularity. Further, to the extent that they are drawn from people's expressions in particular circumstances, they are organized into unique structures of particular *feelings of anticipation or expectation* that can 'work' in guiding all of us in our attempts[34] to speak and to act meaningfully in relation to similar such circumstances.

On the need to raise our 'practical consciousness' into our 'discursive consciousness'

If we are asked: 'What actually is it to be a person?', we cannot give any final, definitive answers; yet the fact is, we can give a whole collection of partial answers: 'To be a human being', 'To have speech', 'Not to be like a wild animal', and so on. The fact that we cannot give a short, synoptic definition or conceptual statement that captures in a unified fashion the essential *essence* of *what* actually it is for us to be a person, leaves us facing total disorientation when told, for instance, to *respect* or to *care* for other people: what *actually* is our respectful activities or caring activities supposed to achieve in our relations to the others around us, why do such activities matter?

Like St Augustine's famous remark about time: "What then is time? If no one asks me, I know what it is. If I wish to explain it to him who asks, I do not know," we are in the same predicament. Clearly, we have an enormous amount of knowledge of *what* a person *is*, along with a sense of the countless similarities to, and differences from, all the other 'things' around us that we might compare a *person* with — for we have no trouble at all in *using* the word with some precision in a variety of everyday contexts — while at the same time, bringing a whole array of other words into appropriate relations with it. And, as Wittgenstein (1969) makes clear, that capacity is exhibited over and over again in many of our untroubled everyday, spontaneous practical acts of speaking and doing; it is only in our more *deliberate* activities, in which are trying to relate ourselves to a fellow being in solely in selected, general terms, that we can find ourselves in trouble (accused of *insulting* or *disrespecting* them for treating them as an *object* rather than as a person).

As Giddens (1984) makes clear, knowing something in our 'practical consciousness' is not to know how to bring it into our 'discursive consciousness', and thus to raise what we can do *spontaneously* into

---

34 Hermeneutical unities cannot provide us with any *certainty* in guiding our actions; their function is to provide us with a sense of the *anticipated consequences* of our actions; the 'point' of our intended actions shows up in what we are *trying* to do.

something we can set out to do *deliberately*. In other words, there is something special in our *ways of acting* out in the world as a member of a socio-linguistic-cultural group with a history to it, i.e., as a person, that is quite different from our being merely a living organism, and utterly different from our being a material mechanism. Yet it seems next to impossible for us to place all our fragments of knowledge of what is to be a person, within the same inner, mental landscape, enabling us to gain an explicit grasp of the function and meaning of each fragment in terms of their relations to each other.

As I see it, this fact has not been at all sufficiently appreciated in our so-called 'objective, scientific' inquiries within the human and behavioural sciences today. In ignoring, not simply the fact of our, mostly, untroubled *use of words*, but also the fact that, as James (1890) puts it, "large tracts of human speech are nothing but *signs of direction* in thought, of which direction we nevertheless have an acutely discriminative sense, though no definite sensorial image plays any part in it whatsoever" (vol.1, pp.252-253), we fail to recognize that in our very speaking and acting, we spontaneously arouse within ourselves a *sense* of 'where next' we should be trying to go in our actions.

Indeed, being aware of what a person is saying, and using that awareness to *sense* what they will say next, what their 'point' is, is a process with which we are all familiar; indeed, as listeners, we can often 'fill in' speaker's next words for them, when they themselves falter. Yet, because of their unique, dynamical, step-by-step, unfolding, transitional nature, we lack an established vocabulary within which to refer to them; we thus refer them as merely *subjective* when in fact such a *sense* is clearly shared[35], and basic to our capacity to understand each other's speech. Clearly, something of very great importance is being missed here.

We also miss the fact that we 'measure up', so to speak, each step we take towards our overall goal in our actions against an "anticipatory intention" (p.253) which, in functioning as an 'inner compass', guides us towards that goal, while also, at each step, relating us *uniquely* to our current circumstances. Failing to notice this, we instead feel — precisely because of their *situated uniqueness* and their pre-conceptual, unnameable nature, along with our assumption that all these 'inner things' *are merely subjective variants of, in fact, more basic objective entities* — that we need to conduct our inquiries within the boundaries of a causal/mechanistic *theoretical* framework (or at best a

---

35 Further, I will talk of the primacy of what I will call *before-the-fact*, objectively shared, "Real Presence[s]" (Steiner, 1989, p.3) or "necessary possiblit[ies]" (p.3), in possession of which we can become "executants of felt meaning[s]" (p.9) intelligible to all the others around us (Shotter, 2003).

living/organic one), if we are to be properly 'scientific' in the conduct of our inquiries, if we are to arrive at 'objective' results that can be shared in by all. But this is to base our inquiries in what is secondary and parasitic for us as members of a social group, sharing a form of life along with its associated language.

We fail to recognize that we must already be living in a world in common with the others around us, prior to some of us forming a special social group of people all oriented toward a sphere of human activity in particular, or else the forming of such groups would be impossible. We would all be speaking at cross purposes, unable to coordinate our own individual actions with those of the others in the group. We thus invent 'theoretical frameworks', 'systems of thought', 'perspectives', etc., for ourselves to *think-within*, when in fact, as Wittgenstein (1953) makes clear, if only we could come to a grasp of the *ways of sense making* already existing in common amongst us, this would be quite unnecessary — although, as we shall see, the immediate practical advantage of our working within such clearly *bounded* spheres of activity provides us with a very strong incentive for working in this way. In the next chapter, we must go further in exploring this issue: what actually is the nature of our humanness, our nature as human bio-social becomings, such that we can — with the help of the others around us — raise our 'practical consciousness' into our 'discursive consciousness', thus to do *deliberately* what at first we can only do *spontaneously*.

3 On our nature as personal beings, as bio-social becomings

"That modern psychology has projected an image of man which is as demeaning as it is simplistic, few intelligent and sensitive non-psychologists would deny.... The mass dehumanization which characterizes our time — the simplification of sensibility, homogenization of experience, attenuation of the capacity for experience — continues apace. Of all fields in the community of scholarship, it should be psychology which combats this trend. Instead, we have played no small role in augmenting and supporting it."

(Koch, 1964, p37-38)

"Every sign *by itself* seems dead. *What* gives it life? — In use it is *alive*. Is life breathed into it there? — Or is the *use* its life?"

(Wittgenstein, 1953, no.432)

Above, I suggested that we cannot achieve the kind of understandings of our everyday 'works' that we seek, by a recourse to *traditional scientific methods alone*, i.e., just by the use of theory-based and/or theory-driven methods. The reasons I gave many years ago (in Shotter, 1975), were that, although modern psychology promised to discover our true nature in its experimental laboratories, in fact it only investigated there what happens when people were, or still are, treated *as if* they are rats, machines, information processors, or some other non-human entity out in the world around us, while the fact of our being responsible for the creation and sustaining of our own human nature — as *persons* living within a *culture* with a long developmental *history* to it — was, and still is, often ignored. Concerned just with solving what, *prima facie*, were taken to be 'psychological' problems, such *similarities* often seemed quite sufficient to provide, at least partially, 'reason-based solutions', where previously mere opinion had prevailed. Thus, the idea of us as persons, as beings living in relation to all the others and othernesses around us, capable of creating in our 'works' so many different ways of actualizing and expressing amongst ourselves our humanness, did not then seem to be needed, and often now, still does not seem to be needed as a central focus in the so-called mainstream social and behavioural sciences[36]. Little attention was paid to the fact of our own activities exerting an influence *in our lives*.

---

[36] A clear exception is *Relational Being: Beyond Self and Community* by Kenneth J. Gergen, Oxford University Press, 2009.

On our coming to possess mental functions in the first place

Yet, even then, it was clear that there was, and still is, a major defect in this approach. As I put it then: Although as natural scientists we are attempting "to discover the nature of things independently of any responsibility that we might have for their behaviour... when we turn this endeavour round upon ourselves, when we attempt to discover our own nature independently of any responsibility that we might have here for our own behaviour, the result is absurd... [For] in our study of ourselves we want to understand in what way we can be[37] responsible for our own behaviour" (Shotter, 1975, pp.68-69). Indeed, to go further, as living beings, "it is only because we can sense, when acting in accord with theories of what the world might be like, whether the results of our actions accord with or depart from the expectations engendered by [a theory], that we can ever put such theories to empirical test... If people were unable to distinguish between what happened as a result of their intentional activity and what just happened, by itself, there would be no basis for scientific inquiries at all... Our sense of our own responsibility is, then, not only a central part of everyday life — it is at the very heart of science itself, and is quite irreplaceable. Scientists without any sense of their own functioning would be unable to do experiments" (pp.86-87).

But how is it that we can become responsible for our own behaviour? The developmental thesis I want to explore here is drawn, primarily, from Vygotsky (1986); as he puts it: "The general law of development says that awareness and deliberate control appear only during a very advanced stage in the development of a mental function, after it has been used and practiced unconsciously and spontaneously. In order to subject a function to intellectual and volitional control, we must first possess it" (p.168). And as I outlined it a while ago (Shotter, 1984, p.69, p.73-74), the process seems to involve the need for another person — someone other than the children themselves, who have enough to do in monitoring their own speech for its *meaning* — who not only can observe the child's *speech forms* and draw a child's attention to them by 'naming' them, but also by, sometimes, also 'spelling them out': **Child**: (around 12-18 months, pointing toward an animal) "Moo-moo." **Mother:** "Yes, 'moo-moo'... it's a "cow," a 'cee-oh-double-u', "cow"!... Now you say it (pointing at the cow): "a cow"!

The service of both reflecting back to one, *the forms* employed in one's *spontaneously* performed actions, and of elaborating them further — thus to treat one's continuously flowing action as a sequence of 'named'

---

[37] I now realize that I should have written that "we want to understand in what way *we can become* responsible for our own behaviour."

and thus 'representable events'— can be provided *only by another person* who is currently, so to speak, 'in touch with' ones intentions, who can *sense* what one is trying to do in ones reachings, pointings, and clutchings, a service that is essential if one's performance is to be later structured into 'components' or 'episodes' which one can, as a set of 'named entities', arrange and rearrange, *deliberately*, as one pleases. Indeed, it is only as we move from a 'practical consciousness' to a 'discursive consciousness', that the possibility of placing our problematic circumstances within a *certain field of comparisons* becomes available to us, thus to see them within a much *thicker* form of objectivity shared with all the others around us — a crucial aspect of our being able to *think-about* and *intend* mentally an action before performing it, deliberately, in practice.

So above, while I was critical of the fact that in the social and behavioural sciences, we continually make use of what I called our everyday *relationally-responsive* usage of words in *conceptualizing* or *formalizing* them in our special *representational-referential* uses of them in our theorizing, here instead, I want to emphasize how important this process is in our becoming able to talk and to act in a deliberate fashion in the rest of our everyday activities. Indeed, it is a major aspect of what is involved in our becoming autonomous, self-determining individuals, able to act as *we* require, rather than our always responding spontaneously in terms of what *our circumstances* 'call out' from us. Further, rather than merely responding spontaneously to the expressions others address to us, we can also learn from them *reasons* for not doing so, for acting towards them on the basis of our own deliberations — for in noting how others have 'replied' to our actions in the past, we can begin to institute a sense of how best it might be to act towards the others before us now. Acting in the knowledge of the socio-cultural consequences of one's actions, rather than simply 'on impulse', is a crucial aspect of one coming to be able to act *prudently*[38].

But all this still leaves unexamined, in the background, the first spontaneously expressed learning exhibited by the child in the course of their engaged, participatory immersion in the many everyday streams of intra-activity occurring around them — their initial calling of cows, 'Moo-moos', for instance.

Indeed, much more is going on between them and all the others and othernesses around them, than them merely learning, as Helen Keller (1990) once put it, as the result of an incident at a water pump, that "everything has a name" (p.15). If we read her account of the incident

---

[38] "... it is thought to be the mark of a prudent man to be able to deliberate rightly... [about] what is conducive to the good life generally" (Aristotle, 1955, p.209).

more fully, we find that at first, the word 'water' finger-spelled into her hand *could not* represent or stand for water as some *already well-defined stuff*, because "earlier in the day, we had had a tussle over the words 'm-u-g' and 'w-a-t-e-r'," she said, "Miss Sullivan had tried to impress upon me that 'm-u-g' is *mug* and that 'w-a-t-e-r' is *water*, but I persisted in confounding the two" (p. 16). Thus at first, she simply did not know *what* that indeterminate 'stuff' *was* that she could feel with her hands.

Her coming to an understanding of it *as* water was clearly a process of a much more hermeneutical, part-whole kind, of being able to 'place' that vague stuff within a whole web of internal relationships as a unique *thisness*, a unique *presence*, in relation to all the other unique *thisnesses* already known to her — she not only became acquainted with it as a 'some-thing' called *water* (but not called *mug*), but much more than this happened to and within her.

Earlier, she had described herself as if "at sea in a dense fog, ... as if a tangible white darkness shut you in... without compass or [depth] sounding-line, [with] no way of knowing how near the harbour was" (pp. 14-15); but after this experience, as the dense white darkness of the fog within her began to lift, and with her strange new sight, she began to understand how to 'move around' within the sea in which she had at first felt 'shut in'. And even more: On learning how words are used by others in a similar fashion, to open up *ways* of moving around in a world shared with others, as she put it: "The beautiful truth burst upon my mind — I felt that there were invisible lines stretched between my spirit and the spirit of others" (p. 22) — her knowing became a *con-scio* knowing, a witnessable knowing along with others (Shotter, 2005a). Rather than being 'lost at sea', 'shut in' without a compass or sounding-line, she began to feel *oriented*, she felt she could begin to *navigate*, imaginatively, within an *open* and *shared in common* sea of worldly 'things' and other people.

Getting oriented — entering into a common-sense

So what was it that Annie Sullivan was 'doing' with Helen Keller in her *personal relationship* with her, that was quite different from teaching her to think deliberately, but basic to teaching her the *proper use* of words? If we return to that basic orienting quote of Vygotsky's (1986): "... that awareness and deliberate control appear only during a very advanced stage in the development of a mental function, after it has been used and practiced unconsciously and spontaneously... [that] to subject a function to intellectual and volitional control, we must first possess it" (p.168), we might find it useful to accept that, at first, we exhibit our possession of a particular mental function only in our everyday, spontaneously responsive, practical activities, when involved in activities with the others around us. And what we can first learn from those around us, is to recognize and move around in relation to 'things' and to the other people around us as *they do* in *their* everyday practices — for such practical recognitions cannot be taught us at this stage by them trying to teach us propositions or by offering us facts formulated linguistically.

Thus we can suggest that what Annie Sullivan is doing — in this early stage of helping Helen to communicate linguistically, in a way that enables her later, to say explicitly: "This is an X (but not a Y)" — is enabling her at this early stage to come to know, *implicitly in her bodily activities*, what X-ness and Y-ness feels like. And this capacity to orient towards the distinctive, unfolding 'movements of feeling' that characterize the particular what-ness of things' in our surroundings for us, thus enabling us to act towards them in the same manner as those around us do so, is crucial to Helen coming to participate in a similar "form of life" to the adult Annie Sullivan.

In other words, as Wittgenstein (1953) puts it, if people are not to pass each other by, and to continually mis-direct the others they address in their talk, it is a matter of them agreeing with those others, "in the *language* they use. That is not agreement in opinions but in *form of life*" (no.241, my emphasis), and he goes on to remark: "If language is to be a means of communication there must be agreement not only in definitions *but also (queer as this may sound) in judgments*. This seems to abolish logic, but does not do so. — It is one thing to describe methods of measurement, and another to obtain and state results of measurement. But what we call 'measuring' is partly determined by a certain constancy in results of measurement" (no.242, my emphasis).

As a mental function, what we call or count as 'measuring' — our comparing something up against something that, in Wittgenstein's (1969) terms, "stands fast" (no.144) for us — is a mental skill that we can come to develop in the course of using an "object of comparison" (Wittgenstein, 1953, no.131) in gaining a sense of its similarities to, and differences from that comparison object. As Vico (1968) puts it, in making such comparisons as those around us do, we are also sharing a *way of sensing*, of *making sense*, with those around us, where: "Common-sense [*sensus communis*] is judgment without reflection, shared by an entire class, an entire people, an entire nation, or the entire human race" (para 142, p.63). Thus, coming to be able to *judge* that this is indeed like an X and not like a Y, is something we can acquire in the course of our spontaneous involvements with those around us, where such shared judgments can both 'set the scene' for our unproblematic talk, while also becoming, sometimes, topics in our more problematic talk.

Coming to think in this way, spontaneously, is something a 'good enough' mother (Winnicott, 1988) can teach us, also spontaneously, in the course of her being attentive to what she senses as our 'needs', the unsatisfied tensions she can perceive us as feeling in the incipient intentions she can see us as *trying* to execute, as she feeds, comforts, plays, and otherwise actively interacts with us[39]. (1) It is our 'tryings' (and 'failings') that are important to her at this early stage in our development, the non-linguistic expressions manifested in our bodily wrigglings, our facial expressions, vocal gurgles, and laboured breathing, not our actual achievements. (2) While at a much later stage, being able to reflect back to us *the forms* we employ in our *spontaneously* performed successful actions, and to elaborate them further, is a help towards our being able to think *deliberately*[40].

Thus, if we seek to go back to the earliest stages of consciousness, to the view that the world is initially experienced as a chaos of unordered sensations, consisting simply in simple objective qualities such as light or dark, warm or cold, spots of colour, fragments of lines, etc., we find it clearly untenable. As Winnicott makes very clear, infants are interested in human faces as early as the middle of the first year, it is not difficult to establish the effect of the parents' facial expressions on the child. Rather than merely a flux of chaotic sensations of lines and colour, of light and dark, changing with every movement of the mother or the child, by the middle of the first year, the child is reacting to a friendly or an angry face, and in such a different way that there is no doubt that the effect is immediate and spontaneous, not something that the child has to 'work out' by a mental effort. Clearly, such phenomena as "friendliness" or "unfriendliness" are extremely primitive[41] — much more primitive than that, say, of discriminating between triangles and squares. Yet, for some reason we persist in thinking that this is not so, that we must 'work out' what we see in people's expressive movements,

[39] As Winnicott (1988) puts it, a mother communicates to her baby: "I am reliable — not because I am a machine, but because I know what you are needing; and I care, and I want to provide what you need. This is what I call love at this stage of your development" (p.97).

[40] Winnicott (1988) states the nature of these two stages, and their relation to each other, very nicely: "... from these silent communications we can go over to the ways in which the mother makes real just what the baby is ready to look for, so that she gives the baby the idea of what it is that the baby is just ready for. The baby says (wordlessly of course): 'I just feel like...' and just then the mother comes along and turns the baby over, or she comes with the feeding apparatus and the baby becomes able to finish the sentence: '... a turn-over, a breast, nipple, milk, etc., etc.' We have to say that the baby created the breast, but could not have done so had not the mother come along with the breast just at that moment. The communication to the baby is: 'Come at the world creatively, create the world; it is only what you create that has meaning for you'. Next comes: 'the world is in your control'" (pp.100-101).

[41] See my later reference to Koffka (1921), who points out the very early differential reactions of children to such expressions, long before they attend to a blued spot.

in the same way that we must make an effort to 'interpret', to make determinate as 'things', other aspects of the ceaseless flux of our experience. Why is this?

From enclosing ourselves within self-imposed boundaries to 'opening-up' to the world itself

Although judgments such as "friendliness" and "unfriendliness," spontaneously have a 'life of their own', so to speak, in our everyday life activities — in that they can 'call out' from us many different ways of responding to them — they cannot be defined in purely *formal* terms, i.e., in terms of similarities of 'spatial shape', they are thus vague, subjective, and not publicly identifiable in undisputable terms; in short, it is assumed that they cannot be properly *objective*.

Descartes (1968), in despair at the lack of any such agreed ways of 'going on' in human affairs, decided to start again from scratch, and in his *Discourse on the Method of Properly Conducting One's Reason and of Seeking Truth in the Sciences* of 1637, proposed to conduct all his *reasoning* as if he was doing geometry — for as he saw it then, in geometry there does seem to be some basic *certainties* of a general kind[42]: "Thus, for example, I very well perceived that, supposing a triangle to be given, its three angles must be equal to two right angles, but I saw nothing, for all that, which assured me that any such triangle existed in the world; whereas, reverting to the examination of the idea I had of a perfect Being, I found that existence was comprised in the idea in the same way that the equality of the three angles of a triangle to two right angles is comprised in the idea of a triangle or, as in the idea of a sphere, the fact that all its parts are equidistant from its centre, or even more obviously so; and that consequently it is at least as certain that God, who is this perfect Being, is, or exists, as any geometric demonstration can be" (pp.56-57).

And Descartes felt able to go on from this to say: "... as far as all the opinions I had accepted hitherto were concerned, I could do no better than undertake once and for all to be rid of them in order to replace them afterwards by better ones, or even by the same, once I had adjusted them by the plumb-line[43] of reason" (p.37) — given his starting

---

[42] Indeed, before the invention of non-Euclidean geometries, Euclidean geometry stood unchallenged as our most 'true' representation of the nature of space, and as a major paradigm for rational forms of thought, it seemed to present a 'rock-solid' foundation to many upon which to base their claims to be talking 'truly' of the nature of reality. The disturbance produced by the invention of non-Euclidean geometries, however, went far beyond the boundaries of mathematics and science; and we were forced to accept that, rather than 'reality' determining our forms of thought, the reverse was the case: our forms of thought and talk comes to determine what we take our 'realities' to be.

[43] As we shall see, what Descartes talks of here as "the plumb-line of reason," is, I think,

point, the kind of reasoning involved here is of a 'calculational' kind based in after-the-fact *identities* of objective spatial shapes, forms, or patterns.

This kind of *objective truth* or *formal truth* seems to have provided us with our sense of the rightness of our shareable conclusions for the last few hundred years — how could we be doing wrong if we were seeking "The Truth"? But, to repeat, in conducting our inquiries in a Cartesian fashion, we are in fact enclosing ourselves within a geometrical image *of the world of our own construction*, we are achieving only a 'partial objectivity' or a 'thin objectivity'; for only features corresponding to those formally represented in our theories can be 'counted as' influencing our 'findings', features not formally represented are being ignored. Thus to achieve a 'full or a thick objectivity', we need to turn ourselves instead towards the already shared, trans-individual world existing within and amongst us, that makes our untroubled, everyday use of language, and our coordination of (most of) our activities, possible, i.e., the world in which people agree in their judgements of 'friendliness' and 'unfriendliness', even though they cannot provide any fully agreed 'definitions' of *what* goes into our arriving at such judgements.

Clearly, we need to distinguish between what is involved in coming to a grasp of the nature of dead forms in contrast to focussing on the *responsivity* of growing and living forms, both to each other and to the othernesses[44] in their surroundings, and on *their* own particular and unique ways of coming-into-Being. Each requires understanding in its own way. While we can come to an understanding of a dead form in terms of objective, explanatory theories representing the sequence of events supposed to have caused it, *a quite different form of engaged, responsive understanding becomes available to us with a living form.* It can call out spontaneous reactions from us in way that is quite impossible for a dead form. It is this that makes these two kinds of understanding so very different from each other. While we can study already completed, dead forms at a distance, seeking to understand the pattern of *past* events that caused them to come into existence, we can enter into a relationship with a living form and, in making ourselves open to its movements, find ourselves spontaneously responding to its *inner* nature.

---

better described an *aspect* of a *particular* hermeneutical unity, and as such, it can function as what Wittgenstein (1953) calls "an object of comparison — as, so to speak, a measuring-rod; not as a preconceived idea to which reality *must* correspond" (no.131). Descartes' plumb-line of reason is not quite as basic as he took it to be.

[44] I use the term 'othernesses' here for, as we will see, much of our talk relates to 'emergent things' that are still emergent, that are in still *in statu nascendi*: they are 'somethings' to which we can allude, but which we cannot at all classify, and which, if we do, we succeed only in falsifying their nature.

Understanding 'cultural objects' or 'works' from within the living contexts from which they have emerged

> "Only the intended picture reaches up to reality like a yardstick. Looked at from the outside, there it is lifeless and isolated" — It is as if at first we looked at a picture so as to enter into it and the objects in it surrounded us like real ones; and then we stepped back, and were now outside it; we saw the frame, and the picture was a painted surface. In this way, when we intend, we are surrounded by our intention's *pictures*, and we are inside them. But when we step outside intention, they are mere patches on a canvas, without life and of no interest to us... it means something to speak of 'living in the pages of a book'".
>
> (Wittgenstein, 1981, no.233).

> "Every sign by itself seems dead. What gives it life? — In use it is alive. Is life breathed into it there? — Or is the use its life?"
>
> (Wittgenstein, 1953, no.432)

In other words, instead of seeking to *explain* a present activity in terms the past, we can *understand* it in terms of its meaning for us, i.e., in terms of our spontaneous responses to it. It is only from within our involvements with other living things that this kind of meaningful, responsive understanding becomes available to us (Shotter, 1993). This entails our displacing our *deliberate* thinking from the centre of inquiries, and, to repeat, beginning to attend to what *just happens to us* in our spontaneous, before-the-fact, dialogically-structured, everyday ways of acting.

Cassirer (2000) puts this issue as follows: "The object [*Objekt*] of nature appears to lie immediately before our eyes. To be sure, keener epistemological analysis soon teaches us how many more and more complicated concepts are required in order to determine this object, the "object" [*Gegenstand*] of physics, chemistry, and biology in its particular nature. But this determination proceeds in a certain steady direction: we approach the object, as it were, in order to get to know it ever more exactly. But the cultural object requires a different observation; for it lies, so to speak, behind us ... And yet it is just here that there emerges a barrier to knowledge that is difficult to overcome. For the *reflexive* process of the understanding is opposed in its direction to the *productive* process; both cannot be accomplished together at one and the same time ... They must treat analytically what was produced synthetically. Thus a continual flux and reflux prevails here ... In Kant's expression, natural science teaches us "to spell out phenomena in order to read them off as experiences;" the science of culture teaches us to interpret symbols in order to decipher their hidden meaning — *in order to make the life from which they originally emerged visible again*" (pp.85-86, my italics).

In other words, without our being self-consciously aware of how they came into existence, we are already making use of certain cultural ways of making sense of occurrences and events happening around us — and it is in this way that we leave such *ways* behind us. Thus unlike the after-the-fact *analyses* we can conduct in arriving at an *objective* account of physical entities, our task in making the life from which our ways of sense making they originally emerged visible again, involves us a back-and-forth process of oscillation between two very different processes: *descriptive analyses* within which our attention to the particular nature of our expressions (Wittgenstein), and *hermeneutical syntheses* within which the particularities are internally-related to each other, or intra-linked into holistic unities without losing their particularity (Gadamer). This also is very much in line with the views of Ingold and Palsson (2013) in which they are critical of the move in mainstream human sciences that "the philosopher Whitehead (1925) called 'misplaced concreteness'[45] — an essentialism that fallaciously assigns a material presence, in human bodies and minds, to *abstractions born of our own analytic attempts to establish a baseline of commensurability* that would render all humans comparable in terms of similarities and differences" (p.4, my italics).

In other words, just as I wish to examine our *coming into being* as human beings in the world, not in terms of the *after-the-fact* theories, idealizations, and conceptualizations we produce in our deliberate thinking, and wish to turn to the *before-the-fact* ways of acting and speaking, so Ingold and Palsson (2013) want also to think of us as *becomings* rather than simply as being already *beings*. As human "bio-social becomings," as they see it, "each of us is instantiated in the world *along a certain way* of life or 'line of becoming' (Deleuze and Guattari, 2004, p.323), understood not as a corpus of received tradition but as a path to be followed, along which one can keep on going, and which others will follow in their turn... human becomings continually forge their ways, and guide the ways of consociates, in the crucible of their common life" (p.8, my italics).

For although we may seem to be always living within *boundaries*, within describable *horizons* and *contexts*, this is not the case. We are the ones who make such *bounded regions* of thought and action for

---

[45] "I shall in subsequent lectures endeavour to show that this spatialization is the *expression of more concrete facts under the guise of very abstract logical constructions.* There is an error; but it is merely the accidental *error of mistaking the abstract for the concrete*" (Whitehead, 1925, pp.50-51).

ourselves for our own practical purposes — and, as a result, find ourselves conducting our practical affairs in terms of *conceptualizations* and *definitions* of not wholly of our own individual creation, but of the "thought collective" (Fleck, 1979) of which we are a member.

Thus what we miss in thinking of ourselves as having 'our own thoughts', and of being able to think what no others before us have ever thought, is the fact that, as Fleck (1979) points out: "What actually thinks within a person is not the individual himself but his social community. The source of his thinking is not within himself but is to be found in his social environment and in the very social atmosphere he 'breathes'. His mind is structured, and necessarily so, under the influence of this ever-present social environment and *he cannot think in any other way*" (p.47) — or better: people find it *very difficult* to think in any other way, and to have those around them find what they have to say as a result of their new thinking intelligible. Unless we can find ways to link what we have to say to experiences that we know that those in the group before us have had, we will not be able to 'touch' them with our words, to arouse anticipations within them as to the 'point' of our utterances, as to 'where' next we (and they) might 'move' within the 'mental landscape' of our shared context.

Thus what is involved in our escaping from, or better, reversing the professional forms of thought imposed on us by our discipline memberships?

Cassirer (2000), as I see it, has stated the issue perfectly: A science of culture should teach "us to interpret symbols in order to decipher their hidden meaning — *in order to make the life from which they originally emerged visible again*" (p.86, my italics). We must, in other words, in considering the *outcome* of a *productive* process, undertake some creative, imaginative work: This seems to entail oscillating between methodical scientific inquiries of analytical kind and non-traditional philosophical forms of a synthetic kind — for, as Cassirer (2000), "both cannot be accomplished together at one and the same time" (p.86).

So the linguistic task we face — in expressing *their* [professional] expressions in *our* [everyday] terms — is to accept that our language is a system of intra-dependent terms in which the linguistic-value of each term, its meaning[46], results solely from its terms being placed in terms of their *differences in relation* to all the others, simultaneously present within the system. Such an arrangement enables us to create (in fact, many) unfolding *time-shapes* in our word sequences that can be

---

[46] Understood as the *anticipations* as what should come next in a particular circumstance of their use.

compared with the unfolding time-shapes of the *movements of feeling* occurring within us as we conduct our step-by-step imaginative explorations of a 'work' of concern to us. So, although, as we saw above, what Cassirer calls "cultural objects or symbolic forms," are always open to being further articulated or specified in countlessly many kinds of differently worded ways, they are not open to just any further specifications. As Saussure (1911/1959) puts it: "even outside language all values are apparently governed by the same paradoxical principle. They are always composed: 1) of a *dissimilar* thing that can be *exchanged* for the thing of which the value is to be determined; and 2) of *similar* things that can be *compared* with the things of which the value is to be determined" (p.115).

In the next chapter, I will explore the radical consequences of this claim, to bring out the fundamental difference between imposing *conceptualizations* upon a circumstance *from outside* of our living involvements with it, and the power of our *difference making* speakings when they are spoken *from within* a living involvement with an other or otherness in our surroundings. As Wittgenstein (1981) notes, a picture "looked at from the outside, ... is lifeless and isolated" (no.233); it becomes a meaningless object; in becoming unrelated to its surroundings, it ceases to 'speak' to us uniquely of itself.

Switching to this new starting point in the *Logos*, in our everyday, spontaneously responsive *ways of speaking* and of *accounting* for ourselves to each other (Shotter, 1984) — *ways* of spontaneously responding learnt in the course of growing up into *this*, *that*, or *some other* linguistic culture — thus works to shift the whole 'centre of gravity' of social inquiry away from the general and eternal, to the particular and practical, to the situated and timely, away from a 'thin' practicality of satisfying an immediate *want* or *desire* to the 'thicker' practicality of 'doing justice' in one's actions to the 'requirements' of one's circumstances, with the need, always, to consider the overall human cost of our human attempts to better ourselves. Instead of enclosing ourselves within our own preferred images of the world, our task now is to turn toward the actual world, the rich, before-the-fact, objective 'cosmos' that is shared in an embodied fashion by all within our languaged social group; it is, we might say, a crucial aspect of our *language-structured* or *discursive consciousness*.

Involved in doing this requires us to engage in what has been called *"participative thinking"* by Levy-Bruhl (1926) and Bakhtin (1993), and what elsewhere (Shotter, 2005b&c; Shotter 2011) I have called *withness*-thinking — the *relationally-responsive* kind of thinking and speaking we do spontaneously in our everyday conversations, in contrast to the kind of *aboutness*-thinking we do in *referential-representational* thought when talking philosophically or theoretically.

Persons who can think "participatively," according to Bakhtin (1993), "know how not to detach their performed act from its product, but rather how to relate both of them to the unitary and unique context of life and seek to determine them in that context as an indivisible unity" (footnote p.19).

In other words, it is a kind of thinking *from within* a particular flowing circumstance in which we open ourselves up to being 'moved' by that flow. Thus, an engaged encounter of this kind is not simply a matter of 'seeing' of objects, for what is sensed is in fact invisible; nor is it an interpretation (a representation), for it arises directly and immediately in the course of one's living encounter with an other's expressions; neither is it merely a feeling, for carries with it as it unfolds a bodily sense of the possibilities for responsive action in relation to one's momentary placement, position, or orientation in the present interaction.

In short, we can be spontaneously 'moved' toward specific possibilities for action in such a way of being. And this where another person's *words in their saying* can be helpful — in entering into our inner dialogues, they can help to orient us, help us to be responsive to what we might otherwise ignore: "Look at this, notice that, think about it this way..., and so on!"

In trying to come to a rich sense of the *before-the-fact*, already instituted, intra-woven form of objectivity, a holistic common-sense that provides to all the participants within it, a shared *sense of the circumstances* they are currently occupying, we can turn to Levy-Bruhl's (1926) account of *participative thinking*. As he sees it, although primitive peoples live and act as we do, in an environment of beings and objects, besides the properties we also recognize them as possessing they are also imbued with *mystic* attributes. Their before-the-fact objective reality is mingled in with another reality: People feel themselves surrounded by countless other imperceptible entities of an awe inspiring nature that are invisible to sight. Levy-Buhl (1926) describes their nature of their experience thus:

"But the collective representations of primitives are not, like our concepts, the result of intellectual processes properly so called. They contain, as integral parts, affective and motor elements, and above all they imply, in the place of our conceptual inclusions or exclusions, participations which are more or less clearly defined, but, as a general rule, very vividly sensed. Why, for example, should a picture or portrait be to the primitive mind something quite different to what it is to ours? Whence comes that attributing of mystic properties to it, of whence we have just had an instance? Evidently from the fact that every picture, every reproduction 'participates' in the nature, properties, life of that of which it is the image" (p.79).

We shall examine the radical nature of *participative* or *withness* thinking, and its role in our more thick, already instituted, before-the-fact forms of everyday objectivity, more fully below.

4   On the priority of the I-thou over the I-it symbolic forms

"*Within* a general process of development, two qualitatively different lines of development, differing in origin, can be distinguished: the elementary processes, which are of biological origin, on the one hand, and the higher functions, of socio-cultural origin, on the other. *The history of child behaviour is born from the interweaving of these two lines.*"

(Vygotsky, 1978, p.46)

"The further back we trace perception, the greater becomes the preeminence of the 'thou' form over the 'it' form, and the more plainly the purely expressive character takes precedence over the matter or thing-character. The understanding of expression is essentially earlier than the knowledge of things."

(Cassirer, 1957, p.63)

Above, we *compared* two ways of orienting, or of relating ourselves to what Cassirer (2000) called "cultural objects or works:" (1) Observing them as if *from the outside* as dead things, and (2) that of coming to an understanding of them *from within* the involvements we enter-into with them. Here, I want to explore the fact that the world of expression — the world of *I-thou* relations within which our 'works' are fashioned — is more primordial than the world of what we take to be physical objects — the world of *I-it* relations. Again, it is a matter of what, in our too easily adopted *after-the-fact* forms of inquiry, we leave ignored in the 'background', influences that are in fact still at work in directing and shaping what we attend to, and how we act.

Thus my purpose in doing this, in highlighting the nature of *I-thou* relations, is to bring to light the fact that what I am calling the already instituted, thick, prospective, *before-the-fact*, holistic common-sense that provides to all of us as participants within it a shared *sense of the circumstances* we are currently occupying, has a deep and often disregarded history to it. As Wittgenstein (1993a) put it: "An entire mythology is stored within our language" (p.133).

Consequently, we need yet again to examine the importance of our disregarding what is already at work within our shared, background common-sense, and our thinking that we can simply start afresh in formulating a 'framework' within which to 'think about' the problems we face. For we can so easily, at the moment in these modernist times, find ourselves (mis)led into relating ourselves to an event or incident *as if* it is existing or occurring in total isolation from all else around it, *as if* it contains all its properties in and of itself (without in fact owing its existence to its surroundings). And we find ourselves spontaneously acting in this manner, because we feel that it is only in a scientific form of inquiry that we can avoid merely *subjective meanings* and arrive at *objective* results that are meaningful and valid for all the different subjects that participate in it. Science, we think, gives us a system of intersubjectively valid propositions, the *language* of science is thus *universal* — that is, it claims can be understood, can be translated into, by all different speakers in the world, we assume.

But is this actually so? If the world is not initially for us a wholly chaotic place, but is in some sense, as a result of our having grown up within a social group of people already sharing a basic common-sense understanding of *their* world, an already orderly place for us, we can now see Science as forming only one mode of an ordered reality, as representing only one dimension of what objectivity *is*. Thus it is for this reason, we cannot turn science around, so to speak, to discover what is involved in our arriving at what we call objective knowledge as such. "For this problem belongs, if we take it in its full generality," as Cassirer (2000) remarks,

"to a sphere that cannot itself be grasped and exhausted by science even taken as a whole. Science is only one member and one factor in the system of 'symbolic forms'. In a certain sense it may be regarded as the copestone in the edifice of these forms; but it does not stand alone and it could not accomplish its specific performance if it were not for the other energies that share with it in the task of 'synoptic vision', of spiritual 'synthesis'. The statement that concepts without intuitions are empty also holds good here. The concept seeks to encompass the whole of the phenomena; and it reaches this goal by way of classification, subsumption, and subordination... But in this kind of logical structure the concept must be tied throughout to intuitional structures. It is by no means the case that 'logic', conceptual scientific knowledge, carries out its work as if it were in the void. It encounters no absolutely amorphous stuff on which to exercise its formative power. Even the 'matter' of logic, even that particular that it presupposes in order to raise it to universality, is not as such structureless" (p.18).

What it is that makes us feel that we are not yet in possession of an objective form of knowledge, i.e., a form that cannot be shared with others, is the fact that we can only exhibit our possession of it in our everyday, spontaneously responsive, practical activities, when involved in such activities with the others around us. We cannot provide an accurate, *representational-referential* account of it. But given the fact that what are sensing is both *like* what we have sensed in the past, as well as *different* from it, in its *uniqueness*, it nonetheless provides us with, to repeat the phrase I used above from William James (1890), "an acutely discriminative sense" (p.253) its nature, such that we can 'measure it up', so to speak, against a number of different "objects of comparison" (Wittgenstein, 1953, no.130) to at least *characterize it metaphorically*, in a way that 'does justice' to its unique nature.

Concepts and speakings

> "*An interpersonal process is transformed into an intrapersonal one.* Every function in the child's cultural development appears twice: first, on the social level, and later, on the individual level; first, *between* people ..., and then *inside* the child. This applies equally to voluntary attention, to logical memory, and to the formation of concepts. All the higher [mental] functions originate as actual relations between human individuals".
>
> (Vygotsky, 1978, p.57)

Thus, what we miss in ignoring our expressive bodily movements and in thinking that our spontaneously spoken language is too vague and ambiguous to be of much use to us, is the fact that as living beings, we can *come to* relate ourselves to events occurring in our surrounding circumstances in *two* fundamentally, very different ways: (1) deliberately, in the traditional metaphysical fashion, by making use of an *a priori* conceptual system or framework to guide us in what we pick out to attend to in our inquiries; or (2) spontaneously, as 'meaningful expressions' in the form of living processes that emerge, step-by-step, in our *dialogically-structured* relations with those around us.

These two processes need to be conducted in a very different fashion from each other: (1) Concepts work 'from outside' a circumstance of our concern; they are 'pre-emptive' in the sense of decreeing ahead of one's inquiries, *the basic entities one is going to discover*; they work to put a *boundary* around of *field* of study, and they work in terms *samenesses*, of 'identities' even; we see the world around us *only through* them, as *corresponding* to definitions of our own devising.

(2) By contrast, our meaningful expressions draw our attention to the acutely discriminative sense that we have of the movements of feeling occurring within us, and present us with the task of expressing what these experienced movement *are like*, what they are similar to, as well different from. As such, we must work 'from within' the sensed circumstance of our concern, 'from within' a phenomenon; we must try to work to 'internally articulate' it into a more richly structured

'landscape of possibilities', of next steps forward into the future.

Our meaningful expressions thus leave the circumstance open to further development; we thus *cannot define* in any precise way its *nature*, but we can by the use of images and metaphors, and other carefully crafted ways of talking, say very precisely *what they are like* so that others can related to their nature. This enables inquirers to inquiry into *this*, *that*, or *some other* particular situation *in terms of itself*, in terms of features within it of relevance to the concerns of those living within that circumstance; our *speakings* thus work on listeners by 'pointing out' features in the listener's surroundings to attend to — features that they themselves may not yet have responded to; where different *intonations* can indicate a speaker's own relations to their own words — confident, hesitant, offered, demanding, etc, etc.

But what is most crucial, though, is both the ethical and political function of our *wordings* in the *speaking* of our utterances, for different wordings can 'point us toward' quite different expectations for the future, ones that we might not at all prefer.

Indeed, as we saw above, although living forms can call out spontaneous reactions from us in way that is quite impossible with dead forms, giving rise to two forms of understanding seemingly very different from each other, they are also related; for it is our adoption of either an *instrumental* or an *expressive interest*[47] in their behaviour, that makes our understandings so very different from each other.

What changes as the child grows up, then, according to Vygotsky — with his modernist interest in *instrumentalism*[48] — is not just a matter of the child being simply able to remember more things, along with a larger number of connections between them. But the child is 'instructed' in the use of various, culturally invented, mediational means, and enabled, in the development of various *interfunctional* relations between them, to develop capacities within which mediated and nonmediated functions are interwoven. Indeed, he claims, the interfunctional relations involved in learning mediated remembering *reverse* their direction:

"*For the young child, to think means to recall; but for the adolescent, to recall means to think.* Her memory is so 'logicalized' that remembering is reduced to establishing and finding logical relations; recognizing consists in discovering that element which the task indicates has to be

---

[47] The function of our *interests* in shaping our actions is a much ignored topic in Social Theory (but see Habermas, 1972), and I will return to it later on in this book.

[48] He thought of 'signs' as 'tools' for use by the child in shaping its instrumental behaviour: "Learning to direct one's own mental processes with the aid of words or signs is an integral part of the process of concept formation" (Vygotsky, 1986, p.108).

found... When a human being ties a knot in her handkerchief as a reminder, she is, in essence, constructing the process of memorizing by forcing an external object to remind her of something; she transforms remembering into an external activity... In the elementary form something is remembered; in the higher form humans remember something. In the first case a temporary link is formed owing to the simultaneous occurrence of two stimuli that affect the organism; in the second case humans personally create a temporary link through the artificial combination of stimuli" (1978, p.51). And in doing so, young children act towards their surroundings deliberately, as they require, rather than spontaneously, as their circumstances require.

Thus as children grow up, "into the intellectual life of those around them" (p.88), says Vygotsky (1978), *"the nature of the development itself changes,* from biological to sociohistorical. Verbal thought is not an innate, natural form of behavior, but is determined by a historical-cultural process and has specific properties and laws that cannot be found in the natural forms of thought and speech" (p.94) — hence our need for what above I called 'before-the-fact' *descriptive accounts,* aimed at bringing into rational visibility the *processes* involved in our arriving at what we are pleased to call 'the facts of the matter' — a topic that I will return to in more detail below.

But let it suffice here to say that, as Cassirer (1957) pointed out above, that "the further back we trace perception, the greater becomes the preeminence of the 'thou' form over the 'it' form, and the more plainly the purely expressive character takes precedence over the matter or thing-character. The understanding of expression is essentially earlier than the knowledge of things" (p.63), and we need to take that into account in our efforts at understanding whether, in fact, there can be, as Cassirer claims, *cultural sciences* that do not have to be distinguished in their conduct from the *natural sciences* — because they are both in fact based, not in *objective subject matters,* but in *distinctive movements of feeling* that can actually guide us in the performance of our actions.

Being born adapted to living 'within expressive communicative relationships' — on learning to act 'instinctively'

> "I want to regard man here as an animal; as a primitive being to which one grants instinct but not ratiocination... Any logic good enough for a primitive means of communication needs no apology from us. Language did not emerge from some kind of ratiocination".
>
> (Wittgenstein, 1969, no.475)

"But what is the word 'primitive' meant to say here? Presumably that this sort of behavior is *pre-linguistic*: that a language-game is based *on it*, that it is the prototype of a way of thinking and not the result of thought".

(Wittgenstein, 1981, no.541)

Here, I want to explore the nature of our spontaneously responsive reactions to events occurring around us, not simply as human organisms, but as persons, as members of a particular linguistic community, sensitive to the *Logos* expressed in its everyday activities within its overall form of life. For, as we shall see, the focal importance of such spontaneous reactions, is that they can provide the only openings for radical, innovative changes in a linguistic community's common-sense. This, in itself, is a radical departure from currently accepted ways of bringing new ways of acting, new social organizations and institutions into existence, through strategic planning, policy making, and forms of legislation.

As we saw above, it is easy to assume that we come into the world as a 'blank slate', a 'tabula rasa', free to be shaped either as we ourselves, or others, desire. And classically, it has been easy for us to assume, in accordance with an assumption of a mechanistically working physiology, that certain sensations are always aroused by certain stimuli. Thus, to this way of thinking, there cannot be the recognition of any strictly creative processes in perception at all: for the whole meaning and content of perception consists in the accurate reflection and reproduction of the relations of the 'entities' constituting a circumstance in the outside world. But is this so? If we go back to the earliest stages of consciousness, to the moment of a baby's birth and the putting of the baby to the mother's breast — a moment of intense expectation and curiosity, of waiting, of looking, listening, of touching, stroking, caressing, of waiting to see, to hear, of sensitive responsivity — we will find the need to reverse every one of these assumptions.

The perception of expression is more primitive than the perception of physical features

The view that the world of the infant is initially experienced as a chaos of unordered sensations, each consisting in a basic objective quality, such as light or dark, warm or cold, loud of soft, red or blue, proves to be absolutely untenable. We see the baby straightaway being responsive to events occurring around it in well-known ways — and furthermore, as the infant grows into the *symbolic forms of life* of those around it, it is almost as if distinct 'instincts', to respond spontaneously in distinctive ways to certain distinctive events, emerge. But are they 'instincts' as such?

Our spontaneously responsive reactions to events occurring around us occupy, as we shall see, a special 'in-between' realm of neither *actions* we individually 'do', nor of mere *happenings* we passively suffer. It is, we might say, a kind of thinking that just comes to happen within us all, spontaneously, as members of a social group who have all shared in the learning a common language — which, as such, provides the basis for the more deliberate thinking we, as individuals, can do. So, although not in any sense inherited genetically, like say blue eyes, it is something we can inherit after birth, in the course of growing into the languaged form of life of all those around us.

As Wittgenstein (1969) puts it: "I did not get my picture of the world [*Weltbild*] by satisfying myself of its correctness; nor do I have it because I am satisfied of its correctness. No: it is the inherited background against which I distinguish between true and false" (no.94) — so, although it seems that our perceptions simply provide us immediately with a *given* situation, the fact is that it is as a result of our language-intra-twined, learned *ways* of looking that we come to *give form* to our circumstances as we do.

Thus, as we saw above, what we miss in ignoring the power of our expressive bodily movements to arouse, spontaneously, responses in the others around us, and in thinking that deliberately spoken language is essentially our primary form of shared communication, is the fact that we primarily relate ourselves to events occurring in our surrounding circumstances, not in terms of *patterns* or *arrangements* of basic objective 'things', but in terms of immediately experienced phenomena — initially indeterminate phenomena whose *meaning* we spontaneously determine in accord with our current immersion within the *Logos* of the forms of life into which we have grown, shared with all those around us.

John Macmurray (1961) puts the nature of this initial, not instinctive but instinct-like state of affairs very nicely in saying: "The baby must be fitted by nature at birth to the conditions into which he is born; for otherwise he could not survive. He is, in fact, 'adapted', to speak paradoxically, to being unadapted, 'adapted' to a complete dependence upon an adult human being. He is made to be cared for. He is born into a love relation that is inherently personal" (p.48); and he goes onto to remark: "That man is social by nature it is true, but highly ambiguous. Many animals are social; yet no species is social in the sense in which we are, for none has the form of its life determined from the beginning by communication. Communication is not the offspring of speech, but its parent" (p.67). And, as I commented above, just as we find here the reverse of what we expect — that speech is an emergent product of communication, not the other way round — so also, we find that, rather than being genetically pre-determined to act in specific ways to specific circumstances, what we too easily call 'instincts' need to be understood as aspects of a linguistic community's (inherited and inheritable) common-sense.

Indeed, as we saw above, with Fleck (1979) and Kuhn (1970), the common-sense of a social community influences in a very primary way *what* we take the very basic nature of our world to be. As Cassirer (1957) puts it: "We do not thereby sink back into a mere chaos, rather, an ideal cosmos once more surrounds us... [But] it reveals certain basic traits which are by no means directed from the outset toward the object of nature or toward the knowledge of the outside world, but which disclose an entirely different direction. Myth, in particular, shows us a world which is far from being without structure, immanent articulation, yet does not know the organization of reality according to things and attributes[49]. Here all configurations of being show a peculiar fluidity; they are differentiated without being separated from one another" (pp.60-61).

Later, we must return to the notion of a shared *cosmos*, and the foundational role of essentially *mythic* accounts of reality — accounts in which we *allude* to possibly 'emergent things' as best we can, poetically, for as 'things' still *in statu nascendi*, classifying them at all will only falsify their nature — but for the moment, let me just repeat Kuhn's (1970) claim that: "Normal science,... is predicated on the assumption that the scientific community knows what the world *is like*" (pp.4-5, my italics); so that various sections of the scientific community can then move on from mere *similarities* (and *differences*), to more precise definitions and conceptualizations in the formulation of specific theories, requiring specific tests for their truth, on the primitive basis of such similarities.

Here, let me return to Macmurray's (1961) remark that we have our forms of life "determined from the beginning by communication" (p.67), and to the fact that we seem to be born physiologically attuned to respond, spontaneously, to certain basic movements occurring in our surroundings in an *expressive* manner. To repeat, although it is easy to assume that we come into the world as a 'blank slate', a 'tabula rasa', free to be shaped either as we ourselves, or others, desire, and that our initial experience of our surroundings is merely a flux of chaotic sensations of lines and colour, of light and dark, changing at very every moment, the fact is that we find infants reacting very early on to the different expressive movements of their caretakers. "If this theory of original chaos were sound," remarks Koffka (1921, in Cassirer, 1957), "we should expect that 'simple' stimuli would first arouse the child's attention: for it is the simple which it will first be possible to separate

---

[49] See my account in the Appendix of Vico's (1968) *Scienza Nuova*.

out of the chaos and which will first enter into other combinations. This is contrary to all experience. The stimuli which most influence the behavior of the child are not those which seem particularly simple to the psychologist because simple sensations correspond to them. The first differentiated sound reactions respond to the human voice, hence to highly complex stimuli and "sensations"). The infant is not interested in simple colors, but in human faces.... For the chaos theory, the phenomenon corresponding to a human face is merely a confusion of the most divergent sensations of light, dark, and color, which moreover are in constant flux, changing with every movement of the person in question or the child himself, and with the lighting. And yet by the second month the child knows his mother's face; by the middle of his first year he reacts to a friendly or, an angry face, and so differently that there is no doubt that what was given to him phenomenally was the friendly or angry face and not any distribution of light and dark... We are left with the opinion that phenomena such as "friendliness" or "unfriendliness" are extremely primitive — even more primitive, for example, than that of a blue spot" (pp.64-65).

So, although the precise nature of such spontaneous reactions take some time to develop — and we might surmise that they develop as such as a result of infants coming to *anticipate the consequences of such expressions*, what in fact they next lead on to — we find that they are very basic to the rest of the child's development. In actively 'shaping' the character of the circumstances we find ourselves attending to, both as children and ourselves as adults, not only do we come to use a whole range of descriptive terms — saying of them, that they are 'strange', 'terrible', 'uncanny', 'forbidding', 'menacing', etc., while others are 'charming', 'attractive', or 'delightful', etc., while yet others are 'awkward', 'energetic', 'puzzling' or 'bewildering' etc. — but we also find ourselves unavoidably driven to spontaneously respond to them in a correspondingly distinctive manner: we find ourselves 'tempted' by what is 'charming', 'intrigued' by what is 'uncanny', and 'repelled' by what is 'menacing', and so on.

The perception of non-objective agential influences

Indeed, to go further, in seeming to find ourselves, spontaneously, 'driven' to act in specific ways, it is all too easy to feel ourselves 'bound' or 'tied' to a *commanding agency* of some kind, to what Bakhtin (1986) calls a *superaddressee*: "... the author of the utterance, with greater or lesser awareness, presupposes a higher *superaddressee* (third), whose absolutely just responsive understanding is presumed, either in some metaphysical distance or in distant historical time... Each dialogue takes place as if against a background of the responsive understanding of an invisibly present third party who stands above all the participants in the dialogue (partners)... The aforementioned third party is not any mystical or metaphysical being (although, given a certain understanding of the world, he can be expressed as such) — he is a constitutive aspect of the whole utterance, who, under deeper analysis, can be revealed in it" (pp.126-127).

Finding ourselves 'driven' to act as we do in relation to such circumstances as these, we are, of course, tempted to ask "*Why?*" — to try to *explain* what *causes* us to want to act in this fashion? And this is where, of course, our current Cartesian forms of common-sense are yet again at work within us.

We can, however, find an alternative in Wittgenstein's (1993) *Remarks on Frazer's Golden Bough* — for he was very critical of Frazer's attempt to *explain* so-called primitive people's beliefs in magic and religion, as if they are *errors* in such people's attempts to come to an instrumental, intellectual understanding of natural events just as a 20th Century scientist might: "I believe that the attempt to explain is already therefore wrong," he said, "because one must only correctly piece together what one *knows*, without adding anything, and the satisfaction being sought through the explanation follows of itself. And the explanation isn't what satisfies us here at all. When Frazer begins by telling us the story of the King of the Wood of Nemi, he does this in a tone which shows that he feels, and wants us to feel, that something strange and dreadful is happening. But the question 'why does this happen?' is properly answered by saying: *Because it is dreadful*. That is, precisely that which makes this incident strike us as dreadful, magnificent, horrible, tragic, etc., as anything but trivial and insignificant, is also *that* which has called this incident to life" (p.121, my italics).

Indeed, as Wittgenstein shows, Frazer 'trips himself up', so to speak, by speaking (writing) in such way, as if *he already knows what will make us feel* that something strange and dreadful is happening; in so doing, he is in fact making use of already shared expressions of feeling existing amongst us. Feeling that something "is" *dreadful*, is something very basic to whom we are, as participants within a linguistic community's inherited form of life. We talk of such responses as being 'instinctive', because we simply *find ourselves* feeling and acting in relation to certain circumstances in *this way*, whether we like it or not.

Yet, to repeat, it is a spontaneous responsiveness inherited *after*, rather then, *before* birth, and as such, not immutable. So how shall we describe such spontaneous, feeling-aroused actions? Wittgenstein (1993) offers the following account: "When I am furious about something, I sometimes beat the ground or a tree with my walking stick. But I certainly do not believe that the ground is to blame or that my beating can help anything. 'I am venting my anger'. And all rites are of this kind. Such actions may be called *Instinct-actions*" (p.137, my italics).

They are 'actions' because in acting in this way, although I feel I have no immediate choice, I am still an agent; thus, although I am a participant within a linguistic community that makes it very difficult for me to "*think in any other way*" (Fleck, 1979, p.47), it is not impossible; once aware of the linguistic circumstances 'shaping' my actions, other possibilities can come into view. And this is Wittgenstein's point; our need for an *explanation* is not the only need we face.

Our "real need" (Wittgenstein, 1953, no.108)[50], as he sees it, is for us to get a sense of the 'distinctive feelings' guiding our (and Frazer's) everyday *uses* of language, for, as he says, "nothing shows our kinship to those savages better than the fact that Frazer has on hand a word as familiar to himself and to us as 'ghost' or 'shade' in order to describe the views of these people" (Wittgenstein, 1993, p.133); Frazer did not choose these words by accident.

He then further suggests that if we "correctly piece together what one *knows*, without adding anything, and the satisfaction being sought through the explanation follows of itself" (p.121); we what we needed, was not so much an *explanation* (in terms of what might have caused the phenomena), as another kind of understanding altogether: "the understanding which consists precisely in the fact that we 'see the connections'[51]" (p.133). Where the value of such an understanding is, that by situating ourselves wholly within our immediately actual circumstances, and attempting to relate ourselves to them as they *are* in themselves — rather than as we *want* to see if them if we are to manipulate them in achieving our own purposes — we can arrive at a *secure sense* of being oriented, of knowing our "way about" (Wittgenstein, 1953, no.123) within the landscape of possibilities available to us, and of how best "to go on" (no.154) within that landscape in ways which others will *see as* intelligible (even if, after-the-fact of having acted, we still cannot give them any good reasons for our having so acted)[52].

Without such a relational understanding, without our being able to relate our own particular actions to the different particular ones of others in our social group in such a way that both we and they can 'see

---

[50] See next section.

[51] Let me call it a "relational understanding."

[52] Of course, we will only be asked to *account* for our actions (Mills, 1940), if the others around us fail to 'see their point', if they do not understand us; if they do understand us, they will simply respond as they see fit.

the connections', we would be unable to join with them in common projects; we would all be speaking and acting at cross purposes, unable to coordinate our own individual actions with those of the others in the group. So, although Wittgenstein (1993) remarks: "Here one can only *describe* and say: this is what human life is like" (p.121); but I must add here that, in our *descriptive utterances*, we need to arouse in our listeners a 'directive sense' (a mental 'compass' or 'gravitational field', one might say), enabling them not only to organize all the steps they might take in relation to each other, but also to judge, at each step they take, whether they are 'on the way' towards aims shared with others or not.

5 Preconceptual speaking — making a 'difference that matters to us' with words

"When we conceptualize, we cut out and fix, and exclude everything but what we have fixed. A concept means a *that-and-no-other*. Conceptually, time excludes space; motion and rest exclude each other; approach excludes contact; presence excludes absence; unity excludes plurality; independence excludes relativity; 'mine' excludes 'yours' ... whereas in the real concrete sensible flux of life experiences compenetrate each other so that it is not easy to know just what is excluded and what not."

(James, 1909/1996, p.254)

"Everything that has been said up to this point boils down to this: in language there are only differences. Even more important: a difference generally implies positive terms between which the difference is set up; *but in language there are only differences without positive terms.*"

(Saussure, 1911/1959, p.120, my italics)

"In a unified whole of this kind, the learned parts of a language have an immediate value as a whole, and progress is made less by addition and juxtaposition than by the internal articulation of a function which is in its own way already complete."

(Merleau-Ponty, 1964, pp.39-40)

My aim in this book is, to repeat, the Wittgensteinian (1953) one of coming to "*a clear view* of our use of words" (no.122). For in our actual, intimate involvements with the others and othernesses around us in our everyday 'worlds' — unlike in our rationally structured reflections — the words we use in relation to the 'things' we experience as occurring in these worlds, come to us spontaneously, for 'worlds' and 'their wordings' are learnt in intimate relation to each other. Thus, as Wittgenstein (1953) puts it: "One might also give the name 'philosophy' to what is possible *before* all new discoveries and inventions" (no.126). "The work of the philosopher consists in assembling reminders for a particular purpose" (no.126) "If there has to be anything 'behind the utterance of the formula' it is *particular circumstances*, which justify me in saying I can go on — when the formula occurs to me" (no.154). What we need is a description that *does justice* to the *particular circumstances* in place at the time of a person's acting within them, if we are to 'enter into' *their* world and to understand *their reasons* for their actions. Along with what it is within them that leads them to organize their relations to their surroundings in the particular manner that they do?

What I would like to explore in this chapter, is what happens when we attempt to conduct our inquiries, not in our own terms, but as a member of a social group, of a "thought collective" in Fleck's (1979) terms, and as a result, finding ourselves conducting our practical affairs in terms of *conceptualizations* and *definitions* of not wholly of our own devising. Among the many different pressures on individuals to sustain the integrity of the group, is the pressure to sustain a common vocabulary. For crucial within such a group is the possibility that everyone is able to act in their own different ways, while at the same time being *oriented* in their investigations towards the same overall goal. In other words, before we can begin to talk amongst ourselves on how to proceed with our inquiries, we need to understand the workings of language in, as C. Wright Mills (1940) put it, "its social function of co-ordinating diverse actions" (p.904). How is it possible that so many diverse activities can come to be *intra*[53]-related to each other in such a way that we feel justified in saying that they all are *expressions* of a common or unitary culture?

Theories do not reach down and anchor themselves in a fundamentally neutral, physical reality — indeed, whenever we speak of atoms and molecules, and the laws of nature, we are speaking of what we mean, by the expressions 'atoms', 'molecules' and 'laws of nature' (Winch, 1958); they are all expressions associated with a particular way of 'seeing' the world and of manipulating it by the means it provides. Theories are grounded, as Kuhn (1962) makes clear, in the activities which give research practices their reproducibility: namely, their *accountability* amongst those conducting them.

But notice how this accountability is achieved. Participants begin by appreciating how, given the practical phenomena confronting them, theoretical categories can be used to constitute them as events of a recognizable kind — the research practice provides an account as to how a theory should be used and applied. Such categories are used as an unquestioned (and unquestionable) resource in organizing one's perception of events within the research paradigm (Hanson, 1958). And it is in this sense that one is *entrapped*: for by conducting all one's further activities in terms of a set of categories — grasped in, as Stolzenberg (1978) puts it, "initial acts of acceptance as such in the domain of ordinary language use" (p.267), and then suspended from all

---

[53] See footnote 8.

further doubt — necessitates one having to assimilate them also to such a pre-established set of categories. There is no possibility of a hermeneutical development of new categories; the transformation of one's perceptual categories in the course of dialogue is denied.

Consider, by comparison, the process of listening to an account: if the facts so far are unsatisfactory, incomplete or even bewildering, one waits for later facts and uses them in an attempt to decide the sense of the earlier ones; what sense there is to be found is not decided beforehand, but is discovered in the course of the exchange within which the account is offered.

Stolzenberg (1978) shows how, as result of such acts of acceptance as such, even mathematicians can *entrap* themselves in closed systems of thought of their own devising to such an extent that, once inside such systems, it is extremely difficult to escape from them. For although "an objective demonstration that certain of the beliefs [within the system] are incorrect" can exist, "certain of the attitudes and habits of thought prevent this from being recognized" (p.224).

From 'reflective' intellectualized to 'spontaneous' everyday talk

In our reflections, we move from functioning within an unbounded, everyday space of yet-to-be-determined possibilities to operating within a well-articulated, single, systematic order of connectedness; from coping with natural-tendencies-in-the-wild, so to speak, to dealing with more 'cultivated' or 'orchestrated' tendencies *organized* in relation to our own *interests* (Habermas, 1972); from intra-twined streams of indivisible, flowing, turbulent activities to ordered *systems* of inter-connected, separately existing, unambiguously nameable 'things' or 'entities'.

To the extent that we must talk and/or to write in ways already intelligible to our fellow beings, if we must express our utterances in words with already *unambiguous* meanings, we must, inevitably, prejudge what we *will find* in our reflections: each of us, subjectively, will find a world of already, separately existing 'things', appreciated by us, we say, from our own 'point of view'. Thus, in turning to the task of 'picturing' or of 'representing in words' what we can 'see' in our reflections, we need to 'see' them as 'hanging together as a unity', to adopt a 'perspective' towards them, to see them as fitting into a pre-existing orderly arrangement of some kind. In short, if we begin with our reflections, with our *speculative* thoughts *about* a circumstance, we find ourselves, so to speak, acting within a hall of mirrors, entombed, literally, within *this* or *that* or *some other* conceptualized reality of our own creation.

The advantage of this, as we saw above, is that coming to an understanding of how diverse actions can become co-ordinated is not at all easy; while establishing a bounded space of *samenesses* makes it perfectly possible. The disadvantage, however, is that *unique* events and happenings which, in fact, present themselves to us as essentially *themselves*, so to speak — and often offer *openings* to novel next steps forward — are easily treated as merely *subjective variants of, in fact, more basic, pre-existing objective entities*, with their novelty being ignored.

If we are to arrive at an understanding of what a person *means* by their actions and/or utterances in a particular everyday circumstance, then we cannot begin our inquiries by, retrospectively, reflecting on what they have said or done. For reflection is a bending back, a re-*flection*, an 'after the fact' process in which we *look back* at something that has, for us, already come into existence as an objective, nameable 'thing', as an instance of a type, as the instantiation of a concept. We continually act as if the future is merely a repetition of the past.

Indeed, as Garfinkel (1967) demonstrated, in episodes in which he asked his students to 'play as scientists' — by asking their friends to give clear, unambiguous definitions for their use of certain words — such requests for clear definitions, rather than improving the process of communication, actually worked to disrupt it, drastically. For instance: A friend tells one of Garfinkel's student-experimenters that she had a flat tire on the way to work the day before. The student responds by asking: "What do you mean, you had a flat tire?" The result as reported by the student is as follows: "She appeared momentarily stunned. Then she answered in a hostile way: "What do you mean, 'What do you mean?' A flat tire is a flat tire. That is what I meant. Nothing special. What a crazy question!" (p.42).

Clearly, that attempts ahead of time to define the meaning of one's words prior to opening one's mouth to talk, will disrupt rather than enhance the possibility of people coming to a clear understanding of each other in their communication," may seem to be a somewhat strange and unexpected conclusion; but, in fact (on most occasions) this indeed seems to be the case.

For what we can be called the "specific vagueness" (Garfinkel), or the "specific variability" (Voloshinov)[54] of our linguistic forms, allows the

---

[54] "... the constituent factor for the linguistic form, as for the sign, is not at all its self-identity as signal but its specific variability; and the constituent factor for understanding the linguistic form is not recognition of 'the same thing', but understanding in the proper sense of the word, i.e., orientation in the particular, given context and in the particular, given situation — orientation in the dynamic process of becoming and not 'orientation' in some inert state" (Voloshinov, 1984, p.69).

meaning of the linguistic forms we use to be determined by the context of their use, such that, in fact, they may be used in many different ways. Indeed, I drew attention above to the fact that, in learning to speak, not only do we become capable of spontaneously using a large (but not infinite) number different words with a fair degree of practical success in describing particular features of the world around us, but also — which is perhaps even more worthy of note — we can bring off an uncountable number of different practical consequences with what is in fact a limited number of words, without in either case needing to pre-define their usage in unambiguous, ideal terms ahead of time.

In other words, in coming to "*a clear view* of our use of words" (Wittgenstein, 1953, no.122), we badly need to distinguish our use of words in our informal, disorderly, non-professional, everyday, unbounded activities — in which people can *still* come to co-ordinate their diverse actions in with each other's in the pursuit of a common goal, while not operating within a pre-established bounded conceptual space — from our use of them in bounded professional and disciplinary contexts.

Indeed, to go further, we must not in our inquiries, ahead of time, assume our circumstances to possess any pre-selected features. For our task in trying to understand how a bounded, stable, orderly *arena of language use* within a particular social group can be, both *constituted* and then *instituted*[55] as required, is that of selecting out of an indeterminate realm of natural tendencies, just those that are relevant to the pursuit of a common goal, or to a focus on the sustaining and elaboration of a tradition or a culture. That is, we must allow for a *particular meaningful whole*, hermeneutically, to emerge amongst us from a set of particular fragmented but nonetheless intra-connected experiences, as we all imaginatively explore them, step-by-step, prior to our assuming that we share a 'topic' (or 'topos') in common to us all.

The performative, 'action-shaping' functions of our 'speakings' — the importance of what we 'care about'

As Garfinkel (1967) puts it: "For the purposes of *conducting their everyday affairs* persons refuse to permit each other to understand

---

55 To *institute* ways of acting within a social group, is to create within it practices and procedures concerned with how, once constituted, they may be sustained by bringing into existence stable, self-sanctioning, disciplinary procedures oriented towards a particular 'subject matter'. As Merleau-Ponty (1970) put it: "What we understand by the concept of institution are those events in experience which endow it with durable dimensions, in relation to which a whole series of other experiences will acquire meaning, will form an intelligible series or a history — or again those events which sediment in me a meaning, not just as survivals or residues, but as the invitation to a sequel, the necessity of a future" (pp.40-41).

'what they are really talking about' in this [idealistic] way. The anticipation that persons *will* understand, the occasionality of expressions, the specific vagueness of references, the retrospective-prospective sense of a present occurrence, waiting for something later in order to see what was meant before, are sanctioned properties of common discourse. They furnish a background of seen but unnoticed features of common discourse whereby actual utterances are recognized as events of common, reasonable, understandable, plain talk. Persons require these properties of discourse as conditions under which they are themselves entitled and entitle others to claim that they know what they are talking about, and that what they are saying is understandable and ought to be understood. In short, their seen but unnoticed presence is used to entitle persons to conduct their common conversational affairs without interference. Departures from such usages call forth immediate attempts to restore a right state of affairs" (p.41-42).

In other words, we live within 'circumstances of practical concern' to us; what we 'care about', what 'matters' to us, works to organize what we attend to and respond to in these circumstances. And as we 'move around' from within our living immersion, from within our engagement with these circumstances — *sensing* a fragment *here* at this moment in time, another fragment *there* at that moment in time — we gradually come to a *unitary sense* of a 'something's' particular nature *in* 'its' mattering to us. We come to adopt an *emotional attitude* towards it. And on certain occasions, we come to sense *something* as mattering to us in an ultimate way; it becomes an ultimate value for us — something we relate to from within the special nature of a *care-* or *concern-* or *love-relation* (see Chapter Eight).

Martha Nussbaum (2001a) puts it thus: " ... *emotions are forms of evaluative judgment that ascribe to certain things and persons outside a person's own control great importance for the person's own flourishing.* Emotions are thus, in effect, *acknowledgments of neediness and lack of self-sufficiency*" (p.22, italics in original). In other words, on such occasions, it is as if a diffuse, unlocatable restriction is at work in limiting one's freedom of action.

As Frankfurt (1998) sees it: "A person who cares about something is, as it were, invested in it. He *identifies* himself with what he cares about in the sense that he makes himself vulnerable to losses and susceptible to benefits depending upon whether what he cares about is diminished or enhanced ... The moments in the life of a person who cares about something, however, are not merely linked inherently by formal relations of sequentiality. The person necessarily binds them together, and in the nature of the case also construes them as being bound together, in richer ways. This both entails and is entailed by his own continuing concern with what he does with himself and with what goes on in his life" (pp.83-84).

But more than with just becoming a good athlete or academic, a highly professional doctor or lawyer, Frankfurt is concerned with those ways-of-being-in-the-world in which persons subject themselves to what he calls a "volitional necessity," that is, with people who have *chosen* to care about an issue so much that it is impossible for them to turn away from taking a particular course of action, irrespective of its costs to them. "It was presumably on such an occasion," he says, "for example, that Luther made his famous declaration: 'Here I stand; *I can do no other*'" (p.86).

Another example Frankfurt offers is an occasion on which Wittgenstein telephones a friend, Fania Pascal, who's just had her tonsils removed, and asks her: "How are you?" "Like a dog that's been run over," she replies. And Wittgenstein replies irritably: "You don't know what a dog that has been run over feels like" — but why does he reply in such an unpleasant manner?

We can only surmise that, because Wittgenstein largely chose to devote his philosophical energies to identifying and combating what he regarded as tempting and insidious forms of "nonsense-talk," i.e., talk in which *we fail to be concerned with* the way the world *is in itself*, and too easily turn to a description of it of our own invention, he felt that even here, with a good friend, he still could not let such nonsense-talk go by. But his strong reaction is not because Pascal is lying to him. She is not trying to deceive him about how she really feels, or about how a dog would feel if run over. Her wrong-doing, Frankfurt (2005) concludes, is not that she conducted a flawed inquiry into how a dog would feel if run over, *but that she conducted no actual inquiry at all.* "It is just this lack of connection to a concern with truth — this indifference to how things really are — that I regard as the essence of bullshit" (p.33), he says. In other words, 'bullshit' or 'nonsense-talk', is an example of the fragmentation- and separation-producing talk that works to 'disconnect' us from "the soil of the sensible"[56] which 'grounds' our after-the-fact 'scientific' forms of inquiry.

If Frankfurt (1998, 2005) is correct, and I think he is, there are certain kinds of *achievements* in all our lives that are of ultimate importance to us, events in our lives in which we say to ourselves 'this is what I do, because *this* is who I am,' achievements without which we could not be ourselves.

---

56 Merleau-Ponty (1962, pp.160-161). Wittgenstein (1980a), in describing the nature of his own work, uses the same metaphor: "I believe my originality (if that is the right word) is an originality belonging to the soil rather than to the seed... Sow a seed in my soil and it will grow differently than it would in any other soil ...." (p.36).

As Bakhtin (1993) puts it: "... this world-as-event is not just a world of being, of that which is given; no object, no relation, is given here as something simply given, as something totally on hand, but is always given in conjunction with another given that is connected with those objects and relations, namely, that which is yet-to-be-achieved or determined; 'one ought to...', 'it is desirable that...' An object that is absolutely indifferent, totally finished, cannot be something one experiences actually... to be exact, it is given to me within a certain event-unity, in which the moments of what-is-given and what-is-to-be-achieved, of what-is and what-ought-to-be, of being and value, are inseparable" (p.32).

Each event-unity is a *particular, unique, unity*, which, as such, is still open to further development, to further internal articulation; it thus needs to be understood *in its own terms*, in terms of itself, rather than in terms of another, external, eternal, *ideal world* of our own creation as academics. This is because the unfolding of its unique time-course in the world cannot at all be likened to the performance of a pre-existing script, but is much more like the way in which, say, a particular seedling works as a structured means mediating the further growth of a particular plant; or the way in which the awareness of what one has just said or done works as a structured means determining the possibilities available as to what one might go on to say or to do next. Indeed, as we move around within a circumstance of concern to us in our efforts to relate ourselves to it, the *movements of feeling* we arouse within ourselves provide us with quite specific *action guiding anticipations*[57] as to our next possible steps — where our task then becomes that of 'going on' to take that step in the circumstance in question, in a way that is *intelligible to all the others around us*. Just acting in a way that is effective for ourselves alone, will not do.

To do this, we must act in an *accountable* fashion; that is, we must intra-weave verbal descriptions of how we are acting into our actions in such a way that others, living within the same 'circumstances of concern' as ourselves, are 'moved' into 'seeing' our actions as 'fitting into' that specific circumstance in an appropriate way, as not in any way untoward. In other words, our 'speakings', our utterances, our

---

[57] Indeed, one of the best accounts of how such anticipations work within us known to me, is William James' (1890) account in his famous *Stream of Thought* chapter: "The truth is," he says, "that large tracts of human speech are nothing but *signs of direction* in thought, of which direction we nevertheless have an acutely discriminative sense, though no definite sensorial image plays any part in it whatsoever... These bare images of logical movement... are psychic transitions, always on the wing, so to speak, and not to be glimpsed except in flight. Their function is to lead from one set of images to another... [These] 'tendencies' are not only descriptions from without, but that they are among the *objects* of the stream, which is thus aware of them from within, and must be described as in very large measure constituted of *feelings* of tendency, often so vague that we are unable to name them at all" (vol.1, pp.252-254).

expressive bodily movements, must work to arouse in those around us, and in ourselves also, "feelings of tendency" (James), "anticipations" (Bakhtin) of what might 'come next', both in our everyday language intra-twined *activities*, as well as in our more orderly, language intra-twined *practices*.

Here, then, we become concerned with what we might call the *functional* or *performative* (Austin, 1970) use of words — as Mills (1940) put it, "what we want is an analysis of the integrating, controlling, and specifying function a certain type of speech fulfils in socially situated actions" (p.905). Performative understandings are not to do with facts or information, but with *what kind of context* we are in, with the 'requirements' our current surroundings exert on us to respond within them in *appropriate* ways, as well as with the opportunities for action they *afford* (Gibson, 1979) us — they involve, then, a kind of knowing that shows up in our *readinesses to respond* in certain ways, spontaneously, according to the anticipations embodied in our *approach*, *attitude*, or *stance* towards the particular circumstances we happen to find ourselves in.

'Discursive formations' and the 'enunciative dimension' — Foucault

> "Instead of being something said once and for all — and lost in the past like the result of a battle, a geological catastrophe, or the death of a king — the statement, as it emerges in its materiality, appears with a status, enters various networks and various fields of use, is subjected to transferences or modifications, is integrated into operations and strategies in which its identity is maintained or effaced".
>
> (Foucault, 1972, p.105)

About what he calls "the task" of the rules within a discipline's "discursive formation," Foucault (1972) remarks that it "consists of not — of no longer — treating discourses as groups of signs (signifying elements referring to contents or representations) but as practices that systematically form the objects of which they speak. Of course, discourses are composed of signs; but what they do is more than use these signs to designate things. It is this *more* that renders them irreducible to the language (langue) and to speech. It is this 'more' that we must reveal and describe" (p.49). The 'more' that Foucault alludes to here, is the 'more' that comes into view as we move from a *representational-referential* use of our words in our theorizing, to what I above called our more everyday *relationally-responsive* use of words, a shift from our words as merely 'standing for things' to them arousing in our listeners and readers "action guiding anticipations" (Shotter,

2005, 2008), a shift from a concern with the *content* of patterns of already spoken words (as word *forms*) to a concern with the arousal of *movements of feeling* by our *words in their speaking*.

Foucault (1972) talks of this shift as a shift to the *enunciative* level, away from viewing the function of our *linguistic formulations* within grammatical and logical levels. In so doing, we arrive at the view that: "A statement is not confronted (face to face, as it were) by a correlate — or the absence of a correlate — as a proposition has (or has not) a referent, or as a proper noun designates someone (or no one)... The 'referential' of the statement forms the place, the condition, the field of emergence, the authority to differentiate between individuals or objects, states of things and relations that are brought into play by the statement itself; it defines the possibilities of appearance and delimitation of that which gives meaning to the sentence, a value as truth to the proposition ... in contrast to its grammatical and logical levels: through the relation with these various domains of possibility the statement makes... a sentence to which one may or may not ascribe a meaning, a proposition that may or may not be accorded a value as truth... One can see in any case that the description of this enunciative level can be performed neither by a formal analysis, nor by a semantic investigation, nor by verification, *but by the analysis of the relations between the statement and the spaces of differentiation, in which the statement itself reveals the differences*" (pp.91-92, my italics).

I quote all this to bring prominence/attention to the power of our *talking*, to the *activity* of it, to the *movement* of it, and to leave in the background the static *forms* of the already *said*, the supposed *hidden ideal entities* — 'standing (in)' for what we call our 'ideas', 'thoughts', 'theories', etc., etc. — that we claim are *really* shaping our actions.

As I see it (along with Wittgenstein, Bakhtin, Merleau-Ponty, etc., etc.) the *meaning* of our *speakings* is 'in' our *speaking*, not in the '*content*' of what is *said*. And this is where we meet all the troubles that our *academic* ways of working get us into. Each *discipline* has a *subject matter* — the "*what*" our inquiries. "How shall we *define* it?" — "How can we *conceptualize* it?" — we also say. And *this* is how we take it *out of* the everyday lives of ordinary people; this is how we *disconnect* it from the lives in which it has its *proper home*; this is how we create a *fantasy world*, which for us as academics, can come to seem more 'real' than the everyday world of ordinary people.

Yet, on certain some occasions, as I intimated above, there *is* a need for unambiguous word-meanings, for clear definitions of word use. It is thus necessary to distinguish between the two realms in question: between what we might call (1) the realm of our professional activities and disciplinary practices, and (2) the realm of our everyday practical projects and of people simply getting and staying in-touch-with-each-other, a realm to do with knowing how-one-is-currently-placed in relation to one's fellows — a realm that I've touched on many times above, in which, as Wittgenstein (1953) puts it, I'm concerned to "know my way about" (no.123). In short, the realm of 'big B' Being that makes available to us *countless* possibilities for our next steps, but which continually confronts us with the fact that although countless they are quite *specific*, not 'just anything goes' — while being clearly 'open' to further specification... they are open only (and this is most important) to further specification of an already specified kind. In other words, at each point in the process, what has been specified so far is known in terms of its already specified further specifiability (Shotter, 1984, p.187).

Our concern here, then, with the use of language in relation to our *everyday* activities and practices, is a concern quite different from that of academics (living *reflectively* and *intellectually* rather than *practically*), who each wish to establish within their particular discipline a "*discursive formation*" (Foucault, 1972) which brings into rational visibility the focal 'subject matter' of the discipline — a subject matter that can be set out, as if exemplifying a Cartesian world order, in terms of a set of 'objects', and a set of rules for the 'ordering' of the relevant objects.

In other words, in moving from realms of social activity within which people *can come to* co-ordinate their diverse actions in with each other's *in the pursuit of a common goal* to realms of activity in which *practical* and *professional* ends as such are not at issue, we must operate in our inquiries within the realm of our informal, disorderly, non-professional, everyday activities. Indeed, to go further, we must not operate within any pre-established boundaries, or assume any pre-selected features, for our task in trying to understand how bounded, stable, orderly *arenas of language use* within a particular social group can be both *constituted* and then *instituted*[58], is that of selecting out of an indeterminate realm of natural tendencies, just those that are relevant to the pursuit of a common goal, or to a focus on the sustaining and elaboration of a tradition or a culture.

---

[58] To *institute* ways of acting within a social group, is create within it practices and procedures concerned with how, once constituted, they may be sustained by bringing into existence stable, self-sanctioning, disciplinary procedures oriented towards a particular 'subject matter'. To repeat, as Merleau-Ponty (1970) put it: "What we understand by the concept of institution are those events in experience which endow it with durable dimensions, in relation to which a whole series of other experiences will acquire meaning, will form an intelligible series or a history — or again those events which sediment in me a meaning, not just as survivals or residues, but as the invitation to a sequel, the necessity of a future" (pp.40-41).

From bounded conceptual realms 'in theory' to unbounded, but articulated spaces, 'in the everyday worlds of our practical activities'

Central to my exploration of our functional or performative or 'directive' use of our words in their speaking so far, is the distinction I have drawn between those *unconsidered* uses that occur to members of a particular linguistic community, spontaneously, and the kind of *considered* talking we do in which we very carefully choose our words in an effort to utter a temporal-sequence of word-forms whose unfolding articulation will express, will re-produce, the unique contours of a particular experience. Where the task at issue here, as I see it, is that of showing that the unfolding of the experience in question is such that, if *worded* differently, it could lead into different continuations. In other words, at issue is the difference between describing 'Reality' *as it is*, and the *'openings* in Reality as it is' for changing it to *how we would like it to be.* Or, to put it differently: How can we break the hold on us of those unconsidered uses of words that occur to us spontaneously, in order to talk in a more considered fashion aimed at revealing such openings?

Currently debate rages (see Schear, 2013) as to whether *all* our relations to reality in fact draw on our conceptual capacities in some way or other (the view of John McDowell, 1998), or whether we draw on non-rational, non-propositional, embodied *coping skills* of a completely non-conceptual kind (Dreyfus' view). As Dreyfus (2013) sees it, "McDowell begins his account of the relation of mind to world *too late*" (p.23, my emphasis), and in this I can only agree. But I want also to add that although Dreyfus agrees with Heidegger and Merleau-Ponty, that "what is required are non-conceptual coping skills that disclose a space in which things can be encountered as what and how they are... [which] by orienting to it... we are absorbed into a field of forces drawing us to keep up our ongoing coping like a pilot staying on the beam" (p.21), he does not supply an account *of the process* within which the kind of *"holistic background"* or *"field of forces"* that we can become *absorbed* into enables us to come to act in ways in which *accountable* to others in our socio-linguistic group, i.e., ways that lead those others to 'see' our otherwise indeterminate, novel activities *as* we intended them to be 'seen', as still 'fitting in with' the 'done things' within our culture. He merely provides an *after-the-fact* phenomenological *description* of the outcome of an earlier process. Thus in another sense, his account is also *too late*; as I see it, a *before-the-fact* account is still required (see Shotter, 2014).

That is, we still need to distinguish between re-arrangements of what we currently take to be pre-existing 'things' and the emergence of the radically new; between the 'seeing' of new *possibilities* for re-relating already determined entities into new configurations — a cognitive-epistemological achievement – and the nature of that radical, first-time activity in which we make what is essentially *indeterminate* take on a form, a *symbolic form for us that is open to further differentiation*, other than that which it would have had if we had not acted. In so doing, in "that moment of Being which is constituted by the transitiveness and open event-ness of Being," as Bakhtin (1993, p.1) puts it, as we orient ourselves differently in relation to our surroundings, we not only *determine* a new set of intra-related actualities, we also *determine* a new range of *possibilities* now open to us that were not previously in existence — a perceptual-ontological achievement.

If our task is to seek to understand what we experience and perceive only in terms of what we experience and perceive, to understand it in terms of itself, rather than in terms of another worded world of our own creation — to explain what is real for us only by what is real for us, and the situated and time-bound only by the situated and time-bound — then we must talk *from within the living* of our lives, rather than from an *illusory* place outside them. To do this, we need to come to a grasp of the difference between difference–, distinction–, and/or relation–making speech, and conceptually-shaped speech.

Concepts, definitions:

- They work 'from outside' a circumstance of concern'
- they are 'pre-emptive' in the sense of decreeing ahead of one's inquiries, the basic *entities* one is expecting to discover[59].
- they also work to put a *boundary* around of *field* of study
- they work only in terms of *samenesses*, 'identities' even
- we see the world *only through* them, as *corresponding* to definitions of our own devising
- their power is supposed to be in their *general* nature, true for *all time*, and *all places*.
- in other words, they work in an 'after-the-fact' manner to decree the *whatness* (ontology) of what we have *already observed* as having happened in a situation or circumstance.
- they are 'in our interest' of *explaining* events in terms of their *causes*
- ordinary people experience themselves as lacking the 'expert'

---

59 "... the world of the [laboratory] experiment seems always capable of becoming a man-made reality, and this, while it may increase man's power of making and acting, even of creating a world, far beyond what any previous age dared to imagine in dream and phantasy, unfortunately puts man back once more – and now even more forcefully – into the prison of his own mind, into the limitations of patterns he himself created" (Arendt, 1959, p.261).

knowledge of academics, but at the same time experience it as *lying outside* of what *matters* to them

- thus academic 'knowledge' can all too easily work to disable those who are already enabled (in many different ways of their own devising)
- indeed, they can very easily lead practitioners into 'gaming' a practice, i.e., acting to achieve their own *interests* as professional practitioners, rather than in working out in the world at large

Is there an alternative? – Yes, the 'difference making distinctions' at work in our speakings

- They work 'from within' a sensed circumstance of concern, 'from within' a phenomenon
- they work to 'internally articulate' it into a more richly structured 'landscape of possibilities'
- they leave the circumstance open to further development
- we can thus *not define* in any precise way the *nature of* the circumstance – but, noting James' comment that "we nevertheless have an acutely discriminative sense" of the "*signs of direction* in thought" it provides us with, we can (by the use of images and metaphors, and other carefully crafted ways of talking, say very precisely *what they are like* so that others can related to their nature.
- but they do not place any boundaries on the *realms* of our inquiry – this means that we are always left with a sense of there being a 'something more' that we might bring into out later inquiries
- most importantly, they work, not in terms of identities, but in terms of similarities *and differences*, thus to produce, to repeat the point made above, an internally articulated landscape of possible ways forward.
- this enables inquirers to inquiry into *this, that,* or *some other* particular situation *in terms of itself,* in terms of features within it of relevance to the concerns of those living within that circumstance.
- they work on listeners by 'pointing out' features in the listener's surroundings to attend to – features that they themselves may not yet have responded to.
- what is most crucial here, though, is both the ethical and political function of our *wordings* in the *speaking* of our utterances.
- different words arouse different *anticipations* of what next might happen.
- different *intonations* indicate a speaker's own relations to their

own words — confident, hesitant, offered, demanding, etc, etc.

- our *textual formations* matter if we are to inquire into the *uniquely particular* situations within which we all live in our everyday lives.
- in other words, they can work in a 'before-the-fact' manner to 'point out' possible steps in a 'developmental trajectory' in our exploratory efforts, aimed at determining, along with the others around us, what collectively we come to call the 'facts of the matter'.

Inside the realm of 'difference-making speech'

Straightaway, we can point to a number of major advantages of such *difference-making* and *relation-making* activities over those working in terms of simply *making-correspondences*: In not putting boundaries around a field of inquiry, they leave the 'space' around us unbounded and open for further exploration. Further, instead of requiring a one-off, fitting-or-not test of correspondence, continuing inquiries can, over time, introduce further inner articulations into the space, thus enabling our inquiries to exhibit an evolutionary or developmental trajectory to them — a time-course, with a from-birth-to-death[60] generational structure to it, with each new generation beginning its life from within the already structured context of its predecessor's cultural achievements, a context that now makes available the satisfaction of *needs* (Todes, 2001) of a kind utterly unknown to previous generations.

I have called these kinds of difference-making inquiries, Wittgensteinian (1953) ones, because, as we saw above, he suggested we can make sense of what is bewildering us by using what he called "objects of comparison" (no.130) — like the notions of "language-game" (no.7), "form(s) of life" (no.19), or a "measuring-rod" (no.131), as itself something with which a comparison is made.

Such objects are objects that cannot in themselves be precisely defined, but whose (in fact countless) features can be used *poetically* or *metaphorically*, as required, in the service of bringing into rational visibility, features or aspects of an otherwise indeterminate circumstance, thus to suggest a *way* of moving on from it. Where, what is crucial here, is that by equating what is indeterminate with what is well-known to us, we can try *acting towards* it *as if* it is amenable to being treated in a similar manner — where the 'test' of our correctness is not in a once-off *formal* correspondence, but in our *gradually*

---

60 Which can be elaborated into birth; growing-into-a-way-of-life; adolescence; courtship; marriage; conception; pregnancy; family; death... and so on...

coming to act in the course of our *trying to act correctly*[61].

As a consequence, and perhaps most importantly, rather than merely working with a once-off, 'thin' correspondence between *shapes* or *forms*, we can now begin to deal with unpacking 'thick' *meanings* over a period of time by working with difference-making speakings which can 'move' us *ontologically*, not just *epistemologically* — that is, in their happening from within an unfolding, pulsating, from-birth-to-death time-course, they can 'move' us in a developmental or evolutionary fashion in our very being-in-the-world.

Indeed, in Shotter (1975), I outlined the process of difference-making thus: "For example, in Fig. 8.1, think of f (flux) as some as yet, say, unanalysed speech noise: stage 1. After experiencing it for a while, we may begin to distinguish between periods of, say, relative variability (A +) and relative constancy (A—): stage 2. Having distinguished the two parts and set them over against one another, we must remember that they are still related to one another as parts of the same whole: stage 3. Within the more constant episodes (A—) we may then notice, say, a relative presence (B +) and a relative absence (B—) of hiss: stage 4. And, again, after having noted the difference we must also remember the relation: stage 5. And so on: the totality of the flux may be differentiated further, or in relation to quite different features, as exigencies demand.

Fig. 8.1 (Shotter, 1975)

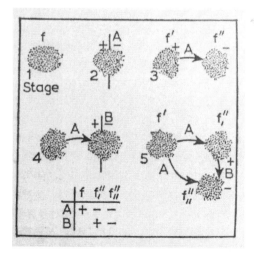

---

[61] I will return to the task of spelling out the unfolding time-course of this process in more detail below.

The process serves to structure a whole into a set of inter-related parts, the character of each part being known in terms of its relations to all the others in the system — they are all still parts of f, but now they are 'characterized' parts. Unlike the attempt to characterize things in isolation from one another by abstracting common features, the parts here are reciprocally determined, all in relation to one another. Each has its significance in the context provided by the rest; one unit cannot be changed without changing the character of the whole. And, while perceptually distinguishable, the parts cannot be physically isolated from one another without destroying the set of relations constituting the whole.

Construing or differentiating a totality into a system of interrelated parts by use of a construct system does two things: (1) it identifies each part just as much in terms of features it does not have in common with others as those it does — things are known both in terms of what they are and what they are not; and (2) parts are defined not by what they are in themselves but by the part they play in relation to all the other parts constituting the whole. Thus we have here then the kind of system discussed by Dewey as an organic structure, in which the parts are known in terms of their *value* or *function,* by what they are doing in the system rather than by any formal qualities they may have when considered in isolation from one another. Such a form of order as this is of quite a different kind to mechanical forms of order, consisting of objective parts" (p.117).

Further, in thinking of the act of distinction in *after-the-fact* terms, it is difficult to avoid thinking of differencing only in terms of *separating one 'thing' from another*, so we come to think of 'distinguishing' and 'separating' as the same. But they are not. We can see that they are not by considering the *before-the-fact* unfolding of the relevant step-by-step process, to get a grasp of the coming into-being of the *relational-structure* so produced.

Thus if our task is to seek to understand what we experience and perceive only in terms of what we in fact experience and perceive, then we must talk *from within our living* of our lives, rather than from an *illusory* place outside them. To do this, we need to come to a grasp of the difference between our everyday *uses of* distinction–, difference–, and/or relation–making speech — as we sense both the particular *movements of feeling* aroused in us, along with our need to phrase our utterances both ethically and politically — and the function of our prior, conceptually-shaped speech, in coming to express the in fact unclassifiable feelings[62] occurring within us in the particular situations

---

62 See footnote 19: Wittgenstein (1953) calls some forms of evidence, "imponderable evidence" (p.228), because they cannot be categorized or classified; they constitute what

we occupy. This task — of considering the nature of speech *before it is actually spoken*, of describing the processes at work in us to do with *bringing an experience to linguistic expression* — is as yet so little appreciated that I want to spend the next chapter in exploring its nature.

Thus, clearly, we do not need to be able to *explain* our everyday utterances and actions scientifically, i.e., analyze them into a certain set of elements that combine in repetitive patterns to produce observed outcomes, to be able, through everyday reflection and inquiry, to improve them, to gain a more deliberate command of them. And to make this claim is not to reject the value of science in our lives. It is simply to note such facts, for instance, that in the course of their everyday involvements with them, in being spontaneous responsive to their children's actions in a living, bodily, expressive manner, parents can (informally) teach their children, not only their mother tongue, but also countless other aspects of acceptable and intelligible behavior, without having any idea of the supposed *laws* or *rules* by which their children's minds and bodies are governed.

---

physicists would call "singularities;" they give rise to experiences occurring as a result of our participation in what Bakhtin (1993) calls "once-occurrent Being-as-event" (p.2).

6 The primacy of 'specifically vague' movements of feeling

"... expressions do not have a sense that remains identical throughout the changing occasions of their use. The events that were talked about were *specifically vague*. Not only do they not frame a clearly restricted set of possible determinations but the depicted events include as their essentially intended and sanctioned features an accompanying 'fringe' of determinations that are open with respect to internal relationships, relationships to other events, and relationships to retrospective and prospective possibilities."

(Garfinkel, 1967, pp.40-41, my italics)

"Actually I should like to say that... the *words* you utter or what you think as you utter them are not what matters, so much as the difference they make at various points in your life... *Practice* gives words their sense."

(Wittgenstein, 1980a, p.85)

What makes the nature of our efforts and struggles to *say something* before we actually *say it* so difficult to describe, is their 'fluid', dynamical, still-in-process nature, the fact that they are always on the way to somewhere else, always in movement, with no clear beginnings or endings, with no clear existence as self-contained and thus nameable 'things'. The difficulty is, as Wittgenstein (1953) puts it — in suggesting that because we often talk in a completely untroubled fashion in our everyday affairs, we must in fact already know how to express our experiences in words — is that if someone claims that "'You know how sentences do it, for nothing is concealed'," you straightaway want to reply: "'Yes, but it all goes by so quick, and I should like to see it as it were laid open to view'" (no.435). In other words, although in practice we *just do it*, spontaneously, it is not a capacity that is available to us to perform *deliberately*; we would like to 'see' a step-by-step, unfolding trajectory laid out from beginning to end, with an account at each step of *where* in the larger scheme of things we *are*, along with an account of *what might be done* next, if we are to achieve an overall goal in concert with all the others in our social group.

In trying to do this, to provide such an account, as I intimated above, what becomes more and more clear to us as we try to 'enter into' the nature of the developmental-expressive process, is that it begins its 'birth' within a particular, concrete, definitive and distinctive movement of feeling occurring within us, within an experience of our current, living relationships to the world around us, that opens up to us, not by our choosing to *think about* it in a particular way, but as we begin to *act* in the course of *trying to do something particular* within it.

It is the *uniqueness* of this originating movement of feeling that makes it so difficult to describe, for, as James (1989) points out: "Sensorial images are stable psychic facts; we can hold them still and look at them as long as we like. These bare images of logical movement, on the contrary, are psychic transitions, always on the wing, so to speak, and are not to be glimpsed except in flight. Their function is to lead from one set of images to another. As they pass, we feel both the waxing and the waning images in a way quite different from their full presence. If we try to hold fast the feeling of direction, the full presence [of the words meant] comes and the feeling of direction is lost" (p.253).

Indeed, without our sense of the *transitions*, of continuities, our sense at each moment of what in particular leads to what next — which holds all the sequenced words of an utterance together as a particular meaningful unity — we would be unable to grasp the *unique* meaning of a speaker's words in *this* situation. And in a moment, giving primacy to our acting rather than to thinking, I will begin to explore the task of expressing our unfolding, temporal, bodily experiences linguistically, in a comparative manner, or artistically, in a more direct manner, in relation to our beginning to *act* or to *speak* in the course of *trying to do something in particular* within a particular situation. But for the moment, let me return to a further exploration of what our *intending to speak* is like *before* we actually speak, and how our 'urge' to 'speak the truth' in our claims as to the nature of a phenomenon can drastically shape the claims we make about it.

William James (1890) brings this out as follows: "Suppose we try to recall a forgotten name. The state of our consciousness is peculiar. There is a gap therein: but no mere gap. It is gap that is intensively active ... We can only designate the difference by borrowing the names of objects not yet in the mind ... If wrong names are proposed to us, this singularly definite gap acts immediately so as to negate them. They do not fit into its mould. *And the gap of one word does not feel like the gap of another, all empty of content as both might seem necessarily to be when described as gaps ... Which is to say that our psychological vocabulary is wholly inadequate to name the differences that exist, even such strong differences as these.* But namelessness is compatible with existence. There are innumerable consciousnesses of emptiness, no one of which taken in itself has a name, but all different from each other. *The ordinary way is to assume that they are all emptinesses of consciousness, and so of the same state.* But the feeling of absence is *toto coelo* other than the absence of feeling. It is an intense feeling. The rhythm of a lost word may be there without a sound to clothe it; or the evanescent sense of something which is the initial vowel or consonant may mock us fitfully, without growing more distinct" (pp.251- 252, my italics)[63], and so on.

We thus face a dilemma: Given our Cartesian heritage, and the ease with which we accept the primacy of our thinking and generalized truth-talk — compared with the difficulty of treating our actions as primary and that of accepting that we can only *gradually come to act correctly* after a great deal of (possibly) risky exploratory activity — it is no wonder that in 'filling in the gap', in satisfying the tension of an "emptiness of consciousness" (James), or the "precise uneasiness in the world of things-said" (Merleau-Ponty, 1964, p.19) aroused in us by our asking ourselves: '*What, actually, is* happening in me?', we feel that we need an account that *clearly distinguishes* that *what* from all else that might be happening to us. Where are we to find that account? As William James (1890) puts it, because "it has ... a nature of its own of the most positive sort," we find it all but impossible to say anything about it "without using words that belong to the later mental facts that replace it." Thus, "the intention *to-say-so-and-so* is the only name it can receive" (p.253).

Such after-the-fact accounts — *explanations* couched in terms of such named entities as being the *causes* of our actions — clearly provide a satisfaction of the felt tensions motivating many of our inquiries. But, as we have seen above, over and over again, we cannot treat such accounts as final, as providing the *last word*, if our overall aim is that of *coming to act as our particular circumstances require us to act*. Perhaps the best thing we can say, is to repeat what John Austin (1970) said about our spontaneous, unconsidered everyday uses of ordinary language, "... that superstition and error and fantasy of all kinds do become incorporated in ordinary language and even sometimes stand up to the survival test (only, when they do, why should we not detect it?). Certainly, then, ordinary language is not the last word: in principle it can everywhere be supplemented and improved upon and superseded. Only remember, it *is* the *first* word" (p.185).

---

[63] "It has therefore a nature of its own of the most positive sort, and yet what can we say about it without using words that belong to the later mental facts that replace it? The intention to-say-so-and-so is the only name it can receive" (p.253); hence our assumption that "they are all emptinesses of consciousness, and so of the same state" (p.252). Merleau-Ponty (1964) makes a similar point: "Signification arouses speech as the world arouses my body — by a mute presence which awakens my intentions without deploying itself before them... the significative intention (even if it is subsequently to fructify in 'thoughts') is at the moment no more than a *determinate gap* to be filled by words — the excess of what I intend to say over what is being said or has already been said" (p.89).

There are, thus, two conclusions that I want to come to in this section: One is to do with the *agential* nature of the felt 'gaps' or 'emptinesses' in our experiences of our circumstances, and the fact that they, so to speak, exert 'calls' and make 'demands' of a very precise kind upon us; the other is to do with how easy it is for us, as Stolzenberg (1978) puts it, to be 'taken in' by "initial acts of acceptance as such in the domain of ordinary language use" (p.267) expressing theoretical claims as to the basic nature of a phenomenon in question, which, once accepted, come to shape our thinking to such an extent that we become inescapably entrapped.

The anonymous agential thinking occurring within me

Above, I distinguished between the kind of thinking that just comes to happen within us — the kind of thinking that is 'done' spontaneously by all those within a social group who have all come to share in the learning of a common language — and the more deliberate thinking we, as individuals, can do, that occurs within us, and is shaped by, the *common-sense* or *sensing* (as an agential activity) we share with all the others in such a group. Merleau-Ponty (1962) brings out its anonymous, agential nature as follows: "Every perception takes place in an atmosphere of generality and is presented to us anonymously. I cannot say that *I* see the blue of the sky in the sense in which I say that I understand a book or again in which I decide to devote my life to mathematics. My perception, even when seen from the inside, expresses a given situation: I can see blue because I am *sensitive* to colours, whereas personal acts create a situation: I am a mathematician because I have decided to be one. So, if I wanted to render precisely the perceptual experience, I ought to say *one* perceives in me, and not that I perceive" (p.215).

But further, we hardly ever just behold a visual scene without a particular practical aim in mind, in surveying what is before me with the purpose of moving forward within it, my as-yet-indeterminate sense of my situation constitutes a bewilderment for my body to resolve: I must find an *orientation*, a *way of relating* myself to my surroundings, which will provide *it* (not me) with the means of determining a pathway forward for me. To do that, I must immerse myself within my situation, and allow 'it' to 'think itself within me', as the anonymous agency it is. Thus rather than what elsewhere (Shotter, 2005c, 2011) I have called 'aboutness'-thinking that functions in terms of features and properties, we need here to practice 'withness'-thinking, a way of thinking in which we permit, allow, or invite the *unfolding time-contours* of our experiences to shape our expressive activities.

Returning to our dilemma: That (1) without a *distinctive name* for the precise kind of 'gap' or 'emptiness' we are experiencing in our current circumstances, we can easily assume that no such 'entities' can be at work in shaping our activities — we thus come to overlook observable phenomena whose occurrence becomes obvious to us all with a little training in how to pay attention to them — but (2) without a distinctive name for them, we have a tendency to assume that our expressions *do* "have a sense that remains identical through the changing occasions of their use" (Garfinkel, 1967, p.40), when in fact they do not.

In resolving this dilemma, I want to turn to the work of John Dewey (1938/2008), who in his *Logic: the Theory of Inquiry*, points out that, while psychological theories take "a *singular* object or event for the subject matter of its analysis. In actual experience, there is never any such isolated singular object or event; *an* object or event is always a special part, phase, or aspect, of an environing experienced world — a situation" (p.72). Indeed, there is an overall pervasive quality to the *situations* within which we conduct our inquiries which not only "binds all constituents into a whole but it is also unique" (p.74), and which also constitutes or determines (in essentially a hermeneutical manner) the particular 'objects' of our studies as the unique kind of objects they are. Thus, for Dewey (1938/2008), the fact that a situation in all its unfolding details is held together as a complex whole by the fact that it is constituted and characterized throughout by a single, unique *quality*, a quality that "is sensed or *felt*" (p.73), is of great importance. It gives rise to a kind of contextualized mode of determination that allows for countless different features or aspects of a circumstance to be brought into visibility as *named entities* as required, rather than it being insisted that they can only be known in terms of a few pre-selected features or properties.

Thus, in opposition to the current mainstream, instead of beginning our inquiries by trying to form theories or conceptual frameworks — which as Dewey sees it are so "fixed in advance that the very things which are genuinely decisive in the problem in hand and its solution, are completely overlooked" (p.76) — we should begin our inquiries (as has been already suggested above) by being prepared to 'go into' our perplexities and uncertainties, to 'go into' our feelings of disquiet at what we already know, to 'go into' our confusions and bewilderments. For strangely, it is precisely *within these feelings*, if we take the trouble to explore them further, that we can begin to find the guidance we need in overcoming our disquiets. For, says Dewey (1938/2008), "the peculiar quality of what pervades the given materials, constituting them a situation, is not just uncertainty at large; it is a *unique doubtfulness* which makes that situation to be just and only the situation it is. It is this unique quality that not only evokes the particular inquiry engaged in but that exercises control over its special procedures" (p.109, my italics).

We can call the kind of inquiry Dewey (1938/2008) outlines, a practice-situated or situation-based kind of research, rather than theory-driven research (the kind of research undertaken in the laboratories of the natural sciences). As he terms it, this kind of inquiry is much more oriented towards overcoming the kind of difficulties we face in our everyday worlds in which we must deal continually with other people, and with the enormously complicated ways in, in the service of our *interests* (Habermas, 1972), we need to seek "the controlled or directed transformation of an indeterminate situation into one that is so determinate in its constituent distinctions and relations as to convert the elements of the original situation into a unified whole" (p.108).

As stated, this may seem to be saying that the human and the behavioural sciences should be seen as being structured and conducted in ways very different from the natural sciences (as should the humanities, as such, be seen also). But if Cassirer (2000) is correct, and I think he is, this means that a common ground for *all* our inquiries, as to how best to live our individual lives *in relation to* the lives of all the others around us, is to be found in our efforts at understanding expressive phenomena and the nature of the thick, before-the-fact objectivity we share with everyone else — for within this larger context, as Cassirer claims, the conduct of *cultural sciences* does not have to be distinguished from that of the *natural sciences*. This fact is unfortunately obscured by our failure to fully recognize the degree to which we make use of what elsewhere (Shotter, 2011) I have called our everyday *relationally-responsive* usage of words, in *formalizing* our special *representational-referential* use of them, later, in our theorizing.

In other words, in simply taking it that our 'words stand for things', and that when we state *what* we are inquiring into, and the others around seem to understand us without any difficulty, we either ignore or simply forget the fact that, in constituting amongst ourselves a sense of *what* the subject matter of our inquiries *is*, that we must first undertake, essentially, shared hermeneutical explorations akin, as Kuhn (2000) points out, to those we go through in our first-language learning.

Entrapment

There are two main ways in which we can come to a grasp of the 'subject matter' of a discipline of inquiry: via conceptualizations and definitions and in essentially a hermeneutical process.

(1) Hermeneutically, participants begin by appreciating how, given the practical phenomena confronting them, theoretical categories can be used to constitute them as events of a recognizable kind — the research practice itself provides 'instructive accounts' as to how a theory should

be used and applied. Such categories are used as an unquestioned (and unquestionable) resource in organizing within the research paradigm one's perception of events. As Kuhn (2000) points out, in this process, in learning Newtonian mechanics, for instance, "the terms 'mass' and 'force' must be acquired together, and Newton's second law must play a role in their acquisition. One cannot, that is, learn 'mass' and 'force' independently and then empirically discover that force equals mass times acceleration. Nor can one first learn 'mass' (or 'force') and then use it to define 'force' (or 'mass') with the aid of the second law. Instead, all three must be learned together, parts of a whole new (but not a wholly new) way of doing mechanics. That point is unfortunately obscured by standard formalizations" (p.44).

(2) In our standard view, via conceptualizations, as Kuhn (1970) points out, we assume that "scientific knowledge is embedded in theory and rules," and students are supplied with problems, "to gain facility in their application" (p.187) — as if 'theories' of the basic entities under investigation, and the 'rules' defining their combinations, will wholly determine what one perceives *as* the relevant phenomena out in the natural world. But, Kuhn adds, "I have tried to argue, however, that this localization of the cognitive content of science is wrong ... In the absence of such exemplars, the laws and theories he has previously learned would have little empirical content" (pp.187-188). What the student needs, rather than mere definitions of such terms, is to be introduced to them by examples of their use — in *this, that,* or *some other* context — by someone who is already a fully-paid-up member of the speech community, the "thought collective" (Fleck, 1979), within which they are current.

In other words, when we learn the *use* of words in this hermeneutical fashion, we find that the practical *meaning* of the terms 'mass' and 'force' are intrinsically intra-related with each other to such an extent that Newton's second law — that force equals mass times acceleration — is a matter of logically implication, not of empirical discovery. For, just as we learn to relate our *use* words to the unfolding contours of our movements of feeling as we act in response to events occurring around us in our first-language learning, so we also learn, Kuhn (2000) suggests, "what categories of things populate the world, what their salient features are, and something about the behavior that is and is not permitted to them. In much of language learning these two sorts of knowledge — knowledge of words and knowledge of nature — are acquired together, not really two sorts of knowledge at all, but two faces of the single coinage that a language provides" (p.31).

Indeed, as we saw above, it is only too easy at the moment to assume that we can establish a social or behavioural science by *defining* a set of independently existing topics — to which we give such *names* as 'attention', 'perception', 'cognition', 'motivation', 'personality', developmental psychology', 'abnormal psychology', and so on — in terms of a *sequence of written words*, a statement assumed to represent, or to 'stand for', the topic in question. But we then go on to find that many of the crucial words that we are using in defining or conceptualizing the topics in question, are also nouns or nominalizations, i.e., *names* 'standing for' (or representing) crucial features in constituting *what*, essentially, the topic in question *is*. And it is, of course, utterly unclear as to whether the *meaning* of *these* words, should be understood in their flexible, everyday, contextualized sense, or whether they also need a special set of distinctive, context-free definitions.

Thus, as Kuhn (2000) points out, we have here the clash between the hermeneutical understanding of a particular term, and its conceptual meaning; the clash between a meaning that is understood by it playing a part or a role within an unfolding meaningful whole, open to a step-by-step differential articulation, and a meaning that is additively expressed by the sequencing of a set of observable features and properties; the clash between an understanding that takes us out into the actual world around us, and an understanding that requires us to relate to the world before us only in terms corresponding to the ones we currently have in our heads. As I noted above, to repeat, it is somewhat obvious that sooner or later, such definitions and conceptualizations are going to be found wanting in our efforts at trying to satisfy our everyday needs in terms of such 'thin', un-situated understandings.

Yet, the fact is, no matter how much thought, critical of this theory-first approach to our inquiries has accumulated over the years, it is the case that our notion of what it is to be a *properly rational* thinker in the world at the moment is still heavily influenced by the Cartesianism implicit in our everyday, taken-for-granted forms of talk and thought. For, to repeat, at the heart of it is our assumption that *systematic thought* must precede *all* our actions, or else others will claim that we are not properly fitting our actions to the requirements of current circumstances. While this *is* a crucial requirement, it is easy to allow it to divert our attention away from the fact that, as users of a common language, *we must be already be living in a world we share with all the others around us*, and it is this that makes it possible for us to orient ourselves, socially, towards organizing ourselves in the performance of tasks in common.

But yet again, as Hanson (1958) notes, in their aversion to dealing with phenomena still in motion, still undergoing developmental or evolutionary change, philosophers of science, by simply taking it for granted, still ignore the importance of the *instituting* activities that draw on the resources made available by this shared 'background', and instead, "have regarded as paradigms of physical inquiry not unsettled, dynamic, research sciences like microphysics, but finished systems, planetary mechanics, optics, electromagnetism and classical thermodynamics" (p.1), and this has, unfortunately, resulted in our arriving at conclusions which are, in fact, the *reverse* of what actually is happening. For like Kuhn, Hanson also questions whether what are often claimed to be empirical discoveries, are not in fact *logical implications* of our concepts. Thus, in outlining what is involved in studying dynamic, research sciences (rather than already instituted sciences), Hanson (1958) cautions: "let us examine not how observation, facts and data are built up into general systems of physical explanation, but how these systems are built into our observations, and our appreciation of facts and data" (p.3)[64].

The importance of this *reversal*, however, is that it does not show up in considering just the facts of the matter; it is thus not open to critical reflective thought. Hanson (1958) gives the example of Ernst Mach and Heinrich Hertz: "Mach construed dynamical laws as summary descriptions of sense observations, while for Hertz laws were highly abstract and conventional axioms whose role was not to describe the subject-matter but to determine it" (p.118). And indeed, as Hanson (1958) shows, in doing calculations, making predictions, and in providing explanations when working with scientific formulae, these two scientists might not differ at all in these activities. The difference between them — to do with the connections and relations they sense as existing within the phenomena of their inquiries — would show up "only in [their] 'frontier' thinking — where the direction of new inquiry has regularly to be redetermined" (p.118).

Indeed, by working simply in terms of pre-established definitions of how one's observations are to be interpreted, are to be made sense of, there is the possibility of one becoming, as Stolzenberg (1978) calls it, *entrapped*. That is, one can find oneself with an *institutionalized* set of attitudes, beliefs and habits of thought that, not only "constitute a closed system but also, and more significantly, (a) that certain of these beliefs are demonstrably incorrect; and (b) that certain fixed attitudes and habits of thought prevent this from being recognized" (p.223). Or, to put it differently: We can find ourselves so strongly committed, institutionally, to what we take to be simply the unquestionable facts of the matter, that we find all alternative proposals simply *senseless*.

How can this come about? In particular, he focuses upon the consequences produced by what he calls "certain unwittingly performed acts of acceptance as such in the domain of ordinary language use" (p.

---

[64] Recollect here, Foucault's (1972) remark that many of our *discursive practices*, "systematically form the objects of which they speak" (p.49).

267). What he means by "acts of acceptance as such" are those occasions when we simply take something for what it appears, or is purported to be, *and proceeds on that basis to some further action*, and if that action is successful, we then, retrospectively, accept them as being true. In other words, initial appearances may serve to structure a whole way of not only acting now, but of further ways of acting in the future based upon accepting them as what initially they appeared to be. Thus in the process, what, originally, were assumptions, become givens, and the idea of calling them into question is no longer intelligible. One is entrapped: for by conducting all of one's further activities in terms of categories and definitions — whose meanings have been grasped in "initial acts of acceptance as such in the domain of ordinary language use" (Stolzenberg) — which are then suspended from all further doubt, necessitates one having to assimilate all further activities to that set of pre-established categories. Having done this, there is no possibility of a dialogical-hermeneutical development of new categories; the transformation/metamorphosis of one's perceptual categories into completely new forms in the course of dialogue is denied.

This is a danger of institutionalization, of conducting one's inquiries within a discipline (Shotter, 2015a). Consider, by comparison, the process of listening to an account of an everyday family event at which one was not present, recounted to one by a family friend: if the facts so far are unsatisfactory, incomplete or even bewildering, in order not to be insulting to one's interlocutor, one waits for later facts and uses them in an attempt to decide the sense of the earlier ones; what sense there is to be found is not decided beforehand, but is discovered in the course of the exchange within which the account is offered — for we assume (i.e., we *trust*) that our conversational partners are *trying* to make sense to us, and will persist so that, sooner or later, they will succeed. For Stolzenberg (1978), then, it is the ease with which we can be influenced by our talk that can lead to our being entrapped. Yet, as Garfinkel (1967) shows, "the anticipation that persons *will* understand... [etc, etc.] are sanctioned properties of common discourse ... their seen but unnoticed presence is used to entitle persons to conduct their common conversational affairs without interference. Departures from such usages call forth immediate attempts to restore a right state of affairs" (p.41-42).

There is thus no simply 'on principle' solution to this dilemma. But I will say this: An intellectualist bias is very apparent in Western Thought, and has been so since the Greeks (and I will explore this in the next and concluding section of this chapter), where the trouble with it, is that it situates or places our perceptual processes — in which we need to transform an indeterminate situation into a determinate one in which all its distinctive, intra-related parts constitute a unified whole — within a Cartesian world of separately existing, self-contained parts in lawful motion.

Instead of continually *instituting* new professions and disciplines, we need to bring into rational visibility the fact that, we are already in our everyday affairs relating ourselves to, and consciously participating in, a 'common world', and that when we do this, an objective order and determinateness becomes readily available to us all. To reiterate what we have already met with above: There is no need to enclose ourselves in images of the world of our own construction; instead, we need to turn outward, toward a world that is already trans-individual, inter-subjective, general, and valid for all. And nowhere is such a trans-individual, inter-subjective world more obviously available to us all than in the phenomenon of language. Spoken words, words in their speaking, always have a 'point'; they reach out beyond the mere noises issuing from speakers' mouths towards 'things' in their surroundings; they 'touch', 'move', or 'arouse tendencies' within listeners to direct their attention in a particular way to what is before them. Thus, if our task is to seek to understand what we experience and perceive only *in terms of itself*, as a unique, unclassifiable entity, then we must talk *from within the actual living* of our lives, rather than from with an *illusory*, pre-organized 'space' outside them. To do this, we need to come to an understanding of how difference–, distinction–, and/or relation–making speech can be used in each particular circumstance we occupy, to fashion a precisely, determinate account of each circumstance in a way that talk of conceptually-shaped generalities cannot.

We achieve precision indirectly, by *allusion*. As Merleau-Ponty (1964) puts it: "By coming back to spoken or living language we shall find that its expressive value is not the sum of the expressive values which allegedly belong individually to each element of the 'verbal chain'. On the contrary, these elements form a system in synchrony in the sense that each of them signifies only its difference in respect to the others (as Saussure says, signs are essentially 'diacritical'); and as this is true of them all, there are only differences of signification in a language. The reason why a language finally intends to say and does say [*veut dire et dit*] something is not that each sign is the vehicle for a signification which allegedly belongs to it, but that all the signs together allude to a signification which is always in abeyance when they are considered singly, and which I go beyond them toward without their ever containing it. Each of them expresses only by reference to a certain mental equipment, to a certain arrangement of our cultural implements, and as a whole they are like a blank form which we have not yet filled out, or like the gestures of others, *which intend and circumscribe an object*[65] *of the world that I do not see*" (p.88, my italics).

---

[65] A particular hermeneutically fashioned unity.

Satisfying our 'desires' is optional, gratifying our 'real needs' is not

7

"The preconceived idea of the crystalline purity can only be removed by turning our whole examination around. (One might say: the axis of reference of our examination must be rotated, but about the axis of our real need.).... We are talking about the spatial and temporal phenomenon of language, not about some non-spatial, non-temporal phantasm... But we talk about it as we do about the pieces in chess when we are stating the rules of the game, not describing their physical properties."

(Wittgenstein, 1953, no.108)

"When philosophers use a word — 'knowledge', 'being', 'object', 'I', 'proposition', 'name' — and try to grasp the essence of the thing, one must always ask oneself: is the word ever actually used in this way in the language-game which is its original home? — What we do is to bring words back from their metaphysical to their everyday use."

(Wittgenstein, 1953, no.116)

Our real need, I want to suggest, as I intimated above, is to 'know our way about' within the particularities of our own human world — a need that is, in fact, *not* satisfied by the presumed discovery of *any* 'ideal orders' hidden behind appearances. As a consequence of ignoring the very fact that we owe our capacity to undertake *scientific* inquiries into our own, everyday human nature, to our having grown-up as active, engaged participants within countless different culturally developed practices and institutions, we now find ourselves bewildered as to *what*, precisely, is the question we are attempting to answer in our current inquiries within the social and behavioural sciences. Clearly, we are just as bewildered now as then as to *what* it really is for us, not just to be *human* beings organically and biologically, but to be *personal* beings, reliant on our relations to others for the nature of our humanness. Indeed, in my little book of 1975, I remarked:

"If men (sic) do make themselves, then, when they lose their grasp on quite how they do it, the process could miscarry, with both theoretical and practical consequences.

Theoretically, the aim of any science is to describe the unity and coherence of its subject matter. We cannot be content with merely accumulating in our journals an indefinitely long list of the empirical traits of man. Yet this is just what modern psychology does do. And in the attempt to find an 'organizing principle' it has taken up and then dropped one idea after another: reflexes, information theory, computer processes, etc., etc. — each new theoretical focus becoming a Procrustean bed into which the facts of man's supposed nature are meant to fit but will not.

The upshot of all this is that perhaps in no other age than ours has man become such a mystery to himself. We have a growing number of different social and biological sciences studying man, and psychology itself fragments almost daily into new specialist disciplines... The explosion in our knowledge has resulted in an ever expanding array of disconnected and fragmented data lacking all conceptual unity — it has provided material appropriate perhaps for the building of a great edifice, but no hint of a plan for its construction. Unless we can find a way of connecting all these scattered facts together, we shall remain buried under the debris of our own investigations... Each new start we make begins (and ends) in the same way as the last — our psychology becomes like a merry-go-round, its tunes and riders changing, but progress upon it largely an illusion" (pp.15-16).

Something was, and is still, missing. For although scientific methods, in the service of satisfying our *desires*, may give us this, that, or some other particular control over our material circumstances, they still leave us 'adrift' without a map or a compass, so to speak, within our larger social and historical circumstances, as to what actually we *need* if we are to succeed in our unremitting task of *humanifying* (Ingold, 2015) ourselves. If we are continually to create and sustain our human-ways-of-being-human-in-a-human-world, what we lack, clearly, is not only an account of what Vygotsky (1978) calls above, the *socio-cultural* dimension, i.e., the nature of the *social-processes* by which we become human, we lack also a 'directive sense' as to whether any of the *desires* we are currently seeking to satisfy are in fact good for us overall, in the long run, or not; we have no way of knowing whether they in fact relate to any of our actual *needs* as *persons*, owing our lives to our living relations with the others and othernesses around us.

As we have seen above, our becoming (and remaining) one or another kind of human being is not something that just happens to each of us, naturally, and individually, without our being 'cared for' and 'responded to' appropriately, by the others around us. Indeed, our becoming 'someone', an autonomous person within a culture, able to account for our own actions if challenged to do so by others, is an unending task, a task that is not only our own responsibility, but also at every moment, the responsibility of others around us, along with our predecessors.

The establishment and maintaining of certain *institutions* responsible for aspects of this task is also required. But it is not always clear to us whether the particular humanifying processes we are currently instituting are in fact contributing to our becoming more human than we are already, or whether they will lead to our sinking down into less well-considered and less socially-well-ordered forms. We at first need an organizing principle, something at work within us as a group of inquirers so that, although we all may explicitly *perform* many different tasks, we all share a yet-unsatisfied-sense of what overall it *is* that we need[66] as the motive for our inquiries; and then, after having taken a few steps, we need a critical appraisal, to do with evaluating the nature of what we have achieved so far.

I emphasize these concerns, because it is often said that we seek knowledge 'for its own sake' — just as it is said that we seek 'art for art's sake'. Whereas, everything above seems to suggest that this is not, or should not, be so. We need to put what appears to us to be *a naturally felt urge to seek knowledge* into a larger context, and to suggest that the urge we feel has its origins in the much more basic fact mentioned above: that we continually *need* to re-create and sustain our humanness in the face of our continuously changing circumstances. And not just any old knowledge will do in that task. Yet strangely, while being able to be very clear about our *wants* and *desires*, so that we can go on to make elaborate plans for their achievement, piecemeal, we find it very difficult to come to a sense of what, in fact, overall, our *needs* are.

At this point, I want to introduce the work of Samuel Todes (2001): As he sees it, on our entry as inquirers into the world around us, "we begin as a creature of *need* rather than *desire*... [Where] a need... is originally given as a pure restlessness; as the consciousness of one's *un*directed activity" (p.176). We come into the world as if we are lost; not as if we have lost something, but as 'lost souls', disoriented, not knowing who or what we are, or where we are. "Our whole quest of discovery is thus," says Todes, "initially prompted by need rather than desire. It is initially 'directed' not to get what we want but to discover what we want to get... The meeting of a need, unlike the satisfaction of a desire, always involves a confirmatory *recognition* of the need met, a recognition that retroactively determines the true nature of the need that prompted the activity culminating in its filling... [A 'desire'] was a 'desire' only because there was no problem of recognition; we recognized what we wanted by it even before its satisfaction... We can thus be disappointed by getting

---

66 As we will see below, Fleck (1979) asks, how is it that "a 'true' finding can arise from false assumptions, from vague first experiments, and from many errors and detours?" (p.78) — it is as if there is a gravitational or magnetic field at work within a disciplinary group, not a unity of opinions or beliefs, but a shared *direction*, a shared way of *characterizing*, but not wholly *determining*, the particulars that can appear within the field.

what we desire... We cannot, in contrast be disappointed by the meeting of our needs. For the whole enterprise of exploration and discovery of the world only makes sense as an attempt to meet our needs; the meeting of our needs is what we *mean* by 'gratification'. Unlike desires, needs as such need to be met" (p.177) — in other words, while satisfying our desires is an optional matter, meeting our needs is not.

Without our being 'cared for' by others when young, without our being able to 'grow into' the mental lives and ways of talking of those around us, we will fail to flourish as fully autonomous *human* beings, not merely with our own, uniquely *personal* way of being in the world, but also lacking in ways of being *accountable* to the others around us, when we act in ways which at first make no sense to them (Shotter, 1984). As I outlined above, an *account* is to do with bringing ordinary everyday words to an otherwise indeterminate flow of circumstances, to constitute it as a sequence of events of a kind already well known within a society's ways of making sense of things. Where it is *the use of the words* in uttering one's accounts that works to arouse in their recipients the "anticipated situational consequences of questioned conduct" (Mills, 1940, p.905).

Thus it is the actual expressing of appropriate wordings that is crucial: "When an agent vocalizes or imputes motives, he is not trying to *describe* his experienced social action. He is not merely stating 'reasons'," says Mills (1940). "He is influencing others — and himself. Often he is finding new reasons which will mediate action" (p.907). Thus, if we bear in mind the *relationally-responsive* use of words, rather than their *representational-referential* use, the actual words we use are important, for we find that within different social groups, members act in terms of a basic, taken-for-granted vocabulary of so-called 'bottom-line' terms. It is as if in our 'inner exploratory conversations' we question ourselves: "If I did this, what could I say? What would they say?" Thus our "decisions," says Mills (1940), "may be, wholly or in part, delimited by answers to such queries... As a word, a *motive tends to be one which is to the actor and to the other members of a situation an unquestioned answer to questions concerning social and lingual conduct. A stable motive is an ultimate in justificatory conversation*" (p.907). The use of motive-talk "in justifying or criticizing an act [works to] link it to situations, integrate one man's action with another's, and [to] line up conduct with norms" (p.907).

Distinguishing lower and higher forms of ourselves: eliminating injustices, eliminating disquiets

"The more narrowly we examine actual language, the sharper becomes the conflict between it and our requirement. (For the crystalline purity of logic was, of

course, not *a result of investigation*: it was a
requirement.)... We have got on to slippery ice where there
is no friction and so in a certain sense the conditions are
ideal, but also, just because of that, we are unable to walk.
We want to walk: so we need friction. Back to the rough
ground!"

(Wittgenstein, 1953, no.107)

A major assumption in the doing of science, is that it can only be done
in terms of *ideal forms*, in terms of inquiries within which we seek to
discover in the natural world, formal correspondences between
patterns of thought of our own devising and observable *patterns* of
events out in the world around us. Indeed, right at the beginning of his
The Principles of Mechanics (orig. German edition, 1894), Hertz (1954)
described the role of symbolic representations in science thus: "In
endeavouring... to draw inferences as to the future from the past... We
form for ourselves images or symbols of external objects; and the form
that we give them is such that the necessary consequents of the images
in thought are always the images of the necessary consequents in nature
of the things pictured. In order that this requirement may be satisfied,
there must be a certain conformity between nature and our thought"
(p.1).

By contrast: beginning from within our already existing institutions and traditions

"Artistic form, correctly understood, does not shape already
prepared and found content, but rather permits content to
be found and seen for the first time".

(Bakhtin, 1984, p.43)

In contrast, my major assumption above is that — in our ordinary
everyday lives, within which we have accumulated an enormous volume
of experiences in dealing with countless different 'things' in different
ways, and within which we have come to possess a sense of the
countless *similarities to*, and *differences from*, that such 'things' have in
relation to all the other 'things' around them — when we use language
spontaneously and unreflectively, we have no trouble in *using* each
word in our vocabulary with some precision in a whole variety of
different everyday contexts. Yet, when it comes to our giving a short,
synoptic definition or conceptual statement that captures in a unified
fashion the essential *essence* of *what* some 'thing' actually *is* for us, we
are at a loss.

And we can now see that this is because, what matters to us is not what
a 'thing' is as an after-the-fact, objective entity in our everyday practical
affairs; it is what its before-the-fact *meaning* is for us that is important

— for, irrespective of its factual objectivity, while we may *say* that we are responding to it as the 'thing' it *is*, we are in fact being responsive to *just some* of its inexhaustible, detailed aspects while unresponsive to others. In other words, we are failing in our intellectual accounts to *do justice* to the *holistic sense* of it that we have in our *spontaneously responsive* relations to it.

This contrast has, of course, been remarked on countless times in the history of Western philosophical thought. As is well-known, Aristotle in his *De Anima*, remarked: "Nothing is in the intellect which was not first in the senses;" while Vico (1968), in building on from Aristotle's claim, went on to suggest that: "Throughout this book it will be shown that as much the poets had first sensed the way of vulgar wisdom, the philosophers later understood in the way of esoteric wisdom; so that the former [poets] may be said to have been the sense and the latter [philosophers] the intellect of the human race [779]. What Aristotle [On the Soul 432a 7f] said of the individual man is therefore true of the race in general: *Nihil est in intellectu quin prius fuerit in sensu*. That is, the human mind does not understand anything of which it has had no previous impression (which our modern metaphysicians call 'occasion') from the senses. Now the mind uses the intellect when, from something it senses, it gathers something which does not fall under the sense; and this is the proper meaning of the Latin verb *intelligere*" (para.363). It is in sensing '*this something*', which is not initially in our senses, that we are now aiming at in our more deliberate 'works'.

Wittgenstein (1953) too, noted that this striving after *ideals* mis-directs us towards illusory goals in our inquiries, for "... it is clear that every sentence in our language is in order as it is'. That is to say, we are not striving after an ideal, as if our ordinary vague sentences had not yet got a quite unexceptionable sense, and a perfect language awaited construction by us. — On the other hand it seems clear that where there is sense there must be perfect order. So there must be perfect order even in the vaguest sentence" (no.98) — that is, if we are really careful in 'doing justice' in wording our experiences in accord with the contours of our unfolding experiences.

All this means that we cannot just acquire the skills we need to flourish as fully personal beings, by trying solely on our own to acquire them, nor can we come to embody them from a small group of other individuals who have managed to acquire a number of useful skills in the course of their lives. We need instead to spend a great deal of time out in the many different everyday 'worlds' of our social lives at large, as well as participating within what we might call its 'ecology', i.e., the larger social context of intrinsically unaccounted for (and unaccountable) interdependencies between people from out of which the more orderly social institutions we 'construct' and 'maintain' can emerge. For what is so crucial about our construction of institutions, is that we can place our 'enduring expressions', our 'works' outside ourselves in our shared surroundings — in our literature, in our graphical representations or plastic forms, or in musical performances, as enduring and repeatable, as well as up-dateable aspects of still developing traditions. And in so-doing, we can create *contexts* for people's individual activities that all can jointly shared in; for, as we have seen over and over again above, it is only in a particular hermeneutical context that particular expressions can take on a particular meaning.

Thus an institution, as Merleau-Ponty (1970) puts it, to repeat, consists "not just [in a set of] survivals or residues, but as the invitation to a sequel, the necessity of a future" (p.41); more than simply a field or sphere of separately existing entities, an institution provides for participants within it, a tradition, a set of motivations aimed at exploring and elaborating more and more ways of giving human expression to our own possibilities of being more human than we already are — or, in Ingold's (2015) terms, as contributions to our unremitting task of *humanifying* ourselves.

So while all those working within the tradition may be 'working' differently, to the extent that they all come to embody within themselves the tradition's basic *vocabulary of motives* (Mills, 1940) — or better, a set of such vocabularies, each belonging to and situated within a number of realms of *instituted* or *institutional* activity — their activities will all 'hang together' due to the common 'gravitational field' at work within it. To return to Heraclitus, it is as if a tradition can speak to us of itself, and within the ways of speaking to which it gives rise, we can hear, i.e., gain a sense of, or feeling for, what its overall aim *is*.

Indeed, as Gadamer (2000) puts it, "... tradition is not simply a process that experience teaches us to know and govern; it is *language* — i.e., it expresses itself like a Thou. A Thou is not an object; it relates itself to us. It would be wrong to think that this means that what is experienced in tradition is taken as the opinion of another person, a Thou.... [It is not] an expression of another person's life, but as meaning that is detached from the person who means it, from an I or Thou... [But still,] tradition is a genuine partner in dialogue, and we belong to it, as does the I with a Thou" (p.358).

Thus, from within our traditions, it is as if we can 'get on speaking terms' with our surroundings, as if they have 'facial expressions', a 'physiognomy'[67] — indeed, it is not at all unusual for us to say: *"Prima*

---

[67] We can recognize the face, the physiognomy of a person familiar to us among a thousand, indeed among a million; yet we cannot usually tell how we do this. Similarly,

facie it seems to me that *this* is the nature of the situation here (going on to give a first account of its meaning)." But more than it being like an individual Thou, MacIntyre (1981) emphasizes that a tradition is a "living tradition" when it consists in "an historically extended, socially embodied argument, and an argument precisely in part about the goods which constitute that tradition" (p.207), and is thus to an extent, both a developed and a still developing tradition, to which a multitude of different expressive-responsive participants continually contribute.

Eliminating disquiets: 'doing justice' to the facts

> "The problems arising through a misinterpretation of our forms of language have the character of depth. They are deep disquietudes; their roots are as deep in us as the forms of our language and their significance is as great as the importance of our language".
>
> (Wittgenstein, 1953, no.111)

Where, then, does all this leave us with our task of judging whether what we *are now doing* is good for us or not, whether what we are doing is merely satisfying specific *desires*, or whether we are in fact gratifying any of our real needs? As we saw above, the meeting of a need always involves a confirmatory *recognition* of whether our needs have been met or not in our actions, a recognition that *retroactively determines* the true nature of the need that prompted the activity culminating in our satisfying it in the first place — that 'hunger' that we feel, is it a hunger for food that can be satisfied by eating, or is it a more existential 'hunger' for company, for friendship? Clearly, it is not easy to judge into the future whether what we are doing now *will* be good for us later.

But we are not wholly 'at sea without a compass', as it might at first sight seem. In giving up our search for *ideal forms*, and in being prepared to begin with our *sensings*, with the *distinctive movements of feeling* occurring within us as we experience the particular situation currently confronting us, we find ourselves with a quite different set of questions, relating to a quite different set of 'background' understandings. For rather than trying to settle questions of a very general kind, once and for all, we find ourselves oriented to much more

---

we can experience an event as having a unique and distinctive quality, a physiognomy, a quality that allows us to recognize it as the 'same event' occurring again. All human expression (and, for that matter, the expressions of all living things), as well as their traces and inscriptions, can have this quality. Like a friend, there is a *livingness* immanent in an event, in a text, in a piece of architecture, such that they can *speak* to us, they can exert an influence on us, not simply as static forms, as pictures or representations of something other than themselves. In *calling out* living responses from us, they can *themselves* exert a living, participatory influence in our living of our lives.

practical issues, situated within one or another particular circumstance.

I would thus like to bring my exploration of the ethical issues I raised above back into view, by returning to where I began: with the basing of our studies in the *acutely discriminative sense* that we can have of the qualitative nature of people's *sensings and feelings* — beginning both with our own sensings, and with our noticing the spontaneous expressions of others, as we both respond to events occurring to us within our common surroundings.

Someone who has been very clear about the need to adopt such a method in which we try to articulate what an experienced phenomenon *is like* — a method that *he* in fact calls a "method of comparisons"[68] — is Amartya Sen (2009) in his book, *The Idea of Justice*. He begins it by quoting Charles Dickens's who, in *Great Expectations*, put these words into the mouth of the grown up *Pip*: "In the little world in which children have their existence, there is nothing so finely perceived and finely felt, as injustice" (p.vii) — where the grown up *Pip* is recollecting a humiliating encounter with his sister, *Estella*. In other words, he wants to begin his inquiries, not by asking what a perfectly just society would look like, but from our *felt sensing of a something being* unjust, from our *disquiets*, from our feelings of *things being not quite right*.

Why? Because: "What moves us, reasonably enough," he remarks, "is not the realization that the world falls short of being completely just — which few of us expect — but that there are clearly remediable injustices around us which we want to eliminate" (p.vii). Thus, as I suggested above, by situating ourselves within a particular practical situation within which we can gain a shared sense — along with all the others around us — of a particular *injustice* at work; there is a real chance of us all, working together, of arriving at a way of remedying it. For we can all find in such a situation both, a guiding motivation, and, as we mentally move about within it, *ways to bring to light* the resources we need to move on from that injustice — where the *ways* we need will involve our *theories*.... to be used, not as explanatory devices, but as *objects of comparison* to help us in coming to a *felt sense* of what the particular injustice in question *is like*.

This will not mean, however, that we can do away with *theory*; we will still need it; but instead of our arguing with others over which is a *best ideal*, all our theories will find a *use* — a metaphorical and/or poetic use — in bringing to light similarities (and differences) within our task of clarifying what a particular sensed injustice *is like*. And in general, in

---

[68] "The idea of justice demands comparisons of actual lives that people can lead, rather than a remote search for ideal institutions. That is what makes the idea of justice relevant as well as exciting in practical reasoning" (Sen, 2009, p.xxx).

facing the question as to whether what we *are now doing* will be good for us or not in the future, we can, I think, positively carry over what Sen has to say about eliminating *social* injustices, to the elimination of *philosophical* injustices[69].

Conclusions: from 'ideals' to 'situated, integrated practicalities'

In setting out the possibility of this new *orientation* for our social inquiries in this fashion, I am reminded of how Thomas Kuhn (1970) ended his account of *The Structure of Scientific Revolutions*; he said: "We are all deeply accustomed to seeing science as the one enterprise that draws constantly nearer to some goal set by nature in advance. But need there be any such goal? If we can learn to substitute evolution-from-what-we-do-know for evolution-toward-what-we-wish-to-know, a number of vexing problems may vanish in the process" (p.170). And this, of course, is what I am proposing here: that we relinquish the still unfulfilled — and, as I see it, *forever unfulfillable* — dream of gaining the very general results we desire in our inquiries, and to be content with the limited, partial, and situated results that we *can in fact obtain* — which, in the end, will, I believe, perhaps surprisingly, turn out to be of far greater practical use and value to us. While bearing in mind that our task is still that of seeking to overcome the *fragmentation* and *separations* we ourselves create by enclosing ourselves within bounded disciplines and professions in making our inquiries (see Shotter, 2015a).

When we do 'enter into' circumstances that bewilder us, to repeat comments already made above, what becomes more and more clear, is that particular, concrete, definitive and distinctive *movements of feeling* begin to emerge as we 'move around' within it. But what is crucial, is that a particular, but still 'open' and 'fluid' experience of our current, living relationships to the world around us is opened up to us, not by our choosing to *think about* it in a certain way, but by what currently we are in the course of *trying to do*[70] within it. Thus given that such *movements* can only make their appearance within a still ongoing context, we need to accept that we can express their partially ordered nature, linguistically (or more directly, artistically), only in a *comparative* or *allusive* manner. As Merleau-Ponty (1964) puts it: "Expressive speech does not simply choose a sign for an already defined signification, as one goes to look for a hammer in order to drive in a nail

---

[69] As Wittgenstein (1993b) points out: "Nothing is so difficult as doing justice to the facts" (p.129).

[70] "Consciousness is in the first place not a matter of 'I think that' but of 'I can'" (Merleau-Ponty, 1962, p.137).

or a claw to pull it out. It gropes around for a significative intention which is not guided by any text ... If we want to do justice to expressive speech, we must evoke some of the other expressions which might have taken its place and were rejected, and we must feel the way in which they might have touched and shaken the chain of language in another manner and the extent to which this particular expression was really the only possible one if that signification was to come into the world. In short, we must consider speech *before it is spoken*, in the background of silence which does not cease to surround it and without which it would say nothing" (p.46, my emphasis).

8 Keeping on 'speaking terms' with our circumstances – the strange nature of the 'present moment'

"That secret of a continuous life which the universe knows by heart and acts on every instant cannot be a contradiction incarnate. If logic says it is one, so much the worse for logic. Logic being the lesser thing, the static incomplete abstraction, must succumb to reality, not reality to logic. Our intelligence cannot wall itself up alive, like a pupa in its chrysalis. *It must at any cost keep on speaking terms with the universe that engendered it.*"

(James, 1996, p.207, my italics)

"The very concept of the human, then, is fundamentally duplicitous: the product of an 'anthropological machine' that relentlessly drives us apart, in our capacity for self-knowledge, from the continuum of organic life within which our existence is encompassed, and leaving the majority stranded in an impasse."

(Ingold & Palsson, 2013, p.8)

"Only in the stream of thought and life do words have meaning."

(Wittgenstein, 1981, no.173)

What is it like to *live* immersed within the unbroken stream of the everyday, *languaged*, communicative, social activities occurring continuously amongst us all, as human beings, as human becomings, living out our lives together immersed also in a larger world that is still, as far as we can tell, in the process of becoming more well articulated than it is already? One *fact* that we have arrived at, I think, is we cannot capture anything of importance in what I have called after-the-fact, representational Cartesian common-sense, or in Plantonic idealized *forms*, or in any closed systems expressed in terms of *selective* and *exclusionary* concepts, perspectives, or frameworks that we try to imposed on our world from an illusory place *outside* of it. Another *fact*, I think, is that by trying to begin our inquiries in the retrospective, reflective manner required of us in 'doing science', means that we miss the fact that 'something else' altogether is actually guiding us in the performance of our actions, influences that we could attend to, but which our current scientized ideology leads us to ignore. Further, although we are not able to theorize in a *positive* manner such guiding influences ahead of time, the fact is, as a result of our imaginative explorations of particular circumstances that bewilder us, we can come to a *negative* grasp of what it is that we might *lack*[71].

Indeed, this is where instances of our use of such *difference-making* and *relation-making* speech can lead to quite different consequences to those working solely in terms of selective concepts. For example, there is much talk currently about people not *showing respect* for each other — there is thus an attempt to *teach* respect by having pupils trying to *define* the meaning of the word "respect," by listing synonyms for the word, like esteem, value, cherish, appreciate, admire, praise, compliment; or share books in which "respect" is a clear theme. What is not appreciated in such programs, is that instead of working in terms of *similarities*, like Amartya Sen (2009) we might find it advantageous to work in terms of *differences*, to consider how we might eliminate those events in which people held each other in *contempt*, in which people acted to *humiliate* each other (see Shotter, 2004), to consider what is *lacking* in their exchanges with those around them.

Inside the moment of acting and speaking

As I see it, all communication begins in, and continues with, our living, spontaneous, expressive-responsive (gestural), bodily activities that occur *in the meetings* between ourselves and the others and othenesses around us. Indeed, as living, embodied beings, we cannot not be responsive in some fashion to the expressions of others (spoken, written, or otherwise), and to other kinds of events, occurring in our immediate surroundings. Much attention in linguistics has been paid to *patterns of already spoken words*, to the spatial shapes or forms of already completed acts of speaking[72]. Here, instead, I want to try to outline some methods for exploring the unfolding dynamics of our utterances *in their speaking* and how they can give rise to a 'shaped' and 'vectored' sense of our moment-by-moment changing placement within the situation of our talk — by engendering in us both unique anticipations as to what-next *might happen* along with, so to speak, 'action-guiding advisories' as to what-next we *might do*. I want to focus on the dynamic ways in which people make *use* of words in the course

---

[71] To repeat, as Todes (2001) pointed out: "Our whole quest of discovery is thus initially prompted by need rather than desire. It is initially 'directed' not to get what we want but to discover what we want to get... The meeting of a need, unlike the satisfaction of a desire, always involves a confirmatory *recognition* of the need met, a recognition that retroactively determines the true nature of the need that prompted the activity culminating in its filling" (p.177). We can also note Sen's (2009) account of the possibility of *recognizing* the causes of *injustice*, thus to try to eliminate them, even when we cannot in any comprehensive sense, say what is identical to *perfect justice*.

[72] "If I had to say what is the main mistake made by philosophers of the present generation... I would say that it is that when language is looked at, what is looked at is a form of words and not the use made of the form of words" (Wittgenstein, 1966: 2).

of their other actions, as well as on the subtle details of how, as their use of words unfolds in responsive relation to those to whom they are addressed, people adjust their expressions accordingly.

In taking this approach, I was influenced early on by a remark of Vygotsky's (1962) about the "basic laws governing human development." As he saw it, "one of them is that consciousness and control appear only at a late stage in the development of a function, after it has been used and practiced unconsciously and spontaneously. In order to subject a function to intellectual and volitional control we must first possess it" (p.90). In other words, long before we are individually consciously aware of deliberately acting to achieve a goal, we are nonetheless coming to act unconsciously and spontaneously in ways intelligible to those around us.

And, as was clear from all the rest of Vygotsky's work, while we might possess as an aspect of our biological inheritance a great range of 'lower' psychological functions, the gradual growth of our volitional ability to organize them into 'higher', more complex forms, comes about through other, already competent member of our verbal community, 'in-structing' us verbally in how do so: "All the higher psychic functions are mediated processes, and signs are the basic means used *to master and direct them*. The mediating sign is incorporated in their structure as an indispensable, indeed the central, part of the total process. In concept formation that sign is the *word*, which at first plays the role of means in forming the concept but later becomes its symbol" (Vygotsky 1962, p.56, my italics) — and one person's words, their bodily voicing of an utterance, their expressions, can exert this immediate and spontaneous (gestural) effect on (and in) another person. And later, the speaking of *their* words *to ourselves* is "the means by which we [can come to] direct our mental operations, control their course, and channel them toward the solution of the problem confronting us" (Vygotsky 1962, p.58).

Indeed, in line with Vygotsky's comments quoted above, from a dialogical point of view, our inner intellectual lives can be seen as consisting in an 'orchestrated', intra-twining of many different kinds of influences, of conscious and unconscious ones, cognitive and affective ones, deliberate and spontaneous, biologically given and culturally developed ones — and in fact, many others of a much more occasional or momentary kind that are at work in the immediate practical surroundings of a particular utterance.

And what is of crucial importance is, as William James (1980) noted in his famous "The Stream of Thought" chapter, that in discussing the nature of such dynamic forms, we have failed to register "the transitive parts" of the stream and succumbed to an "undue emphasizing of [its] substantive parts [i.e., its resting-places]" (p.237). In so doing, we have tended to confuse "the thoughts themselves... and the things of which they are aware... [For while] the things are discrete and discontinuous... their comings and goings and contrasts no more break the flow of thought that thinks them than they break the time and space in which they lie" (p.233).

In fact, as he puts it: "The truth is that large tracts of human speech are nothing but *signs of direction* in thought, of which direction we nevertheless have *an acute discriminatory sense*, though no definite sensorial image plays any part in it whatsoever" (244). In other words, while speaking, we have an *immediate*, felt sense of the dynamically unfolding 'time-shape' of the situation we are engaged in — what it 'calls for' from us — a time-shape that makes available to us, in an acute discriminatory sense, the *anticipatory tendencies* in fact available to us for our next steps in our thinking (or acting) in relation to it. Such a sense constitutes, as Merleau-Ponty (1964) puts it, to repeat: "a *determinate gap* to be filled by words" (p.89).

To break the strangle-hold of the compulsion we feel to, in fact, break up the flow into separately exists 'bits', James entreats us thus: "Now what I contend for, and accumulate examples to show, is that 'tendencies' are not only descriptions from without, but that they are among the *objects* of the stream, which is thus aware of them from within, and must be described as in very large measure large measure constituted of *feelings of tendency*, often so vague that we are unable to name them at all" (p.246). And, in being *aware of them from within*, i.e., of the *transitory parts* of the inner stream of thought occurring within us, we find that as they unfold they provide us with both a 'shaped' *and a 'vectored' sense* of our moment-by-moment changing placement within our current surroundings. In short, we find such responsive feelings engendering in us both unique anticipations as to what-next might happen, along with, so to speak, 'action-guiding advisories' as to what-next we might do — in Wittgenstein's (1953) terms, they can provide us with an immediate sense of how to "go on" (no.154) in our current, practical circumstances.

To get a sense of how important it is to a thinker to come to a realization that, like Heraclitus, like James, like Bergson, like Wittgenstein, that although all is *in flux*, we can still find the guidance we need for our thinking within the dynamics of our own *movements of feeling*, we can turn to the example of David Bohm (1980), the quantum physicist — notable for his idiosyncratic account of the undivided wholeness of physical reality as being *holographically* organized (in contrast to our Cartesian assumption of its *mechanistic* nature).

He notes that: "Understanding a fact by assimilating it into an already existing order of things could perhaps be called the normal way of doing scientific research." While an alternative way of working is "to give primary emphasis to something similar to *artistic perception*. Such perception begins by observing the whole fact in its full individuality, and then by degree articulates the order that is proper to the assimilation of this fact. It does not begin with abstract preconceptions as to what the order has to be, which are then adapted to the order that is observed" (p.141).

In thinking in this manner, he set out what he called a *"new order of fact"* (p.144), to do with *orienting* or *relating* ourselves to our circumstances in a way very different from our past ways. Indeed, he continued: "Fact and theory are thus seen to be different aspects of one whole in which analysis into separate but interacting parts is not relevant. That is to say, not only is undivided wholeness implied in the *content* of physics (notably relativity and quantum theory) but also in the *manner of working* in physics. This means that we do not try *always* to force the theory to fit the kinds of facts that may be appropriate in currently accepted general orders of description, but that we are also ready when necessary to consider changes in what is meant by fact, which may be required for assimilation of such fact into new theoretical notions of order" (p.143).

What is it that enables him to think in this manner, and to be so sure of it 'doing justice to the facts'? David Peat, a colleague, recounts the following story from Bohm's childhood: "David certainly wanted to move and play like other boys, and around the age of seven or eight, he decided that by watching what they did, he should be able to work out in his head the various bodily movements involved in catching a ball or climbing a tree ... A few years later, at around ten or twelve, he was walking in the woods with a group of boys when they came to a stream traversed by a series of rocks. Again, it was the sort of situation that troubled him, he would now have to plan ahead, note the position of the rocks, and decide where and how to place his feet. For David, physical security came in assuming trusted positions: he would move only when he had developed sufficient confidence. Yet as soon as he jumped onto the first stone, he realized that it was impossible to stop long enough to plan the next step. Crossing the river, jumping from stone to stone, could be done only in one continuous movement. If he tried to stop or even think about what he was doing, he would fall in. His only hope was to keep moving. This moment of insight became so significant to him that he told the story many times during his life. Up to that point, David had assessed each situation in his life, never fully committing himself, always fearful of being pulled along by "irrational currents".... At that moment, however, he suddenly realized that security does not require control and stillness but can come in a freely flowing movement...."[73]

---

73 Downloaded from: http://www.fdavidpeat.com/bibliography/books/infinite1.htm,

We can find the 'direction' we need, as William James (1890) points out, for the execution of our next step, *in* the taking of our present step. In other words, what Bohm seems to have achieved in re-orienting himself to 'staying in movement' on the stepping stones, is to have moved from an indirect, *external relation* to his circumstances, to an immediate, direct, *internal* 'in touchness' with them, as he 'lived out' his practical involvements *with* them and *on* them. Thus, what it is for Bohm to be "on speaking terms with the universe," is for him to do all his thinking *in conversation with* a special *organizing sense* sitting within him: A single, unique, felt sense or quality within whatever situation he encountered, of that situation being constituted and characterized throughout its coming into being as an instance of *undivided, freely flowing movement,* within a total context of wholeness.

Important unacknowledged influences at work in our speakings – what some call 'intuition'

> "... the difficulty – I might say – is not that of finding the solution but rather that of recognizing as the solution something that looks as if it were only a preliminary to it. 'We have already said everything. – Not anything that follows from this, no, *this* itself is the solution!' This is connected, I believe, with our wrongly expecting an explanation, whereas the solution to the difficulty is a description, if we give it the right place in our considerations. If we dwell upon it, and do not try to get beyond it. The difficulty here is: to stop"
>
> (Wittgenstein, 1981, no.314)

As I noted above, we need to distinguish between the thinking that just happens within us, and the thinking that we, as individuals, do deliberately. The distinction is important because, more than simply providing, as we have seen, the basis for the more deliberate thinking done by all those within our social group who share in speaking a common language (Fleck, 1979; Kuhn, 2000), the kind of thinking that just comes to happen within us, spontaneously, is also shaped by all kinds of unacknowledged influences at work within it. Indeed, as we have already seen, rather than trying to separate thought from feeling, and to prize thought over feeling (supposed as 'mere emotion'), we need to take note of the fact, *in their spontaneous performing,* our expressions arouse, both in ourselves and in all those to whom they are addressed, both *feelingful thoughts* and *thoughtful feelings,* along with all the other characteristic elements of impulse, resistance, and tone (relational attitude) that can be spontaneously exhibited in our everyday, common-sense expressions.

In other words, at work in the *before-the-fact* emergence of our still-in-process social experiences, are a whole set of anonymous, agential influences, influences that can in fact put us 'in touch with' the 'reality' of what is before us, that are unavailable to us in any other way. Merleau-Ponty (1964) states the issue thus: "I inevitably grasp my body as a *spontaneity which teaches me what I could not know in any other way except through it*" (p.93).

Someone who has described his experience of this process — of letting his body teach him what he could not know in any other way — in some detail, is Tom Andersen (1992), a Norwegian family therapist: "When life comes to me," he remarks:

"it touches my skin, my eyes, my ears, the bulbs of my tongue, the nostrils of my nose. As I am open and sensitive to what I see, hear, feel, taste, and smell I can also notice 'answers' to those touches from myself, as my body, 'from inside,' lets me know in various ways how it thinks about what the outside touches; what should be concentrated on and what not. This state of being open and sensitive to the touches from the 'outside life' and at the same time being open and sensitive to the answers from the 'inside life' is what I prefer to call 'intuition.' At this point in time my intuition seems to be what I rely on the most. In re-walking my professional tracks, my intuition tells me that I shall take part first, and then sit down and think about the taking part; not sit down and think first and thereafter take part. As I am sure that my thinking is with me as I take part, I have felt comfortable following what my intuition has suggested to me" (p.55).

In reversing the usual way of approaching bewildering circumstances — by first taking part, rather than first thinking about taking part, and then taking part some more — Tom is, in fact, following precisely Bergson's (1955) *method of intuition*, the opposite of using "concepts with fixed outlines" (p.51) in trying to capture the nature of a flowing reality in their terms *from the outside*.

However, as both Bergson and Bakhtin note, the process is not an easy one to implement. Usually, our deliberate, practical activities are conducted, as we have seen above, *step-by-step* in successfully achieving a practical outcome, and we seek knowledge in a similar fashion. We try to understand the *content* (meaning) a person's utterances by *analyzing* the sequence of word-forms by imposing a pre-established order on the speech flow *from the outside*, thus to separate it into a sequence of "immobilities" (Bergson), in the hope of seeing patterns and repetitions within them indicative of future occurrences. But as we have already seen above, there are two kinds of difficulties we can face in our lives, not just one. Wittgenstein (1953) has made it very clear to us that many of our difficulties are *not* of the form of *problems* that can, by the application of a science-like methodology, be solved by reasoning; nor are they are "empirical problems" that can be solved by discovering something currently unknown to us. They are difficulties of a quite another kind, difficulties *of the will* rather than of the *intellect*[74]. They are *orientational* or *relational* difficulties, to do with the how we spontaneously respond to features in our surroundings with appropriate expectations and anticipations as to how next to 'go on' with our activities *within them*, thus to find our 'way about' without (mis)leading ourselves into taking an inappropriate next steps[75]. Clearly, to the extent that we are *not* in fact living in an already determined, Cartesian-Newtonian world of discrete particles in motions, but immersed in an indivisible stream of everyday, communicative, social activities, living out our lives in a larger world that is still, as far as we can tell, in the process of becoming more well articulated that it is already, if we are to explore a person's *orientation* to their lives, what see as of importance within it, how they make sense of their relations to the others around them, then, we must try to place ourselves *within* that flow.

For an example of how such a process might be conducted in practice, we can turn to a case Tom Andersen (2008) presents in which he was asked to talk with a father who got easily irritated, and in such situations, often hit his son. He began by asking the father the following rather strange question: "*If your hand, on its way to hit, stopped and talked, what might the words be?*" He had difficulties to comprehend the question, so it was repeated three times[76]. But finally he said: "*Stop doing what you are doing. What you do is not right.*" He was then asked: How he would say those words? (and that question also had to

---

[74] "What makes a subject hard to understand – if it's something significant and important – is not that before you can understand it you need to be specially trained in abstruse matters, but the contrast between understanding the subject and what most people *want* to see. Because of this the very things which are most obvious may become the hardest of all to understand. What has to be overcome is a difficulty having to do with the will, rather than with the intellect" (Wittgenstein, 1980a, p.17)

[75] Vygotsky (1978), clearly, is aware of the difference between these two kinds of difficulty, and articulates it in terms of the differences between 'signs' and 'tools: "A most essential difference between a sign and a tool, and the basis for a real divergence of the two lines, is the different ways that they orient human behaviour. The tool's function is to serve as the conductor of human influence on the object of activity; it is *externally* oriented; it must lead to change in objects ... The sign, on the other hand, changes nothing in the object of a psychological operation. It is a means of internal activity aimed at mastering oneself; the sign is *internally* oriented" (p.57).

[76] As it happened, Andersen said to himself in his 'inner dialogue': "*It is not surprising that he cannot find words ......for some in some situations (may be most often men?) it might be more easy to beat than finding words.*"

be repeated several times); but he then said: "*I would say it calmly, slowly and firmly.*" During this talk, where the father was brought back to *situating himself in the hitting moments* several times, it was extremely important to go slow and all the time see if he followed the movements of the talk, or stopped, and, so to speak, stood at a distance from them. For, as Tom Andersen saw it, it was only when he was back in the hitting moments, could he take part in investigating other expressions of his irritation and anger than hitting.

Speaking: its emotional-volitional tone and historical factuality

> "Historically language grew up in the service of participative thinking and performed acts, and it begins to serve abstract thinking only in the present day of its history. The expression of a performed act from within and the expression of once-occurrent Being-as-event in which that act if performed require the entire fullness of the word: its content/sense aspect (the word as concept) as well as its palpable-expressive aspect (the word as image) and its emotional-volitional aspect (the intonation of the word) in their unity ... Being-as-event and the performed act that partakes in it are fundamentally and essentially expressible, *but in fact it is a very difficult task to accomplish*, and while full adequacy is unattainable, it is always present as that which is to *be* achieved".
>
> (Bakhtin, 1993, p.31, my italics)

We must now turn to a further exploration of other such rationally unacknowledged influences at work in our social exchanges with each other: What Bakhtin (1993) calls the "emotional-volitional tone" of people's utterances is of importance to us. It can work to guide us in understanding how to *orient* or to *relate* ourselves to *what* a speaker — from within the midst of their immersion within an unbroken stream of the everyday, *languaged*, social activity — is *trying* to say, i.e., to get a sense of its 'point' and 'purpose', their degree of commitment to it, and why they are motivated in such an aim, and so on. It is what a person *is trying to do*, not what they are *stating* in their utterances, that is important. Thus, the

> "mere fact that I have begun speaking about [an object] means that I have already assumed a particular attitude toward it — not an indifferent attitude, but an interested-effective attitude. And that is why the word does not merely designate an object as a present-to-hand entity, but also expresses *by its intonation* my evaluative attitude toward the object, toward what is desirable or undesirable in it,

> and, in doing so, sets it in motion toward that which is yet
> to-to-be determined about it, turns it into a constituent
> moment of the living, ongoing event. [Thus] everything that
> is actually experienced... as something given and as
> something-yet-to-be-determined,   *is   intonated*,   has
> emotional-volitional tone, and enters into an effective
> relationship within the unity of the ongoing event
> encompassing us" (pp.32-33, my italics).

What Bakhtin is suggesting here, is that at every moment, as we voice
an unfolding utterance, there is a degree of personal choice as to the
selections we make, the intonational time-contouring we give our
utterances. So, although "the word in language is half someone else's,"
he notes (Bakhtin, 1981); "It becomes 'one's own' only *when the speaker
populates it with his own intentions*, his own accent, when he
appropriates the word, adapting it to his own semantic and expressive
intention. Prior to this moment of appropriation, the word does not
exist in a neutral and impersonal language (it is not, after all, out of a
dictionary that the speaker gets his words!), but rather it exists in other
people's mouths, in other people's contexts, serving other people's
intentions: it is from there that one must take the word, *and make it
one's own*" (pp.293-4, my italics). Thus what makes a person's words
their own words, are the *efforts* they exert in *trying* to make their talk
conform to 'a something' they are *trying* to express — and we can hear
these *efforts* 'in' their utterances, in their time-contouring of the
emotional-volitional tone of their expressions.

This why Tom Andersen could be satisfied, when he heard the hitting
man say: "*Stop doing what you are doing. What you do is not right.*"
He could sense that the man was, so to speak, taking 'ownership' of
those words, and that he would abide by them[77]. But to go further, and
to explore whether the man was now beginning to understand how to
move away from finding it more easy to beat than uttering words, Tom
asked: How he would say those words? And he finally got the reply: "*I
would say it calmly, slowly and firmly*" — again, with its intonation
orienting Tom Andersen to relate to the man in a satisfied manner. He
seemed in himself, *in fact*, to be changed in his being-in-the-world.

As Bakhtin (1993) notes: "*From within*, the performed act sees more
than just a unitary context; it also sees a unique, concrete context, into
which it refers both *its own sense* and *its own factuality* and within
which it attempts to actualize answerably a unique truth [*pravda*] of

---

77 In his very way of talking, Tom could *sense* that the hitting man *meant* what he said.
As Bakhtin (1986) puts it: "Such intimate speech is imbued with a deep confidence in the
addressee, in his sympathy, in the sensitivity and goodwill of his responsive
understanding. In this atmosphere of profound trust, the speaker reveals his internal
depths" (p.97).

both the fact and the sense in their concrete unity. To see that, it is of course necessary to take the performed act *not* as a fact contemplated from outside or thought of theoretically, but to take it *from within*, in its answerability ... The performed act has, therefore, a single plane and a single principle that encompasses all those moments within its answerability" (p.28, my italics).

Why is what happened here so important? Why did Tom Andersen have to resort to such a strange way of speaking to the hitting man? Why did he confront him with such a difficult task? Because he was (although Tom himself would never put it in this fashion), in short, taking the hitting man (and himself) into the realm of *participative* or *withness* thinking. With each strange question, Tom Andersen's purpose was to 'motivate' the father to take himself 'back into' the hitting moments, to re-live them again and again as if in 'slow-motion', so to speak, to imagine his hand 'on its way' to hitting. Unfolding the hitting event step-by-step, slowly in time, gave the father the *possible* opportunity to move from the *impulse* that drove its outgoing expression, to consider the incoming responses to it from his son (and wife and son's mother) — the 'relational meaning' of his impulsive expression — a possibility that, with Tom's persistent prompting, he engaged with.

But why did Andersen go further and ask the father about his tone of voice? Because it was a way of inviting the father to explore the *relational* or *participatory* meaning of his actions even further — to explore what Bakhtin (1986) calls a speaker's "evaluative attitude" (p.85) toward the subject of his or her speech, to explore the degree of his commitment to his claims. But it was not easy. As Bergson (1955) notes, to repeat, the move into such a realm "is extremely difficult. The mind has to do violence to itself, has to reverse the direction of the operation by which it habitually thinks, has perpetually to revise, or rather to recast, all its categories" (p.51). Usually, we turn to what *rationally* we assume is needed: to conduct a de-contextualized *analysis* of the *content* of a person's words within the framework of a particular theory in order to arrive at their meaning. Whereas, what we lose in de-contextualizing people's utterances, and tying to re-constitute their meaning within an imposed framework, is not what their words mean, but what *they meant* in *using* them.

"It is an unfortunate misunderstanding (a legacy of rationalism) to think that truth [*pravda*] can only be the truth [*instina*] that is composed of universal moments," says Bakhtin (19930, "that the truth of a situation is precisely that which is repeatable and constant in it" (p.37) — in fact, the reverse is the case, the truth of the situation is to be found in particular *details* of the circumstance, and the precise way in which they *relate* to the context within which they occur.

Expression organizes experience, not the other way around

"Can I talk with you Cherrie (Nurse Manager of a Secure Unit)?"// "Yes, but Dr Ashong is your psychiatrist, why don't you talk with her?"// "I can't find my words when I'm with Dr. Ashong."

If it was merely a matter of putting already well-formed thoughts into well-formed expressions, the patient in the secure unit above would not be facing the difficulty she describes. But our thoughts have their own flowing structure, and the transition from them into speech is no easy matter; the flow does not consist in separate units; it consists in, says William James (1890), "psychic transitions, always on the wing, so to speak, and are not to be glimpsed except in flight" (p.253). Indeed, in our daily lives, what we call 'things' are radically indeterminate, and the development of our *sensitivities* to 'thing-like' structures in our surroundings develops only slowly as we come to be able to *judge* that *'this'* is indeed *like an X* and *not like a Y*, as we come to know *implicitly in our bodily activities* — like Bohm with his sense of *undivided, freely flowing movement* — what X-ness and Y-ness feels like. We acquire these judgments in the course of our spontaneous involvements with those around us, and this capacity to orient towards the distinctive, unfolding 'movements of feeling' that characterize the particular 'what-ness of things' in our surroundings for us, enables us to act towards them in the same manner as those around us do so; such shared judgments both 'set the scene' for our unproblematic talk, while also becoming, sometimes, topics in our more problematic talk. All these sensitivities and capacities all *co-emerge*, spontaneously, in the course of our practical involvements with the others around us.

Speaking in our own words — being limited by the 'expressive context'

We do not, and cannot as infants (*infans* ~ without speech), set out deliberately to become *this* or *that kind* of person, as if the possibilities for what we can become already exist. We gradually become a unique, autonomous individual of a certain kind by *showing in our behaviour* as we grow up, that we know *what* matters to those around us: that we know *what* 'play' *is*; *what* 'toys' *are*, and what 'things not to play with'; *what it is* to be 'rude' and what is 'proper' behaviour; *what* emotionally 'hurts' another and *what is* being 'kind' to them is like; what it is to assume that one has been *'born to rule'* (or not, as the case may be); and so on, and so on. Thus in our everyday exchanges we find ourselves making a certain kind of sense — a mostly *relational* sense of things — spontaneously, without our ever having explicitly set out to do so.

In other words, as I noted above, what happens in a particular situation depends upon its *detailed* nature, and on the precise way in which the detailed nature of the context 'sets the scene' for what can occur within it.

Regarding the patient in the secure unit, Goldstein (1995/1933) might describe the situation within which she finds herself thus: "Every unbiased and exhaustive examination of a case repeatedly teaches us that alteration of a given performance even if at first sight it appears to be very prominent, is not necessarily of primary significance for understanding the underlying functional disturbance. On the other hand, a trifle that barely attracts notice may be of the utmost importance... [For instance], the difficulty in finding words, formerly regarded as the main symptom [of aphasia], retreated into the background. The theory of the reduced evocability of speech images became obsolete ... The inability to find and use words voluntarily is not due to the primary defect of the speech mechanism but to *a change in their total personality which bars them from the situation in which meaning is required*" (pp.37-38, my emphasis).

In other words, by simply adopting a 'testing' or 'categorizing' stance — rather than an 'appreciative' or 'exploratory' stance — a psychiatrist can so strongly 'set the scene' for what can possibly be expressed in a situation[78], that the patient feels only the need to find the words *required* by the psychiatrist, and to disregard the need to express *her own* words.

> "Thought does not express itself in words, but rather realizes itself in them"
>
> (Vygotsky, 1986, p.251).

Vygotsky (1986), like Bakhtin (1986, 1993), also explores the task we face in *articulating* or *realizing* our thought in speech as follows: "Thought, unlike speech, does not consist of separate units," he says:

> "When I wish to communicate the thought that today I saw a barefoot boy in a blue shirt running down the street, I do not see every item separately: the boy, the shirt, its blue colour, his running, the absence of shoes. I conceive of all this in one thought, but I put it into separate words. A speaker often takes several minutes to disclose one thought. In his mind the whole thought is present at once, but in

---

[78] "After all, there is no such thing as experience outside of embodiment in signs... Furthermore, the location of the organizing and formative center is not within... but outside. It is not experience that organizes expression, but the other way around — *expression organizes experience*. Expression is what first gives experience its form and specificity" (Voloshinov, 1986, p.85).

speech it has to be developed successively. A thought may be compared to a cloud shedding a shower of words. Precisely because thought does not have its automatic counterpart in words, the transition from thought to word leads through meaning. In our speech, there is always the hidden thought, the subtext. Because a direct transition from thought to word is impossible, there have always been laments about the inexpressibility of thought" (p.251).

In our speech, there is always the hidden thought, the 'subtext', what we are *trying* to do, to achieve, in what we are saying, our 'point'. While Bakhtin (1993) claims that this is expressed in the 'emotional-volitional tone' of an utterance, Vygotsky (1986) suggests that "behind every thought there is an affective-volitional tendency" (p.252), a movement of feeling that also arouses in us an anticipation of what a speaker is *trying to do*, to achieve, in their speaking. Thus, says Vygotsky (1986):

"We come now to the last step in our analysis of inner planes of verbal thought. Thought is not the superior authority in this process. Thought is not begotten by thought; it is engendered by motivation, i.e., by our desires and needs, our interests and emotions ... To understand another's speech, it is not sufficient to understand his words — we must understand his thought. But even that is not enough — we must also know its motivation. No psychological analysis of an utterance is complete until that plane is reached" (pp.252-253).

Speech is expressive of different 'tryings' or of different 'points' — the hidden 'subtext'

Thus, in the simple statements, with different words emphasized, as follows: (a) "I want to *tell* you something" — *what* I say is important; (b) "*I* want to tell you something" — this is important to *me*; (c) "I want to tell *you* something" — this is important to *you*; and so on with many other emphases, each *volitional* tone, each emphasis, leads you to relate or orient yourself toward me differently in listening to what I have to say. And indeed, as I intentionally shape at least some aspects of the unfolding time-contour of my utterances, so can you as a listener, in being continuously 'moved' or 'touched' in *this* way and *that*, sense the 'inner' turns I take, the choices I make at each moment in *populating* these very common, shared words with *my* intentions.

Indeed, we can have an immediate responsive sense of similar such 'inner turns' or choices, not only in people's non-verbal expressions, but also 'in' the 'expressive' movements of non-human animals. In other words, what we talk of as the pragmatics, the politics, the art and the ethics of our communications with each other, are expressed, and bodily appreciated, i.e., *felt*, within the invisible but personally shaped time-contours of the events occurring between us: the authority, the care, the espoused, the inflexibility or flexibility, the precision or looseness, the sympathy, the insults, the humiliations, etc., are all felt in listening to the emotional-volitional tone expressed in another person's utterance.

And this is not something tacked onto a person's utterance as an optional extra, but is crucial to organizing the pragmatic conduct of all our communicating — one cannot give another person a piece of information (without insulting them) until one has set up an *information giving* relationship with them — an expectation-orientation toward something yet to come. Indeed, all complex human activities which involve in their organization, both the sequencing and the simultaneous combining of a whole multiplicity of different (often) individually performed activities, require (as in the performance of a piece of music by an orchestra) the continually re-orienting and re-relating of these many different activities with each other. Thus, to repeat: "Everything that is actually experienced... as something given and as something-yet-to-be-determined, is intonated, has emotional-volitional tone, and enters into an effective relationship within the unity of the ongoing event encompassing us" (Bakhtin, 1993, p.33).

In other words, our talk always points beyond itself to a not-yet-determined something, to a 'world', to the unity of an event encompassing us, within which it *will* have its meaning.

As illustrative here of what can occur in the intoning of an utterance, let me attempt two little experiments: 1) Let's take a few lines from T.S. Eliot's *Four Quartets*: "What we call the beginning is often the end/ And to make an end is to make a beginning. /The end is where we start from..." (Eliot, 1944, Little Gidding, p.47):

a): [Quick with flat 'astronaut' intonation] "What we call the beginning is often the end, and to make an end is to make a beginning. The end is where we start from..." [An attempted 'factual' reading that provokes the reply: "What!? Surely that's garbled nonsense; it's not logical!"]

b): [With Social Constructionist emphases]: "What we *call* the beginning... is often the *end*..., and to *make* an end... *is to make* a beginning... The end is where we start from..." ["That's interesting, I've not seen it in that way before — does that mean that once we read the first line, all the rest is just an elaboration?"]

c): [Realist]: "What *we* call the *beginning*... *is* often the end, and to make an *end*... *is* to make a beginning. The end *is* where *we* start from..." ["That's interesting, I've not seen it that way before — does that mean the, until we have arrived at the end of the poem, we don't really know what was meant by the beginning?"]

Invisible in each of those three readings, but nonetheless hearable in each reading, is what Bakhtin (1984) would call a different "form shaping ideology" (p.83)[79].

2): Another little experiment:
a): [Quick with flat intonation] "The cat sat on the mat. The mat was red, the cat was black" – I get the picture... so what?
b): [A hesitant, uncertain, apprehensive tone] "The cat... sat... on the mat... the mat.. was *red*... the cat... was *black*..." – the beginning of a ghost story, a detective story?

Clearly, it is in arousing anticipations of the not-yet-said — vague and undifferentiated ones in the first case, and more well differentiated ones in the second — that the two very different ways of intoning these words arouse two very different transitory understandings of these words, two very different ways of 'going on' from them. The first arouses us to say: "OK, I get the picture, but... so what? Why do I need this information?" While the second tantalizes us into suspenseful waiting for what will come next.

The 'something more' that 'being on speaking terms' can reveal

"Our fields of experience have no more definite boundaries than have our fields of view. Both are fringed forever by a *more* that continuously develops, and that continuously supersedes them as life proceeds" (James, 2003/1912, p.37).

"Certainly, the reader of *The Waves* needs to swim, to trust to the buoyancy of the eye and the suppleness of the understanding. It is no good panicking when sequence seems lost or persons are hard to pick out. The rhythms of the work will sustain us comfortably as long as we do not flounder about trying to catch hold of events. The events are there, sure enough, but they are not sundered from the flow. This is to say that the form of the waves is acted out in the actual reading experience, and the reader must trust the medium. The rhythmic patterns of the book, this 'play-poem', provide the clues for performance" (Gillian Beer, *Introduction to the Waves*, 2008, pp.xxxv-xxxvi).

---

79 "The deeper layers of this form-shaping ideology," says Bakhtin (1984), "which determine the basic generic characteristics of artistic works, are traditional; they take shape and develop over the course of centuries" (p.83). What is special about Dostoevsky's form-shaping ideology is that it works in terms of internally related 'parts', that is, parts that owe their very character to their relations with others parts, a dynamic, growing, changing network of intra-relationships...

It is in the temporal unfolding of an utterance that each new word uttered gains its individuality, comes to play its distinct role in constituting an utterance's *meaning*, both by contrasting with, and by relating to, the words already said in a way spontaneously responsive to the circumstances of their *use*. Our thoughts are *realized*, then, come to be shaped or organized in a step-by-step process, as expressive of a certain state of affairs. Yet, there are no instant like silences separating two successive words in an utterance; for in moving from one configuration of our vocal tract to another — as with any other bodily movements — we cannot move in any other way than *continuously*. Thus two 'successive', or 'passing', or 'transitional moments' in an utterance are not simply separated[80] by *their qualitative differences*, i.e., by the differences made by a speaker that are indicative of a speaker's intentions, but are *also related to each other* in that the earlier parts of an utterance function to *motivate* the later parts[81].

In Bakhtin's (1993) terms: "From within, the performed act sees more than just a unitary context; it also sees a unique, concrete context, an ultimate context, into which it refers both *its own sense* and *its own factuality*, and within which it attempts to actualize answerably the unique truth [*pravda*] of both the fact and the sense in their concrete unity" (p.28). But in being *answerable in this way to the circumstances of its utterance*, "the act sets before itself its own truth [*pravda*] as something-to-be-achieved..." (p.29). In other words, our utterances are always *fringed*, as William James (2003/1912) put it, by a *more* "that continuously supersedes them as life proceeds" (p.37). And this *more*, this 'reaching beyond' present circumstances either in pursuit of as *desired end* or in *resolution* of a 'disquiet', is a crucial aspect of what a speaker is *meaning* in what they are saying.

But as we have seen, in trying to describe the nature of people's activities retrospectively, in terms of de-contextualized generalities of a kind already familiar to us, we will fail to grasp the unique *meanings*, the invisible 'subtexts' hidden in a speaker's acts and utterances; we will miss *the precise intention they were trying to express* in acting and speaking as they did; we will miss their 'point'. And perhaps of even

---

[80] The very word "separation" as such is misleading; it suggests separation in a spatial sense — we need to realize that the qualitative differences of successive moments cannot be captured in spatial imagery; to differ qualitatively and to be distinct in space are two quite different notions.

[81] As Mead (1934) notes: "That process... of responding to one's self as another responds to it, taking part in one's own conversation with others, being aware of what one is saying and using that awareness of what one is saying to determine what one is going to say thereafter-that is a process with which we are all familiar. We are continually following up our own address to other persons by an understanding of what we are saying, and using that understanding in the direction of our continued speech. We are finding out what we are going to say, what we are going to do, by saying and doing, and in the process we are continually controlling the process itself" (p.140).

greater importance, we will also miss attending to the larger *cultural context* of established institutional forms of life making it possible for people to *try* to express in their actions and utterances such 'something mores'. Indeed, what has become clear above, is that if we conduct our inquiries in this manner — by enclosing ourselves within a theoretical chrysalis of our own devising (as William James puts it above) — we will remove ourselves from being 'on speaking terms' with the world processes which, have not only engendered us, but upon which we still rely in maintaining ourselves as the persons we are in relation to all the others around us.

9 Reversals — 'particular detailed beginnings' are more important than 'finalized generalities'

"A person must actively meet his environment in such a way that he co-ordinates his outgoing nervous impulses with those that are coming in. As a result the structure of his environment is, as it were, gradually incorporated into his outgoing impulses, so that he learns how to meet his environment with the right kind of response ... (This fact would also be evident if it were not for our habitual notion that perception is a purely passive affair.)"

(Bohm, 1965, p. 211)

As we saw at the end of the last chapter: Life is a task. Nothing just springs into existence in an already fully-formed manner. As has been emphasized over and over again in this book, everything *comes into existence* in a to-and-fro, back-and-forth, dialogically-structured process — every 'thing' *has its being in movement*. And further, "things do not settle or endure out of their natural order," as Vico (1968, para.134) has it; we need to sustain *what matters to us* in existence. Our vigilance is required. This shift from thoughtful understandings gained while in motionless contemplation to practical understandings gained only while moving about in action, clearly, is quite revolutionary. Everything we thought we understood and had the vocabulary to describe, changes.

For instance, while many may still see philosophy as primarily oriented toward gaining a kind of knowledge (or wisdom) that ultimately is recorded in a book, Wittgenstein (1953) suggests a much more practical definition. As he sees it, "a philosophical problem has the form," he says, "[of] 'I don't know my way about'" (no.123). And it is (re)solved, he suggests, when we can say to someone (and to ourselves), "'Now I can go on!'" (no.151). I mention these more practical less intellectual, more poetic reformulations of our disquiets here, as these two metaphorical expressions — the one of a kind of difficulty, and the other of what is involved in overcoming it — are central to what I want to offer in this book. For, after all, as a critique of *intellectualism*, it can only be as a contribution to a better understanding of our everyday practical activities that this book can be seen as of use; no matter how much one feels the urge, we need to resist the tug to return to a standpoint in reflective thought.

Having begun with Cassirer's (2000) concern with the fragmentation of our knowledge and understanding of ourselves and our world, as a result of our obsessive urge always to begin our inquiries in the formulation of theories and hypotheses, I now want to turn to what he had to say in a later (his last) work. As Cassirer (1996) put it there:

"As needed and fruitful as this perspective — this clear and conscious concentration on the pure 'telos' of theoretical knowledge — proves to be, the "philosophy of symbolic forms" cannot stop here. Its concern is not merely to take stock of forms, to assess them, so to speak, for what they are as static magnitudes. *It is concerned, rather, with the dynamics of the giving of meaning, in and through which the growth and delimitation of specific spheres of being and meaning occur in the first place.* It seeks to understand and illuminate *the riddle of the becoming of form as such* — not so much as a finished determination but rather with determination as a process. *This process does not follow a single, predefined course leading from a specific beginning to an equally fixed end, which has been determined in advance.* Thought does not flow here in a finished riverbed which has been made for it; rather, it must find its own way — it must first dig its own bed for itself. This *movement of thought* searching for itself is not limited at the outset to a single, particular direction. Instead, distinctly different approaches emerge in it, different centres of power and different tendencies" (pp.4-5, my italics)[82].

We are reminded here of Fleck's (1979) image, of the rain falling here and there on the land, but eventually finding its way, via streams and rivers, into the sea, in spite of flowing in roundabout ways and generally meandering. As he sees it, the field of gravity corresponds to a dominant and directing disposition, organizing the fragmentary rainfall into a holistic (hermeneutical) unity.

Ingold and Wittgenstein on 'reversals' — from dead 'outcomes' to living 'doings'

The riddle, then, we face is that of *the becoming of form as such*, and *the movement of thought* we need to go through with, is that of *reversing* the *after-the-fact* professional forms of thought we allow to be imposed on ourselves by our disciplinary memberships. Our *science of culture* should lead us into making the *before-the-fact* living activities from which the symbolic forms of interest to us originally

---

[82]We can connect here with what Fleck (1979) has to say in Chapter Two about how "the problem of how a 'true' finding can arise from false assumptions, from vague first experiments, and from many errors and detours?," and about how it can, perhaps, "be clarified *by a comparison*" (p.79, my italics) — provided a 'field of gravity', i.e., organizing *tendencies* exist, all the separate, mistaken efforts combine to create a particular, hermeneutical unity.

emerged, visible again. Both Ingold (2008) and Wittgenstein (1953, 1980a, 1981) suggest reversals in our attitude to living events; we need to see them in relation to their surroundings, not simply as having their lives solely encased within themselves.

Figure 1. A drawn circle. Is the line the trajectory of a movement or the perimeter of a figure?

(1) Ingold: Beginning at a particular moment in time, Ingold (2008) applies a piece of chalk to a chalk board, and proceeds in a few seconds to leave a trace behind on it of his movements (as displayed above in Fig.1). He then remarks: "With this figure we seem to have set up a division between what is on the 'inside' and what is on the 'outside'" (p.1796). But equally well, an observer could have said: "Ingold simply made a continuous movement over time in such a way that the trace *on this occasion* happened, towards the end of his movement, to cross over his starting point; with many other movements, this might not have happened" — no mention of the trace being *like a circle* need be made. And indeed, Ingold (2008) himself wishes to go along with the observer's assessment: He sees the *interpretation* of the movement as actually creating a figure with an 'inside' and an 'outside' (and not simply as hand movement with a beginning and an end) as the application of a preferred *logic*, a logic that is pervasive in all our *styles* of western thought. He calls it "the logic of inversion."

"In a nutshell," he says (Ingold, 2008), "what it does is to turn the pathways along which life is lived into boundaries within which life is contained. Life, according to this logic, is reduced to an internal property of things that *occupy* the world but do not properly *inhabit* it. A world that is *occupied*, I argue, is furnished with already-existing things. But one that is *inhabited* is woven from the strands of their continual coming-into-being" (pp.1796-1797, my italics).

Our task in this chapter, then (yours as a reader, and mine, and Ingold's), is to put the logic of inversion *into reverse*. Rather than seeking to find the *life* of 'things' hidden inside them somewhere, we need to restore to these 'things' to the *intra-mingling streams of life* within which they have both their *being* and their *becoming* — a switch from seeking to understand what goes on *inside people* to an inquiry focused on what people go on *inside of*.

I say both *being* and *becoming* above because, in fact, we need to distinguish between spatial 'things', that can have 'boundaries' and exhibit a *self-contained* existence, and temporal 'things' that are always 'unbounded', 'unfinished', 'incomplete', and thus open to further development — but on occasions, we can place temporary, temporal boundaries around them.

Indeed, this was the case when Ingold could be *seen as* having drawn a circle. These temporary boundaries allow temporal things and events to have, for practical purposes, momentarily, a unique wholeness to them. In fact, our ability to pick out for notice certain *dynamic stabilities* within the overall flow of activities within we are immersed, with a *likeness* to experiences already well-known to us, is not only is a very basic ability, but a very important one as we grow into the mental lives and ways of talking of those around us.

However, as we saw above in Chapter Five, because our *common world* seems to be an unfinished, still evolving, not yet fully differentiated, flowing world, rather than trying to determine it *conceptually*, in an enclosed manner, within boundaries, we can, instead, from within the overall flow of intra-mingling activity within we are immersed), differentially specify its nature in terms of the *distinctive features* that it possesses in relation, and distinct from, everything else around it.

Crucially, in contrast to conceptualizations, we can undertake processes of progressive *differencing* or *articulation* work, one the one hand, to arrive at the identification of sustainable *dynamic stabilities*, i.e., organized, hermeneutical unities of a particular kind, while on the other, leaving the unities in question *open* to yet further differentiation(s)[83] as required — in other words, as *beings* such unities can be open to further *becoming*.

(2) Wittgenstein: Wittgenstein (1953, 1980a, 1981) does not see the task of philosophy as that of seeking to create a new, ideal language (as an aid to our doing of science) that will reveal what was at first hidden from us, nor as that of replacing our seemingly inadequate, ordinary everyday understandings with *better* ones, but as we have seen over and over again, as trying to lay out for view the 'workings' of our actually existing quotidian language. And to do this, Wittgenstein realizes that we cannot begin simply by focussing on *what* we find problematic, and

---

[83] An undifferentiated flux may be articulated in terms of many different schemes of *distinctive differences*.

talking to ourselves about it in our reflections upon it. Our current, more deliberate, intellectual ways of talking (in contrast to our spontaneous, everyday ways of talking), mislead us into treating the situation as *containing* all its important *properties* within itself[84].

About this entrapment in our language, he observes: "A picture held us captive. And we could not get outside it, for it lay in our language and language seemed to repeat it to us inexorably" (1953, no.115). As a countermove to the realization that we cannot 'get outside' of our *languaged* activities, he remarks: "When you are philosophizing you have to descend into primeval chaos and feel at home there" (1980a, p.65). In other words, as both participants in, and partakers of the world's differential becoming, we not only create *facts*, we can also give a determinate form to what prior to our acting lacked determination — our task is to make the life from which such determinations originally emerged visible again.

How might we do this? Again, as we will see, a *reversal* is required: we need to move from seeking what is *contained* in the problematic circumstance to what it is *contained in*, or *surrounded by*. Wittgenstein (1981) expresses this in the following remark: "'Only the intended picture reaches up to reality like a yardstick. Looked at from the outside, there it is lifeless and isolated — It is as if at first we looked at a picture so as to enter into it and the objects in it surrounded us like real ones; and then we stepped back, and were now outside it; we saw the frame, and the picture was a painted surface. In this way, when we intend, we are surrounded by our intention's *pictures*, and we are inside them. But when we step outside them, they are mere patches on a canvas, without life and of no interest to us" (no.233).

In switching over from what a problematic circumstance *contains*, to what it is *contained in* or is *surrounded by*, requires us, so to speak, to see it as *emerging from* its embedding within the larger flow of intra-twined, living, still developing activities within which we are also embedded. As such, our everyday, communicative task is to see its 'point', to 'see' what it *means for us* in terms of how we might 'go on' to act next within it, in relation to all our other everyday activities. Wittgenstein (1981) puts it thus: "When one has the picture in view by itself it is suddenly dead, and it is as if something had been taken away from it, which had given it life before. It is not a thought, not an intention; whatever accompaniments we imagine for it, articulate or inarticulate processes, or any feeling whatsoever, it remains isolated, *it does not point outside itself to a reality beyond*" (no.236, my italics).

---

[84] This is, of course, Ingold's (2008) point above.

In their expressions, in their 'works', painters, writers, speakers are trying to arouse in us momentary movements of feeling within which we can 'get an anticipatory sense' of how our expressions can bring the structure of our circumstances to light, can work to *characterize* the nature of our circumstances, while our circumstances can bring the *meaning* of our expressions to light. In other words, a step-by-step *process* of mutual illumination, between our expressions and the circumstances in which we *naturally* and *unproblematically* express them, can result in our coming to a precise understanding of *what* it is that the painter, writer, speaker is trying to express.

It is when we deliberately focus on a picture (or an utterance) outside of its 'workings' in our everyday lives that we lose, not what the painting, sentences, utterances mean, but what a painter, writer, speaker was trying to express in their paintings, writings, speakings. And we cannot make up for this loss (as we have seen many times before), by *trying to analyse* an utterance's *content*, no matter what the occasion of its being uttered, or who is making the utterance, or why they are making it — for that is always to take it *outside* the particular circumstances of its *use*. To come to a grasp of what someone *meant* by what they expressed in a particular everyday circumstances, to repeat, instead of an *analysis*, we need a particular kind of speaking, a *telling* (Shotter, 1981) — an utterance that is not a *report*, a retrospective account of a past state of affairs — but a *prospective* account of a circumstance that commits me to going on in the future in a way different from my relations to the circumstance in the past (see pp.159-160).

A prospective account? What might such an account, as an aid to perception, be like? "*What* you mean — how is that to be discovered?" asks Wittgenstein (1981). "We must patiently examine how this sentence is supposed to be applied. What things look like *round about it*. Then its sense will come to light ... [When] you do not understand your own transactions, ... you do not [yet] have a synoptic view of them ..." (nos. 272, 273), he replies.

In other words, what is needed are short, evocative *vignettes* portraying particular events occurring in our everyday circumstances which, in their telling, arouse in us, distinctive movements of feeling that work to direct our attention to the fact that — to *remind* us that[85] — in our acting, certain *detailed* features of the situation play crucial roles that we would not otherwise notice. In one direction, attention to them will bring the precise *meaning* of our expressions to light, while in the other, the *reverse direction*, they will work to *characterize* the nature of the circumstances within which that meaning has its use.

---

[85] "The work of the philosopher consists in assembling reminders for a particular purpose" (Wittgenstein, 1953, no.127).

Beginnings, noticings, and moments — two consequences of being 'struck'

> "A main source of our failure to understand is that we do not *command a clear view* of the use of our words. — Our grammar is lacking in this sort of perspicuity. A perspicuous representation produces just that understanding which consists in 'seeing connections' ... The concept of a perspicuous representation is of fundamental significance for us. It earmarks the form of account we give, the way we look at things".
>
> (Wittgenstein, 1953, no.122)

> "A great weakness, no doubt, for a person to consist entirely *in a collection of moments*; a great strength also; it is dependent upon memory, and our memory of a moment is not informed of everything that has happened since; *this moment which it has registered endures still, lives still, and with it the person whose form is outlined in it*".
>
> (Proust, *A la recherche du temps perdu*, my italics)

As we have seen, over and over again, we *cannot* begin our inquiries into how to act for the best in our lives from 'good ideas', or 'concepts', or knowledge' we already possess. As Hannah Arendt (1959) noted long ago, it leads to our being imprisoned within "the limitations of patterns [we ourselves have] created" (p.261). Mere information doesn't do it; we need to be 'touched', to be 'moved', to be 'arrested', to be 'struck'; and when we are struck, it is not by what is *familiar* to us, but by what is *unfamiliar*; by a *rare* occurrence (Nussbaum, M. 2001b; Taleb, 2007) that can in fact *dislocate*, or *disorient* us in our everyday assumptions, and leave us at first bewildered as to how to 'go on' in the circumstance in question[86] — but sooner or later, open up to us something uniquely new, unclassifiable, yet closely related to the circumstances within which it emerged. For what seems to be so special about our being 'struck', is that we seem to experience the coming into being of a 'particular inner event within the flow of time', a 'particular unfolding moment', an 'event' that is separate from what came before it and after it, a certain *thisness* with its own duration and quality that is not only noticeable, but also deeply memorable, in a sense that it can provide an inexhaustible range of features that we can draw on in formulating a

---

[86] Rather than being *rare* and always taking us 'by surprise', it might be more appropriate to accept that such moments 'strike' us because they are unusual in that we cannot be *anticipate* them — but this means that we can in fact learn on purpose to 'notice' them. See Katz and Shotter (1996) for an account of how such 'moments', once 'worded' appropriately, can provide therapeutic openings for clients taking new steps forward in moving out of otherwise entrapping circumstances of their own making.

description of its nature.

From 'seeing patterns' to 'sensing openings' — experiencing transitions

But, as we will see, there are two ways in which we can be 'struck': (1) In one, in mathematics, for instance, we can look over arrays of *representational symbols* which at first seem disorganized and utterly confusing, until suddenly, one begins to 'see a pattern' in them; what was a puzzle of unrelated facts can turn in an instant into clarity and order: this is an after-the-fact way of being struck, a *seeing* of something in terms of an image or picture. (2) But there is another before-the-fact way, less to do with seeing *patterns* (repetitions) than with 'noticing' the momentary, spontaneous occurrence of unique *openings* to a next step forward into the future, an event that arouses a *feeling* or a *sensing* within us of a still-not-fully differentiated, particular 'something'.

Such 'momentary events' *matter to us* in our everyday practical exchanges with each other — not in terms of their 'contents', but in terms of their *meanings* for us, in terms of *what* they spontaneously express — for, in our being responsive to just to *some* features in their expressions, while being unresponsive to others, we can begin to act in relation to the 'expressive time-shapes', the 'expressive contours' of a person's inner life, and to what *really matters* to him or her (although they are often unaware of its *mattering* to them). And in so doing, in providing a 'resting moment' (a 'stopping point' that one can return to time and again), we can provide people in a therapeutic situation with a moment for reflection and further articulation, thus allowing them to further articulate the uniqueness of their own lives in ways useful to them (Katz & Shotter, 1996).

Indeed, ironically, this way of relating ourselves to the others and othernesses around us is quite familiar to us in our everyday lives, in which we are continually dealing, not with mechanical repetitions — as in most current Social Theory — but with uniquely new situations for another first time. In shifting our attention to *striking moments*, we are shifting our attention from product to process, from the content of already-spoken words to the moment-by-moment "orchestration" of words in their speaking — a stance that moves us beyond 'think-talk' towards a new body-oriented vocabulary expressed in terms of 'sensings' and 'movements of feelings', 'emergence' and 'articulation', and 'differencing'.

Central to our experiencing this shift, is our being prepared to experience, not a *form* or a *spatial shape*, but a *movement*, a *time-shape* — a transition. Owen Barfield (1999), in talking of what is involved in readying oneself to reading poetry, describes what he calls a "felt change of consciousness," by which he means that the poetic mood "is kindled by the passage from one plane of consciousness to another. It lives during that moment of transition and then dies, and if it is to be repeated, some means must be found of renewing the transition itself" (p.79).

William James (2003) describes the *movements of feeling* we experience in the living of our everyday live in a similar fashion: "We live, as it were, upon the front edge of an advancing wave-crest, and our sense of a determinate direction in falling forward is all we cover of the future of our path ... Our experience, *inter alia*, is of variations of rate and of direction, and lives in these transitions more than in the journey's end. The experiences of tendency are sufficient to act upon — what more could we have *done* at those moments even if the later verification comes complete?" (p.69).

Some 'striking moments' — a 'listing'?

While *experiences of tendency* are sufficient to act upon, when it comes to our giving a short, synoptic definition or conceptual statement that captures the essential *essence* of *what* some event actually *means* for us, we are often at a loss. Beginning by sensing the *unique time-contours* of such experiences, we can only begin to say what such experiences are *like*: and we can either describe them *metaphorically*, or by drawing on particular *turns of phrase* people actually use in remarking on the occurrence of such events. Let me list some of these turns of phrase: (1) We do, of course, all the time talk of being 'struck' or 'touched' by an event or by someone's expression; (2) we often talk of "telling-moments," moments when we suddenly learn that 'this' is how things are 'done around here'; (3) or of "defining-moments," those moments when we knew we wanted to be an X, say, rather than a Y; (4) Moments of excitement, when we sense there is a 'something' here of importance, but we are not yet sure of what it is; (5) Proto-incipient beginnings of a later expert skill — is it the case that our playful exchanges with our infant children can be called "proto-conversations" (Malloch & Trevarthen, 2002); (6) The emergence of a 'style', a 'modus operandi', a 'world-view' (a *Weltenschaunng* and/or *Weltbild*); (7) The recognition of an 'elephant in the room'... what we can hear 'not being said'; (8) Disquiets ... something is not right, but yet I know not what.

The major point about such moments is, to repeat, that — in *them* striking us and not *we* going out to seek them — they can 'move' us, they can 'change' us, they can bring something into us that we would not realize on our own. As Steiner (1989) puts it: "The 'otherness' which enters us makes us other" (p.188).

Talk in a before-the-fact, flowing world of emerging events

When, currently, when we talk of such entities as 'society', 'social relations', 'history', 'the individual', 'the self', 'persons', 'language', 'communication' — as well as 'ideology' — we can no longer assume that we all know perfectly well what the 'it' is that is represented by the concept of the entity we are talking about. It is not just that these concepts are "essentially contested" concepts and involve "endless disputes about their proper use on the part of their users," as Gallie (1962, p.123) claims. It is that the entities they are supposed to represent are not 'already there' in existence in a wholly determinate form, prior to our talk 'about' them. Thus the disputes involved are deeper than just with matters of the proper use of language, for they are not about what already exists. They are to do with attempting to make new forms of human being/becoming possible — for "to imagine a language is to imagine a form of life" (Wittgenstein, 1953, no.19).

Besides all the topics I have already listed above that we need to reconsider in a before-the-fact fashion, I would like to list a number of others: International Politics; National Politics; Organizations; Management; Leadership; Process Studies; Health Care; Mental Health Care; Psychiatry; Psychotherapy; Academic Psychology; and many, many more.

If Karen Barad's (2007) account of *intra-action* is correct, as opposed to our more usual assumption of inter-action, then this also entails that the organizational "things" that we *name* as topics of importance in organization studies — such things as "organizations," "leadership," "communication," "innovation," "management," etc., and think of as existing out in the world, along with a number of other 'things' that we take to be important in our inquiries, such 'things' as "language," "ideas," "theories," "knowledge," "meanings," or "observations" (as the products of processes hidden within the heads of individuals) — are *all* better talked of as emerging within material *intra*-actions occurring within the flow of activities occurring out in the world at large.

In enacting what Barad (2007) calls *"agential cuts"* (p. 140), i.e. taking some aspects of our situation as subjective and others as objective in different ways at different times as we are acting within a particular situation, "we do not uncover pre-existing facts about independently existing things" (p. 91); instead, we "enact *agential-separability* — the condition of *exteriority-within-phenomena*" (p. 140), a functional separation appropriate just to the purposes at hand.

In their lack of a spatial form, and in their existence as dynamic stabilities, sustained by the larger, flowing context around them, they are not thing-like at all; they cannot be "pictured"; yet we continually give names to them as if they can be (Billig, 2013). And as we talk amongst ourselves *about* such things, we assume we are all talking about the *same thing* when we are not. The fact is, the reference of these terms can be identified only within the instance of discourse within which they are contained. This is why a new realm of inquiry — that is clearly oriented towards inquiring into the strange, invisible nature of relational things — is required, a realm of inquiry focussed on "relational things" (Shotter, J. 2015b) that exist only as *dynamic stabilities* sustained in existence by the flowing activities occurring in their surroundings.

Reversals: the back-and-forth, two-way processes at work in our dialogically-structured, everyday activities

In the past, in adopting a *monological,* one-way, cause-and-effect, outside relation to our surroundings, we thought of our understandings as coming into existence as a result of our "thoughts" or "ideas," i.e., as a result of a certain nameable causal processes. But as we saw above, such processes can *only* be seen as *having been at work* in people's performances *after* they have been completed. Consequently, rather than as external agents, trying to *control* the unfolding processes of importance to us, we need to see ourselves as being *internally related* to a still-in-process world of flowing streams of intra-mingling activities — activities that affect us (because of the two-way, *dialogically-structured* relations we have with them) as much as we can affect them.

To take account of this in our inquiries, of the fact that we are *always in a two-way process* with our circumstances, we need to begin them *from within the midst of our embedding in the complicated flow of our local circumstances.* Thus instead of starting downstream, with *after-the-fact,* idealized, theoretical simplicities, and building up to complexities, we need to find *before-the-fact* starting points for our inquiries, upstream. And, as we will see, this is not as bewildering a starting point for our inquiries as at first we might think. For, after all, we are not like, say Oliver Sacks's (1985) Dr.P — the man who mistook his wife's face for a hat — in that we do not continually have to 'figure out', solely on the basis of fragmentary evidence, as to whether the tall, human height shapes around us, covered in cotton, woollen, and other fabrics, are actually living human beings or not. We come to sense that fact, *immediately and directly,* along with many, many others, as we gradually learn, without any explicit, classroom teaching, to become fully responsible, enculturated members of the society into which we have been born.

To repeat a phrase of William James (1890) already mentioned above: The fact is we have "an acutely discriminative sense" (p.253) of the unique (music-like?) 'time-shapes' of the dynamic, unfolding movements aroused in us by events occurring within our surroundings, even when no particular nameable 'things' as such come to mind.

What, in effect, *before-the-fact* accounts of the processual circumstances look like, is the *reverse* of *after-the-fact* accounts. But we must be careful, a two-way developmental *process in time* is involved, from which a *product that can be located in space* emerges: While an after-the-fact account is a named 'thing', a before-the fact account (as we have seen above) is a *portrayal* which, in its telling, arouses within us a distinctive movement of feeling that works to direct our attention to details in the situation that we would not otherwise notice; it works not only to bring the precise *meaning* of our expressions to light, but also, in the *reverse* direction, to *specify* the nature of the larger circumstances within which our expressions can play their part.

As there are countless relevant *reversals*, I will from now on just list ones that I have noticed over the last few years (as the topic has come to interest me), whilst offering a commentary on just a few. Given my assumption of the primacy of *bodily activity*, over that of *thinking*, the first is from Maxine Sheets-Johnstone (2011):

- Our bodily movements out in the world are more important to us than our thinkings: "In effect, *movement forms the I that moves before the I that moves forms movement*" (p.119).

For Sheets-Johnstone, her emphasis on the primacy of movement is radical. She notes a comment from Merleau-Ponty (1962) that: "The problem of the world, and, to begin with, the body, consists in the fact that *it is all there*" (p.198), and profoundly disagrees with it. As she sees it, as infants, by our movements, we awaken in ourselves what she calls a "kinesthetic consciousness" — movements of feeling (experiences) arise in sense organs both in the membranes lining the joints, and from *the sense of effort* (from our tryings) in voluntary movement. And what is so special about such movements is, that in being *spontaneous*, they need not be in any way 'goal-directed'; indeed, in assuming an end-state in the before-the-fact developmental process, we are pre-supposing what we what we are trying to explain: *What emerges dynamically* as we learn to move ourselves *this way* and *that*, is an 'I' *that can move* as desired, and an expanding repertoire of 'I cans'[87], of 'personal powers' (Shotter, 1974) derived from our 'natural powers'. This means that:

- Our activities shape our brain as much, if not more than, our brain shapes our activities; we are not born as *thinkers*, we only become so later in life.

---

[87] "Consciousness is in the first place not a matter of 'I think that' but of 'I can'" (Merleau-Ponty, 1962, p.137).

This is so, because our bodily movements occur to us *spontaneously*, we do not at first initiate them *on purpose*; this means that:

- What *just happens* to us is much more important to us than what we achieve in our *wanting* and *doing*, it provides the 'background' from out of which our *wantings* and *doings* emerge as "interpretations"[88], and into which they return to exert their influence.
- We think that we give meaning to words, whereas in the first place it is words that give meaning to us" (Bortoft, 2012, p.139).

Words, or wording a circumstance, brings it into rational-visibility, so to speak, in a way that is of necessity shared with others; indeed, in living our lives in continual communication with all those others and othernesses around us, means that:

- "Mind arises through communication by a conversation of gestures in a social process or context of experience — not communication through mind" (Mead, 1934, p.50).
- "... humans do not converse because they have inner thoughts to express, but they have thoughts to express because they converse" (Billig, 1987, p.111).

Rather than 'thoughts' or 'ideas', we are often expressing 'feelings' in our spontaneous expressions — "I feel rather upset that we disagree," "I feel, *prima facie*, that we are facing a difficult situation here" — and in expressing our feelings, we are offering an *evaluative judgment*; this means that on many occasions:

- In a bewildering circumstance, we begin with feelings rather than calculations ... we begin with feelings as judgments ... we begin with a sense of there being a 'something' of value to us, and thus of importance to us... even if we don't yet know *what* its nature *is*;
- What is initially *indeterminate* is initially of more interest us in our inquiries than what is already well-known to us... rather than the continual re-discovery of sameness, our interest is in exploring, in 'dwelling in relation to' what is not in any way foreseeable *from the outside*.

As I explore it further, we come to experience:

- A hermeneutical reversal — experiencing a work of art as itself a

---

[88] Gadamer (2000) intended *Truth and Method* to be a description of what we always do when we *interpret* a circumstance (even when we are unaware of doing it): "My real concern was and is philosophic: not what we do or what we ought to do, but what happens to us over and above our wanting and doing" (p.xxviii).

living agency that is able to 'enter into' us and to make us other ... we become receptive subjects for a meaning which just happens to appear.

- What I as an agency thought I was 'bringing forth' begins to act within me as itself an agency that can teach me a new 'way of looking', or a 'new way of thinking'... a new style of painting comes on the scene, we are at first disoriented, but later we find that it has taught us a new 'way of looking' (see Shotter, 2010, 2011 on 'withness'-thinking).

What is special about 'withness'-thinking, is that it is the *reverse* of 'aboutness'-thinking, of cause-and-effect, mechanistic thinking:

- Mechanistically we talk of stimuli *causing responses, yet it is the living responses of organisms that constitute, i.e., give not only form but also value to the stimuli that they orient us towards;*
- Rather than *regularities, or repetitions, or rhythms, we need to work with singularities, particularities, or contextualized details* (what are usually dismissed in scientific psychology as arm-chair 'anecdotes').

But as we saw above, 'anecdotes' are *tellings* (not *reportings*), and a telling has a *tone* to it that arouses a particular quality of feeling within us — "she began in a conversational tone;" "he spoke in a nervous tone of voice;" "she spoke in a hesitant manner;" "he chose his words very carefully" — a tone of voice that *tells us* what the speaker is feeling in relation to the theme or topic of their talk:

- Thus it is useful to distinguish 'active' or 'working' meaning as the *reverse* of 'objective' or 'finished' meaning ... *upstream*, we do not find a meaning already 'there', but the beginning of 'the happening of meaning' — we can catch it 'in the act of coming into meaning', where the happening of meaning is the happening of understanding ... *downstream* our attention shifts to *what* is being understood... it shifts to the facts of the matter.

Kuhn (1977) gives a very nice example of a couple of important *reversals* in his thinking as he began to look into the *history* of revolutions in the development of the physical sciences: He began with the (1) sequencing of *which data* first to take into account; before then (2) moving on to explore the nature of the context *it needs to be contained in* for it to make sense (rather than seeking to find what it contains, its *properties*). He states the realizations he came to thus: "What I as physicist had to discover for myself, most historians learn by example in the course of professional training. Consciously or not, they are all practitioners of the hermeneutic method. In my case, however, the discovery of hermeneutics did more than make history seem consequential. Its most immediate and decisive effect was instead on my view of science ... When reading the works of an important thinker, look first for the apparent absurdities in the text and ask yourself how a sensible person could have written them[89]. When you find an answer, I continue, when those passages make sense, then you may find that more central passages, ones you previously thought you understood, have changed their meaning" (Kuhn, T. 1977, p.xv).

In other words, the form of life from which Aristotle's style of physical thinking emerges, for example, can be brought into rational-visibility, and thus become amenable to critical, intellectual discussion by taking the (hermeneutical) trouble to explore *his fragments* over some long period of time, until they form themselves into their own kind of unity.

---

[89]Kuhn's (2000) concern was with Aristotle's physics. Reading him through Newtonian physics made him seem not only ignorant of mechanics, but a dreadfully bad physical scientist as well; but then Kuhn, after 'dwelling in' his writings for a considerable time, suddenly found the *details* he was focussed on, sorting themselves out in a new way: "When the term 'motion' occurs in Aristotelian physics, it refers to change in general, not just to the change of position of a physical body. Change of position, the exclusive subject of mechanics for Galileo and Newton, is one of a number of subcategories of motion for Aristotle. Others include growth (the transformation of an acorn to an oak), alterations of intensity (the heating of an iron bar), and a number of more general qualitative changes (the transition from sickness to health) ... In Newtonian physics a body is constituted of particles of matter, and its qualities are a consequence of the way those particles are arranged, move, and interact. In Aristotle's physics, on the other hand, matter is very nearly dispensable ... A particular body, a substance, exists... [as] a sort of sponge ... impregnated with qualities like heat, wetness, color, and so on to give it individual identity. Change occurs by changing qualities, not matter, by removing some qualities from some given matter and replacing them with, others" (pp.17-18).

The amazingness of the ordinary
– Love, Actually
10

"The loved being is recognized by the amorous subject as "atopos" (a qualification given to Socrates by his interlocutors), i.e., unclassifiable, of a ceaselessly unforeseen originality/ The other whom I love and who fascinates me is *atopos*. I cannot classify the other, for the other is, precisely, Unique, the singular Image which has miraculously come to correspond to the specialty of my desire."

(Barthes, 1978, p.34)

"Those who treat love as a merely consequential 'reaction' to a value already felt, have failed to recognize its nature as a *movement*, ... Love does not simply gape approval, so to speak, at a value lying ready to hand for inspection. It does not reach out towards given objects (or real persons) merely on account of positive values inherent in them, and already 'given' *prior* to the coming of love. For this idea still betrays that gaping at mere empirical fact, which is so utterly uncongenial to love. Love only occurs when, upon the values already acknowledged as 'real' there supervenes a *movement*, an intention towards potential values still *'higher'* than those already given and presented."

(Scheler, 1952, pp.153-154)

"You might say: The work of art does not seek to convey *something else*, just itself."

(Wittgenstein, 1980a, p.58)

To repeat, my aim above, and in all that follows below, has been and still is the Wittgensteinian (1953) one of coming to "*a clear view* of our use of words" (no.122), of trying "to see it as it were laid open to view" (no.435). But rather than with the study of the *content* of patterns of already spoken words (in their existence as word *shapes* or *forms*), my concern has been with the arousal of unfolding *movements of feeling* occasioned within us as speakers, listeners, and readers, by our *words in their speaking*, and with the "action guiding anticipations" (Shotter, 2005b, 2008) to which they give rise. For, in the course of our actual, intimate involvements with the others and othernesses around us, the words (or wordings) we use in relation to the 'things' we experience as occurring in our everyday 'worlds', come to us spontaneously, as a 'matter of course' — unlike in our rationally structured reflections — for we have learnt our 'worlds' and 'their wordings' in intimate relations to each other as we have grown up into them.

My concern with unfolding movements of feeling, rather than with patterns and repetitions, due to the unremitting flow of time, is to do with the fact that we always find ourselves facing a never-before-happening, novel circumstance, with its own, unique *thisness* — a circumstance that we need to grasp as uniquely *itself*, and not as *identical* to something else already well-known to us. This, as we have seen, not only entails our *reversing* our usual ways of conducting our inquiries — by turning away from reflection and analysis, and situating ourselves *within* the very circumstance of our bewilderment, thus to experience *tendencies* within flowing streams of intra-mingling stream activities which, as such, have not yet been distinguished — which also confronts us with the fact that linguistically *characterizing* our circumstances is not only a difficult task, but also, one with political and ethical implications.

Situating ourselves in the 'extraordinary', the 'unique', the 'unforeseen'

In the previous chapter, in line with my concern with the *uniqueness* of each situation within which we find ourselves having to act, I explored the 'somethings more', the 'feelings of disquiet', the sense that our talk always points beyond itself to a 'not-yet-determined something or other', to another 'world' within which it *will* have its meaning. If we are to remain 'on speaking terms' with the intra-mingling currents of activity that, in fact, influence us more than we can influence them, then we must face the task of understanding the role such uniquenesses or singularities play in our lives. Clearly, our current, after-the-fact 'Newtonian-Cartesian' common-sense is utterly oblivious to their existence and their importance. Like all 'science-influenced' philosophy generally, it is reductionist, concerned to analyse and describe complex phenomena in terms of their most simple or basic constituents in the service of providing a sufficient explanation — an approach only too easily adopted, to repeat, because of the remarkable success of the natural sciences in extending the whole realm of our practical activities into now quite novel, and previously unthought of, spheres of concern.

Yet we must not ignore the fundamental fact that the 'real' world is always 'richer' than any after-the-fact 'reality' couched in general terms of our own devising. We still need to acknowledge that, very originally, Descartes (1968) — while beginning with "clear and distinct" ideas, ideas which in "being real things and coming from God, in so far as they are clear and distinct, cannot to this extent be other than true" (p.58) — saw the whole *point* of his "methods" as to do with "mak[ing] ourselves, as it were, masters and possessors of nature" (p.78). Whereas, our overall aim here is the quite different one to do with our coming to an understanding of *what*, as 'human beings' (in our after-the-fact ways of talking), it is still open to us to *become*.

Still entranced by the ease with which we can find our way about within the Newtonian-Cartesian 'world', it is only too easy, mistakenly, to feel that all the *difficulties* we face in life are like *problems* that we can *solve* by getting to *know* something currently unknown to us.

Whereas, as we have seen above, many of the difficulties we face are of an ontological, not an epistemological kind, to do with our coming to *be* a certain kind of person: "Should we be oriented towards simplifying and reducing the circumstances we face by *conceptualizing* them, in the *interest* of practical efficacies?" Or: "Should we be oriented towards looking into the *details* of different particular situations, with an *interest* in coming to an understanding of them as *uniquely themselves*?" Clearly, Descartes' aim — still often expressed in Academic Psychology as the task of describing, explaining, predicting, and controlling the behaviour and mental processes of others, within the context of a mechanistic world-view — is a much more intelligible (and communicable) task than that of coming to a grasp of a person or circumstance as uniquely *itself*.

It is at this point that I would like to return to Ingold and Palsson (2013), and their account of "bio-social becomings." For one of my central issues in this book — to do with the before-the-fact, evolutionary and developmental processes in which unforeseen *emergents* emerge — runs in exact parallels with theirs; for they also see 'something else', quite different from the influences represented in our after-the-fact theories and conceptualizations, as actually being at work in shaping the developmental activities that give rise to the *living forms* we observe.

Thus, for them: "Neo-Darwinism is dead. The paradigm that has long dictated the terms of accommodation between the sciences of life, mind, society and culture has been brought down by the weight of its own internal contradictions, by the manifest circularity of its explanations" (p.1) — its accounts need turning back-to-front, and inside-out, so that we come to focus, not on nameable *forms*, but, as they say, "to give primacy to the processes of ontogenesis — to the fluxes and flows of materials entailed in making and growing — over *the forms that arise within them*" (p.7, my italics). In other words, what they recommend here, as we have already seen above, is the overcoming of a fallacy by simply reversing the order in which we consider the 'steps', in an unfolding step-by-step process, to be taking place[90] — a solution that

---

[90] I will provide an extensive list of relevant 'reversals' in the next chapter. But for the moment, the most obvious reversal is that of beginning our inquiries, not with what is

"may be simple," but as they say, "the implications are profound" (p.7). Not least, is its effect on the tendency towards fragmentation produced by our use of methods of inquiry structured in after-the-fact terms, which "relentlessly drives us apart, in our capacity for self-knowledge, from the continuum of organic life within which our existence is encompassed" (p.8).

Living, then, as we do, within 'circumstances of practical concern' to us, what we 'care about' or 'matters to us' works, as we have seen, to organize what we attend to and respond to in these circumstances. And, as we saw with Frankfurt's (2005) account of 'bullshit' — as an indifference to how 'things' really 'are' in reality *itself* — it is just such a kind of talk that can 'disconnect' us from what in fact 'grounds' our later, after-the-fact, 'scientific' forms of inquiry.

Emergent, uncontrollable, unforeseeable events — love, and understanding other minds

It is at this point that I would like to turn to the important work of Max Scheler (2009/1923) for three reasons: one minor and two major: About being phenomenological, Scheler remarks: "Let us remember, however, that there is nothing of which the philosopher must be more wary than of taking something to be self-evident, and then, instead of looking to see what *is given*, turning his attention to what 'can be given' according to some supposed realistic theory. For it will be evident that the foregoing assumptions involve a complete departure from the phenomenological standpoint, replacing it — and covertly at that — by a realistic one" (p.224). Indeed, as we noted above, it is not at all unusual to hear in academic meetings, participants questioning each other about the subject matter of their inquiries: "How can we *define* it?" "How can we *conceptualize* it?" — and then going on to exclaim, given the *data* they have gathered — "This allows us to say... X...," while failing to notice, as Scheler points out, that they have slipped from 'being in touch with' a thick, before-the-fact, reality in their lived-experience, to describing things in terms of their own, thin, after-the-fact definitions and concepts. This is the minor point to which I want to draw attention.

(1) A first major point for Scheler (2005/1923), however, is the fact that our naturalistic approaches to reality are "utterly oblivious to the fundamental fact that the 'real' world is always 'richer' than any 'given' one" (p.182), and we thus tend to ignore *rare* and *uncontrollable*

---

familiar to us (as in problem-solving), thus to determine an unknown quantity in terms of its relations with known ones, we need to immerse ourselves, and to 'move around' within an unfamiliar and indeterminate situation, thus to become *familiar* with it, to be able to say in detail *what it is like*.

events[91], events that *emerge*, that *just happen* and cannot be — as is the case with all dialogically-structured activities — planned in advance and then deliberately 'brought of'.

Currently, instead of attending to what *could happen*, but has not yet done so, we continually attend to already-happened events that we suppose can been *repeated* in search of *patterns* within them. But, as Scheler (2009/1923) points out: "It is true enough that such things are easiest to grasp from the point of view of a 'human understanding' bent on controlling and dominating the world, simply because they are the most tractable, widespread and easily communicable, as compared with the more complex and valuable factors; but that is no reason for supposing that being and value are arranged to suit the convenience of an intelligence operating in terms of practical ends" (p.182).

However, very much in line with my assumptions above — to do with the fact that we live immersed within an ongoing, temporally unfolding, still largely undifferentiated flux of activity, in which we can *use* our words, literally, to *determine*, or to *determine*, or to *bring attention to*, features or aspects of the flux to which we can, as needs be, respond — Scheler (2009/1923) makes a very similar set of assumptions. He draws attention to our tendency to suppose that we need to begin our inquiries by assuming other people's experiences are very similar to our own — an assumption that fails to take account of their *otherness*, and the fact that they occupy a place in reality quite different from ours. As Scheler (2009/1923) puts it: "What occurs, rather, is an immediate flow of experiences, *undifferentiated as between mine and thine*, which actually contains both our own and others' experiences inter-mingled and without distinction from one another. Within this flow there is a gradual formation of ever more stable vortices[92], which slowly attract further elements of the stream into their orbits and thereby become successively and very gradually identified with distinct individuals" (p.214).

In other words, there is a gradual formation of what I have called above, *particular hermeneutical unities*. Take *honesty*, for instance: while

---

[91] See the discussion in the Appendix about such events.

[92] Such a flow of experiences is always in the process of becoming other than what at any moment it already *is*. Its growth is an essential and irreducible aspect of its nature; it cannot be separated out and 'added in' later, when convenient. Truly temporal processes are continuous or indivisible in the sense that the very process of differentiating them into phases of before and after serves, not to separate them into a "patchwork of disjoined parts,", as Dewey (1896) puts it, but on the contrary, to relate their phases as aspects of the same dynamic unity. It is a unity which is perceived as a unity, not in spite of its novelty in every moment, but because of it: For while it is clearly changing in one sense, like a swirl or eddy in a stream it remains recognizable in another sense as continually the same. Its unity is that of a stability within a flow rather than that simply of a static object.

anyone can, in principle, report on whether a person is behaving honestly or not, only the person herself can say whether *she is aware* of being honest, and is in fact *trying* to be honest — as if *deliberate honesty* is the only kind of honesty that matters. Thus it seems that two distinct kinds of criteria are involved here, one private and a matter of a thin, *after-the-fact* objectivity, and the other public and a matter of a thought, *before-the-fact*, expressive objectivity. And in the past both philosophers and psychologists have supposed that, as the seemingly private criteria are not open to scrutiny, only the public ones can be used as a basis for ascribing psychological predicates to people.

But if Scheler is correct, this is mistaken; both criteria are necessary and *are* available for scrutiny. For the fact is, due to their *intentional* nature, our feelings, moods, beliefs, aims, and goals *are shown in our actions*, and although they may not involve reference to objective criteria, they do nonetheless involve readily observable criteria which can be made into an "objective" event, a 'thisness' or a 'thatness' of a distinctive kind that people can not only 'point out' to each others, but can also tell others of their possible *meanings*, i.e., what they could lead to[93]. It is 'in' the ability of agents to specify, in a moment-by-moment fashion in their actions and utterances regions of the world beyond their actions, that they can reveal the 'direction' of their actions, and thus make both their intentions, and their personalities, manifest.

Above, I mention explicitly the *expressive* nature of before-the-fact objectivity made available to others in what a person *shows* in their activities and utterances, to make contact with the material explored in chapter three. Coming to an understanding of other people *from within* the involvements we enter-into with them, is of quite a different kind to that of coming to an understanding of them by observing them as if *from the outside* as dead things — clearly, the world of *I-thou* relations within which our 'works' are fashioned, is more primordial than the world of physical objects, the world of *I-it* relations.

(2) This leads me onto the second major reason for my focus on Scheler's (2009/1923) work: As an exemplar of an emergent, unplanned, and uncontrollable event, Scheler (2005/1923) takes the "Love" we can have for another person (as well as, of course, the love we can have for many other particular *othernesses* we encounter in our lives, in particular, the *vocations* to which we devote our personal lives — the ultimate values that we find ourselves to have adopted as a *part of ourselves*, that we cannot give up or betray without ceasing to be who we take ourselves to be, what Frankfurt (1998) calls "volitional necessities").

---

[93] As we have seen, Garfinkel (2002) calls such an event a "witnessable recognizability or recognition" (p. 68),

As we have already seen in Barthes' (1978) epigraph quote above: For us, a loved one is "unclassifiable," a source "of a ceaselessly unforeseen originality" (p.34). But it is not just what a loved one can do for us, that matters to Scheler; crucially, it *a matter of what we can do for them*: "Love does not simply gape approval, so to speak, at a value lying ready to hand for inspection. It does not reach out towards given objects (or real persons) merely on account of positive values inherent in them, and already 'given' *prior* to the coming of love. For this idea still betrays that gaping at mere empirical fact, which is so utterly uncongenial to love. Love only occurs when, upon the values already acknowledged as 'real' there supervenes a *movement*, an intention towards potential values still '*higher*' than those already given and presented. These additional values are *not* yet manifested as positive qualities, being merely envisaged concurrently as potential ingredients of a corporate structural pattern. In so doing, love invariably sets up, as it were, an '*idealized*' *paradigm of value* for the person actually present, albeit conceiving this at the same time as an embodiment of his 'true' nature and 'real' value, which only awaits confirmation in feeling" (pp.153-154).

In other words, if we love any person at all, we not only love them for what they already *are*, but also for what they *might* be[94]. Our love of someone or something is the most effective influence that can 'move' an *otherness* towards potential values still '*higher*' than those already given and presented. As Werner Stark (2009/1923), the editor of Scheler's text describes the influence a lover can have on 'moving' a loved one to a 'higher' level: "Our eyes are fixed upon his ideal image which we grasp in, through and behind his empirical traits; yet we are indifferent as to how far it is reflected and realized in his actual state. At the same time, our love is the most potent force that can lift him from one to the other. It carries before him his own purified, and, as it were, redeemed and transfigured likeness, as a challenge to follow and to reach it; it is like a voice calling: become what you are! become in reality what ideally you are in design!" (p.xli).

---

[94] This is especially true for mothers (and fathers) with their children, or for teachers with their students,

11 A unifying, 'before-the-fact' philosophy

> "One might also give the name 'philosophy' to what is possible *before* all new discoveries and inventions."
>
> (Wittgenstein, 1953, no.126)

> "The work of the philosopher consists in assembling reminders for a particular purpose."
>
> (Wittgenstein, 1953, no.126)

> "If there has to be anything 'behind the utterance of the formula' it is *particular circumstances*, which justify me in saying I can go on — when the formula occurs to me."
>
> (Wittgenstein, 1953, no.154)

I began this book with Cassirer's (2000) concern: That as research began in many different fields, and as each progressed inexorably, their inner unity became problematic; philosophy was unable to put a stop to the growing fragmentation. What 'broke up' the unity of the deep understanding of the 'reality' in which we live, is the unprincipled division of what needs to be a holistic enterprise into a countless number of different 'social scientific' modes of inquiry, each one with its own controversies as to what "the *proper object* of its study" actually *is* (Shotter, 2015a). What I want to examine here, is what we can do to regain that lost unity.

What, temporarily, 'stands fast' for us in our meetings with others

> "An 'inner process' stands in need of outward criteria".
>
> (Wittgenstein, 1953, no.580)

> "What is happening now has significance — in these surroundings. The surroundings give it its importance".
>
> (Wittgenstein, 1953, no.583)

In making these remarks, Wittgenstein is drawing our attention to the fact that — when speaking to an Other, and wishing that we could 'see' what they are thinking, we should not think that it is hidden in some special 'inner space' within their heads — we can 'see' it in how they relate themselves, step-by-step, to the *particular details* of their surrounding circumstances. In other words, if we are to 'enter into' *their* world and to understand *their reasons* for their actions, then we need to understand them, not in terms of generalities, but in relation to particular, holistic unities we fashion, hermeneutically, from our fragmentary experiences of them as we and they 'move around' in relation both to each other, and in relation to *our* circumstances. In other words, we need a description that *does justice* to the *particular circumstances* in place at the time of the person speaking and acting.

In seeking a grasp of the 'inner landscape' of another person's life, we seek to know what it is at work within them that leads them to organize *their relations to their surroundings* in the particular manner that they do; we need to know the larger *context* within which their particular utterances can take on their particular meaning. In relation to my own experience, my concern here is not with what 'comes to mind' *in the course of my reflections,* as I turn, retrospectively, to a past experience to think *about* it, but with how it is that the words and phrases needed to bring the from-to movements of feeling occurring within me when I am *trying* to express myself, "recommend themselves to me, when I am speaking," says Merleau-Ponty (1964), "in such a way that my spoken words surprise me myself and teach me my thought. Organized signs have their immanent meaning, which does not arise from the 'I think' but from the 'I am able to'" (p.88). As I suggested above, our ordinary, everyday ways of acting in the world, in which we *just do* spontaneously what is required, are amazing.

Why is it that we have ignored the practicalities involved in the unproblematic conduct of our daily lives to such an extent? Clearly, it is the *intellectualism* implicit in the power of 'the I think' as a starting point for all our inquiries, that has stood, and still now, stands in the way of our recognizing the extent and the power of the anonymous, agential influences at work in our bodies such that we find — as a result of a to-and-fro, subject-object dialogue occurring within us spontaneously — a 'world' arrayed around us that, as it were, 'speaks' to us in our own terms, and hermeneutically gives our 'thoughts' their place in that 'world'.

And further, to reiterate, within the global expressiveness of that dialogue, its physiognomy[95], we can experience an agential 'it' with its own unique and distinctive character, an 'it' that can not only make 'calls' and 'demands' upon us, but which can 'sit there within us' — as an unchanging standard, as a *superaddressee* (Bakhtin, 1986) — in terms of which we can 'measure' the satisfactoriness (or not) of our attempts at explicitly expressing aspects of its meaning for us.

Once we accept that we do not live in an already-made world, but in an indeterminate world that we can make determinate in countless

---

95 See footnote 67.

different ways, then it becomes clear that prior to any *thought* about the difficulty or difficulties we face, we need to formulate the *subject matter* of our inquiry, initially at least, in the shared common-sense terms available to us in our ordinary, everyday language — for initially at least, we need to find it intelligible, open to our explorations of its meanings for us. For us to be able to make such investigations, we must be able to draw on *the ways of making sense* shared with those around us, that is, on the anonymous, agential ways of thinking that *come to happen within us* as a result, as we saw above, of our growing up as a member of a *particular languaged social group*. Where, in making use of a shared *way of making sense* we are making use of, to repeat Vico's (1968) way of putting it, a "judgment without reflection" (para 142, p.63), i.e., we are *in deed* judging that what is before us is an X and not a Y.

This is where, as I see it, our inquiries *must* in fact begin. For although such judgments are clearly not, as Austin (1970) put it, "the last word" (p.185), they must be our "first word" for at least the two following reasons: (1) Firstly, unless we formulate the subject matter of our inquiries in such a way that those around us can 'go on' to act on our claims as we mean them to be acted upon, they will remain indeterminate and ambiguous; and (2) secondly, to the extent that we do not know at first *how to doubt them*, our initial judgments can function as "hinges" (Wittgenstein, 1969, nos. 152, 341), as stable 'points of entry' or 'starting points' that can "stand fast" (no.152, 234) for us in relation to the overall fluid and dynamical nature of our everyday, practical, socially-embedded activities. Where, in standing fast for us, we can return to them time and time again in an inner process of exploratory movements aimed at gradually *differentiating* the diffuse movements of feeling occurring within us into an articulated and articulable structure of intra-related features.

By acting in this way, by 'grounding' or 'contextualizing' our initial questions and claims in the already existing common understandings at work within the life of the linguistic collective within which we expect our questions and claims to have their currency — in what Vico (1968) calls the *certa* (the certains) existing within a particular *sensus communis* — we can *both* 'set the scene' for our inquiries in unproblematic talk of an everyday kind, *while at the same time* — to the extent that the subject matter of our talk can be made to "stand fast" for everyone concerned to inquire into its nature — make it also a topic open to further exploration. Thus, in speaking in a specific context, we are making (i.e., enacting, creating) specific determinations within an otherwise indeterminate, holistic circumstance.

Intellectualism and the 'conceit' of scholars

> "Intellectualism in the vicious sense began when Socrates
> and Plato taught that what a thing really is, is told us by its
> *definition*. Ever since Socrates we have been taught that
> reality consists of essences, not of appearances, and that the
> essences of things are known whenever we know their
> definitions. So first we identify the thing with a concept and
> then we identify the concept with a definition, and only
> then, inasmuch as the thing *is* whatever the definition
> expresses, are we sure of apprehending the real essence of it
> or the full truth about it".
>
> (James, 1909/1996, p.218)

However, recognition of the importance of this fact is not new: Vico
(1701/1988), in his *On the Most Ancient Wisdom of the Italians*, noted
that "for the Latins, *verum* (the true) and *factum* (what is made) are
interchangeable, to use the customary language of the Schools, they are
convertible" (p.45) — what has come to be known as his *verum-factum*
principle. While later, as an extension of this principle, he began to see
certum, 'the certain', as an ineradicable part of *verum,* 'the true',
certum est pars veri — where *certa* are the unreflective judgments as to
the 'what-ness' or the 'is-ness' of what is actually occurring around us,
judgments that we have *all* constructed between us, spontaneously,
which now constitute aspects of the everyday, taken-for-granted, shared
background to our shared social lives.

Thus we arrive at the view that the shared background to our shared
social lives — as a structure of feelingful thought and of thoughtful
feelings, as a constellation of symbolic forms and of social practices,
with its customs and laws, its arts and its sciences and other
institutions, as they are actively lived and felt — depends for its
intelligibility and legitimacy, just as much, if not more, upon the
common and collective sense of ordinary people than on the refined
ideas of those we think of as intellectuals.

Indeed, Vico takes the seemingly radical view that, if we examine what
has been written so far in the attempt to arrive at an orderly and
consistent account of the principles of human knowledge, we will find
"that it is a tissue of confused memories, of the fancies of a disordered
imagination; that none of it is begotten of intelligence, which has been
rendered useless by ... two conceits ... For on the one hand the conceit of
the nations, each believing itself to have been the first in the world,
leaves us no hope of getting the principles of our Science from the
philologians. And on the other hand the conceit of the scholars, who will
have it that what they know must have been eminently understood from
the beginning of the world, makes us despair of getting them from the

philosophers. So, for purposes of this inquiry, we must reckon as if there were no books in the world" (para.330, p.96). Words in their speaking, our spontaneously responsive expressions, are basic.

But, as Foucault sees it, more than the conceit of scholars was at work in seeking to replace the creative power of *speaking within a context*, with the decontextualized authority of what has been *said*: The ordering and stability of our established social institutions is at stake. As he puts it: "I am supposing that in every society the production of discourse is at once controlled, selected, organised and redistributed according to a certain number of procedures, whose role is to avert its powers and its dangers, to cope with chance events, to evade its ponderous, awesome materiality" (Foucault, 1972, p.216).

Indeed, as he sees it, this was an aspect of Plato's achievement in *The Republic* (written around 380BC). In it, while insisting on the importance of *The Forms* (of Ideals hidden behind appearances) — so that for Plato, the 'Republic', as outlined in his account of it as an Ideal Form, is more 'real' than any State actually in existence — he judged poetry (the tool of the sophists) to be artful language that tended to seduce the unwary into merely seeking pleasure, instead of lifting the soul to contemplate *true* virtue. Judging it solely in terms of its effects, he saw it as *persuading* us to accept a speaker's preferences, rather than what is *true*.

Thus, as Foucault (1972) recounts it, "a century later, the highest truth no longer resided in what discourse *was*, nor in what it *did*: it lay in what was *said*. The day dawned when truth moved over from the ritualised act — potent and just of enunciation to settle on what was enunciated itself: its meaning, its form, its object and its relation to what it referred to. A division emerged between Hesiod [and Homer as poets] and Plato, separating true discourse from false; it was a new division for, henceforth, true discourse was no longer considered precious and desirable, since it had ceased to be discourse linked to the exercise of power. And so the Sophists were routed" (p.218).

Along with the claim that the really 'Real' sources of influence shaping our conduct are the radically hidden *Forms*, goes the concomitant claim that they can nonetheless be wholly represented (mirrored or pictured) within the logical structure of a systematic theory — or at least, they can be if what is represented by a theory of what 'might be' the case is *warranted* as being what in fact *is* the case, by our being able to claim, for instance, that others saw it that way too, or, that it is so because of our possession of a special (professional) competency, etc., i.e., that it is supported by evidence. Indeed, crucial to the power of "pure theory-talk," at least in the recent past, is the way in which almost all of us have been institutionalized into accepting it — if it is appropriately warranted

— as *true* of reality, irrespective of who utters it or the context in which it is uttered.

As Dreyfus and Rabinow (1982) say, in discussing the importance of Foucault's (1972) account of such autonomous discourse: "By passing the appropriate tests statements can be understood by an informed hearer to be true in a way that need make no reference to the everyday context in which the statement is uttered. This exotic form of speech act flourished in especially pure form in Greece around 300 B.C., when Plato became explicitly interested in the rules that enabled speakers to be taken seriously, and, by extrapolating the relative context independence of such speech acts to total independence, invented pure theory... This systematic, institutionalized justification of the claim of certain speech acts to be true of reality takes place in a context in which truth and falsity has serious social consequences" (p.48). Indeed, those with competence in such procedures can construct their statements as 'factual statements', and claim authority for them as revealing a special 'true' reality behind appearances, without any reference to the everyday context of their claims.

The danger in this process, however, is that it can produce, and for us in the social sciences, *does* produce, what we can call *ex post facto* fact fallacies: the fallacious retrospective claim that, for present events to be as they are, their causes *must have been* of a certain kind. Fleck (1979) outlines its general nature as follows: "... once a statement is published it constitutes part of the social forces which form concepts and create habits of thought. Together with all other statements it determines 'what cannot be thought of in any other way'... There emerges a closed, harmonious system within which the logical origin of individual elements can no longer be traced" (p. 37). In attempting retrospectively to understand the origins and development (and the current movement) of our thought, we describe their nature within our to an extent now finished and systematic schematisms. But in doing so "we can no longer express the previously incomplete thoughts with these now finished concepts" (p. 80).

And so it is that we end up, still today, seemingly, with the unresolved tension between an *intellectualism* at the heart of most of our institutionalized practices (in government, the professions, the schools and universities, the law, and so on), and the ordinary, everyday, contextualized use of language, in which the same word can have both a different sense in a different context of use, as well as the same sense in different contexts.

Beginning with 'anomalies', with 'disquiets', with an 'unease'

I say, seemingly, because, as soon as we distinguish between the thinking that just happens within us, and the more deliberate thinking we do as socialized individuals — which is shaped by the *common-sense* or *sensing* (as an anonymous agential activity) we share with the others in our social group — we realize we need to take into account, specifically, the *affective* elements of consciousness and of our relationships: Rather than excluding feeling in favour of thought, or of thought in favour of feeling, we need, to repeat, to take note of feelingful thought and of thoughtful feeling, along with all the characteristic elements of impulse, resistance, and tone (relational attitude) we exhibit in our everyday, common-sense expressions — that is, all the anonymous, agential influences at work, *before-the-fact*, while emergence of our social experiences are still-in-process.

So, although we may think that in order to be 'scientific' we must put our reflective thinking first, and adopt an *intellectualist* or *theoreticist* approach as our guiding orientation at the start of our inquiries, is that where *in fact* they actually *do* begin? Although we may feel that we should purge our rational, 'calculational' thought of all its emotional baggage as soon as possible, the fact is, as we saw above, we find ourselves *feeling motivated* to turn to a particular inquiry — something is still at work within us 'calling us' to undertaking an inquiry of some kind. What might it be?

In the sciences, if Kuhn (1970) is correct, it is our *noticing of an anomaly*, our having our anticipations upset that occasion the beginning of our inquiries. Where, as both Kuhn and Dewey point out, the upset we feel is not just a general upset, but arises, as Kuhn (1970) puts it of our "knowing *with precision* what [we] should expect" (p.65); or as Dewey (1938/2008) puts it, out of "a *unique doubtfulness* which makes that situation to be just and only the situation it is" (p.109); or as Merleau-Ponty (1964) puts it, when we sense that there is "as yet no more than a precise uneasiness in the world of things-said" (p.19).

The unresolved tension between an *analytical intellectualism* at the heart of most of our institutionalized practices and the ordinary, everyday, contextualized use of language, still remains unresolved, and we can see the consequences of it in our political life everyday, especially just at the moment — for I am writing just at that moment in history when the United (?) Kingdom (UK) is said to have voted in a referendum to leave the European Union (EU), i.e., at the moment of 'Brexit'.

But in recent years, there has been no shortage of political projects that have not turned out as people have expected. When this happens, the more exasperated the 'theorists' become, the more they try to force the facts into some preconceived mould, or to create after-the-fact excuses for their non-happening. While their critics, seeing that the 'thin' simplicities of the 'theorists' come nowhere near to satisfying the 'thick' realities influencing the living of fully human lives, try to resist their (shocking and awesome) plans.

But then, the more resistance the 'theorists' experience, the more violent and less grounded in reality are their efforts at overcoming that resistance; and in the middle of the confusion, the greater the reaction the greater the confusion and untold suffering is caused to ordinary people, largely uninvolved the original decision making. And as the process spirals out of control, the original ends are lost sight of, and the consequences of what were, in fact, 'experiments' (proposed outcomes) escalate beyond what anybody had ever wished or planned or expected. Where now should we turn?

Wittgenstein's efforts to return us to the 'everyday' as the primordial, face-to-face, human reality

> "What *we* do is to bring words back from their metaphysical to their everyday use. / You say to me: 'You understand this expression, don't you? Well then — I am using it in the sense you are familiar with'. — As if the sense were an atmosphere accompanying the word, which it carried with it into every kind of application".
>
> (Wittgenstein, 1953, nos.116&117)

> "Mere description is so difficult because one believes that one needs to fill out the facts in order to understand them. It is as if one saw a screen with scattered colour-patches, and said: the way they are here, they are unintelligible; they only make sense when one completes them into a shape. — Whereas I want to say: Here *is* the whole. (If you complete it, you falsify it)".
>
> (Wittgenstein, 1980b, I, no.257)

Above, I introduced and explored Wittgenstein's (1980a) distinction between difficulties "having to do with the will, rather than the intellect" (p.17), and I suggested that we could think of such difficulties as having to do with how we *relate* or *orient* ourselves toward the others and othernesses in our surroundings — how we, so to speak, approach or address them. Indeed, to go further, we understand the *difficulty* as a difficulty having to do with the particular *structure of anticipations* (Mills, 1940) aroused in ourselves, and in those around us, by our *speaking* of an action as being like *this*, rather than like *that*[96]. Thus how we act in response to a person's experience of an event, is not a matter of arriving at an *objective representation* of it that has to be *thought about*, but a matter of understanding its *meaning* in relation to a 'inner landscape' of next possible ways of acting in relation to it.

A classic example here might, perhaps, be Martin Buber's (1970) account of his different relations to a tree: After having listed all his relations to it as an 'It' — as a picture; as a movement; as an instance of a species, of a law, of a numerical pattern, and so on — he goes on to describe a special kind of sudden switch that can occur in his relations to it, the switch from an "I-It relation" to an "I-Thou relation."

He describes it thus: "But it can also happen, if will and grace are joined, that as I contemplate the tree I am drawn into a relation, and the tree ceases to be an It. The power of exclusiveness [its uniqueness] has seized me. This does not require me to forego any of the modes of contemplation. There is nothing that I must not see in order to see, and there is no knowledge that I must forget. Rather is everything, picture and movement, species and instance, law and number included and inseparably fused" (p.58).

In other words, in an I-It relation to the tree, we not only relate to it within what we might call a *single order of logical connectedness* in which, as we look in an orderly fashion from one selected feature of the tree to another and find our orderly expectations satisfied, we can begin to see it as an instance of a general type — a possibility that can only become available to us, after-the-fact.

But once we give up our deliberate gazing at the tree, i.e., give up the orderly way of looking we adopt when we direct our looking according to such an orderly inner system, and allow ourselves, like Buber, to be spontaneously responsive to whatever aspects of the tree that happen to 'move' us, then that is when the tree ceases to be a mere 'it', and becomes a 'Thou', an expressive, *living*, otherness. And in 'calling out' unexpected responses from us spontaneously, the tree can begin to 'say' things to us that can surprise us; so that, for instance, a painter can catch an extra-ordinary aspect of trees that those of us observing trees with only ordinary expectations in mind, would ignore: "Cypresses are on fire since Van Gogh," says Steiner (1989, p.188).

---

[96] Appreciating a word's meaning in relation to such a 'structure', is to understand it as playing a particular 'part' within "an atmosphere accompanying the word" (no.117), a particular 'part' (a *use*) that can change as the circumstances within which it is used change.

But, as Buber comments, this is not to forego any of the other modes of contemplation; it is to realize that everything, picture and movement, species and instance, law and number included, are all inseparably intermingled with each other within a dynamically unfolding, unitary whole. Indeed, in 'working back' from our single orders of connectedness to more comprehensive *ways of looking*, we can do so by switching within ourselves from one orderly way of relating to the tree to another and to another, and in so doing, we can begin to create an "inner dialogue" within which each way of thoughtful looking can become *dialogically related* to the next, and the next, and to the next[97]. And as we relate each way of looking to the next, we can begin to form a whole network of connected ways of relating to the tree, we can begin to see the tree, comprehensively, as a 'Thou'.

In making the comments above, about 'working back' from a set of seemingly disconnected elements toward a comprehensive whole, I was writing with one of Wittgenstein's (1953) methods in mind: His insistence that before coming to any final conclusions as to the nature of one of our concepts, we need to survey a large range of examples of its use. For, in his words, "a main cause of philosophical disease — a one-sided diet: one nourishes one's thinking with only one kind of example" (no. 593). He displays this method at work early on *Philosophical Investigations*, in considering our *situated use* of the word "game" in describing a whole collection of very different activities.

We can feel very tempted to say: "There *must* be something common, or they would not be called 'games'." But, he says, if you take the trouble to look and see if that is the case, you will find that *that* cannot be so: "Look for example at board-games, with their multifarious relationships. Now pass to card-games; here you find many correspondences with the first group, but many common features drop out, and others appear. When we pass next to ball games, much that is common is retained, but much is lost. — Are they all 'amusing'? Compare chess with noughts and crosses. Or is there always winning and losing, or competition between players? Think of patience. In ball games there is winning and losing; but when a child throws his ball at the wall and catches it again, this feature has disappeared. Look at the parts played by skill and luck; and at the difference between skill in chess and skill in tennis. Think now of games like ring-a-ring-a-roses; here is the element of amusement, but how many other characteristic features have disappeared! And we can go through the many, many other groups of games in the same way; can see how similarities crop up and disappear" (no.66).

---

[97] We explored the process involved in arriving at a particular hermeneutical unity in Chapter One.

From 'thinking' to 'moving around'

To get clear about philosophical problems, it is useful to become conscious of the apparently unimportant details of the particular situation in which we are inclined to make a certain metaphysical assertion. Thus we may be tempted to say 'Only this is really seen' when we stare at unchanging surroundings, whereas we may not at all be tempted to say this when we look about us while walking" (Wittgenstein, 1965, p.66).

In other words, his earlier quoted admonition to us[98] is: "don't think, but look!" and if we do, then "the result of this examination is: we see a complicated network of similarities overlapping and cries-crossing: sometimes overall similarities, sometimes similarities of detail" (no.66). This is what the *before-the-fact* reality within which we actually live is like. And he continues: "I can think of no better expression to characterize these similarities than 'family resemblances'; for the various resemblances between members of a family: build, features, colour of eyes, gait, temperament, etc., etc., overlap and criss-cross in the same way. — And I shall say: 'games form a family" (no.67). It is not that they remain an unconnected set of disparate fragments, but the whole they form is not one that can be captured within a single, logical order of connectedness either. They are intra-twined, intra-connected in the hermeneutical fashion I explored above; the particular differences amongst them, are just as undeniable as their similarities to each other[99].

If we are to cure ourselves of the "grammatical illusions" (Wittgenstein, 1953, no.110) that (mis)lead us into assuming that 'things' (nameable objects) in fact pre-exist their expression in language — illusions that

---

[98] See footnote 6.

[99] With regard to 'family resemblances', we may be tempted once again to say that all the members of a family *must* possess features in common with each other, and that is why we can 'see' them *as* a family. But that is to organize them into a family by imposing a framework of our own devising on them — when, in fact, they are already related in their own way. But this is to ignore the importance of the *differences* amongst them. As Bortoft (2012) points out, what we need here is not the idea of *self-sameness*, the assumption that all organisms grow in the same way, but the idea of *self-differencing*, that although they may all be very similar at the start of their grow, in their *coming-into-being* they can become very different from themselves whist still remaining themselves, instead of becoming something else. And what is especially important about this idea, about *family resemblances*, is that, as Bortoft (2012) expresses it: "There is no separation here (if we find it in our thinking, it is because we have 'fallen downstream' without noticing, i.e., started after-the-fact thinking: js): the self-differencing is the unit and concomitantly the unity *is* the self-differencing. This dynamic unity is evidently the very opposite of the unity of the finished products, which is the static unity of self-sameness that is reached by the *exclusion* of difference" (p.71).

arise within us when we say something to ourselves *unconnected to anything in our surroundings* — then we must begin to try to teach ourselves how to think and to talk *while still somewhat disoriented*, and while still trying to make sense of our not-as-yet-well-specified circumstances.

We must teach ourselves, not only to act, intellectually, as best we can in relation to states of affairs *in statu nascendi*, that are still coming into being, but also, to accept that what we are trying to deal with *can never in fact be fully finalized* and must be left *open* to yet further development. Consequently, if we do not, we may still leave others with circumstances to which they cannot contribute, and they will feel excluded and alienated. We need to be aware of this, and be prepared to continue to help them come to a *resolution* of their bewilderment.

But this is not easy to do. As experts, as intellectuals, *working within boundaries of our own devising*, we can become very well versed in thinking and talking about understandings gained from a static standpoint; it is thus easy for us to feel that *they* should come to think as *we* do. The idea of us as being immersed in ceaseless streams of flowing movement is very unfamiliar to us, while *they* feel they are 'playing catch up', or they are being 'overtaken by events'. But we, unlike practitioners immersed in disjointed streams of different projects, almost always talk of seeing some 'thing' from a particular 'standpoint', a place, a position, or point of view, or *from within* a perspective or framework, in terms of static shapes, forms, or pictures. We are still very unused to talking of 'things' from within our ongoing, unfolding relations within the circumstances within which they are still *coming into 'big B' Being*.

Indeed, the shift from thoughtful, reflective understandings gained in while in motionless contemplation to practical understandings gained while moving about in action is, clearly, quite revolutionary.

Everything we thought we understood and had the vocabulary to describe, changes. For instance, while many may still see philosophy as primarily oriented toward gaining a kind of knowledge (or wisdom) that ultimately is recorded in books, Wittgenstein (1953) suggests a much more practical definition. To repeat what has been said many times above, as he sees it, "a philosophical problem has the form," he says, "[of] 'I don't know my way about'" (no.123). And it is (re)solved, he suggest, when we can say to someone (and to ourselves), "'Now I can go on!'" (no.151). I mention these more practical less intellectual, more poetic reformulation of our disquiets here, as these two metaphorical expressions — the one of a kind of difficulty, and the other of what is involved in overcoming it — are central to what I want to offer in this book. For, after all, as a critique of *intellectualism*, it can only be as a contribution to a better understanding of our everyday practical activities that this book can be seen as of use; no matter how much one feels the urge, the tug to return to a standpoint in reflective thought.

Conducting our 'inner conversations' in a different idiom: from nouns to 'verbings', from 'inquiries' to the 'happening' of 'humanifying'

"To human is a verb" (Ingold, 2015, p.115).

But the fact is, now more than ever before, the unresolved tension between an *analytical intellectualism* at the heart of most of our institutionalized practices and the ordinary, everyday, contextualized use of language, still remains unresolved, and we can see the consequences of it in our political life every day, especially just at the moment — for I am writing just at that moment in history when the United (sic) Kingdom (UK) is said to have voted in a referendum to leave the European Union (EU), i.e., at the moment of 'Brexit'!; at the time of Donald Trump's rise to adoption as a Presidential Candidate; at a time when Syria and the Middle East is a complete mess. We seem to be devoid of any certainties of any kind.

Our task, if we are to resolve that tension, is to find *a prior common ground occupied by all professional practitioners that, in fact (without them being aware of it) grounds their claims to their professional skills.* That common ground is to be found, I think, in what Bortoft (2016) calls an *upstream* state of affairs, and I call the *before-the-fact* circumstances that all professionals confront *prior to the particular sense they make of them.*

Currently, given the primacy of our thinking over acting, we take it that prior to acting we need to make a *decision*; we can think of it as occurring in four stages: (1) First, we perceive a situation; (2) then we think of possible courses of action; (3) we then *calculate* which course is in our best interest; and (4) we then take that course of action — *justifying* it by our calculational reasoning if challenged — but is it in fact the making of a *decision*?[100] Being already caught up in a ceaselessly ongoing processes, we *can only act* in relation to the constraints and limited resources our circumstances afford us, as well as what they 'call on us' to do, thus we often just act as best we can — in other words, we hardly make any decisions at all! We simply act in terms of our experienced judgment.

Making inquiries

Clearly, as we have seen over and over again above, the Cartesian view that proper reasoning is based in *calculation* has led professional intellectuals to assume above that stage three (3) is obviously the most important stage: Indeed, entire social science disciplines have been premised on the assumption that people are mostly engaged in rationally calculating and maximizing their own self-interest as the professionals they are (see Shotter, 2015a). Economists and Policy Analysts, in particular, have worked in this way, in terms of *idealized* mathematical models.

But during the recent financial crisis, that way of thinking clearly failed spectacularly. As the former Federal Reserve chairman, Alan Greenspan conceded in his Congressional testimony on Oct, 2008[101], the global financial crisis has exposed a 'mistake' in the free market ideology which guided his 18-year stewardship of US monetary policy. In prepared remarks before the House of Representatives, Greenspan, 82, who retired in 2006, called the financial crisis a "once-in-a-century credit tsunami" and said it had "turned out to be much broader than anything I could have imagined." He was "shocked" that markets did not work as anticipated. "I made a mistake in presuming that the self-interests of organizations, specifically banks and others, were such as that they were best capable of protecting their own shareholders and their equity in the firms." And he went on to suggest that his trust in the responsibility of banks had been misplaced: "Those of us who have looked to the self-interest of lending institutions to protect shareholders' equity (myself especially) are in a state of shocked disbelief."

This, perhaps, should have been the moment when we professional intellectual people began to alter our view of decision-making in

---

[100] "Coming to a judgment, then, is not a matter simply of decision making — as if the possibilities from which we must choose can be clearly laid out before us – nor is it about providing 'an interpretation' of an otherwise bewildering situation (for an uncountable number of interpretations is possible), but a matter of coming to, or resolving on, a clear perception of a circumstance and its performative meaning for us — what it calls upon us to do within it" (Shotter & Tsoukas, 2014, pp.389-390).

[101] See: https://www.theguardian.com/business/2008/oct/24/economics-creditcrunch-federal-reserve-greenspan

general: When, as professional practitioners, we should have begun to shift our focus from step three (3) — arriving at *after-the-fact conclusions* as a result of *calculational reasoning* — to exploring the nature of the *before-the-fact processes* involved in *coming to a specific perception* of WHAT the situation, that we are 'in', *is like*, to examine step one (1), our perception of the situation we are in.

In Chapter Two, we explored the nature of this process from the outside, from a methods-point-of-view rather thoroughly, so I will not repeat that account here, except to say that, rather than problem *solving*, our task seemed to be that of achieving a *resolution*; we needed to bring a *particular determination* to an otherwise, particular indeterminate situation, without losing its particularity — a particular determination oriented towards achieving a particular end-in-view (Dewey, 1928, p.12, and Wittgenstein,1953, no.132).

Here, instead, I want to try to say something about how the whole unfolding, step-by-step process *feels* in our living experience from-within our experiencing of it, and then to go on to say something about the influences at work in us as we try to go about *wording* our expression of these *feelings* or *sensings*, given that the words we use will take us (and others) into the future.

As I made clear above, such states of affairs are always *in statu nascendi*, they are still coming into being; as such, we can characterize them in terms of three features: (1) they are in motion; (2) still indeterminate and thus open to many further determinations; and (3) directed toward the future. In other words, rather than 'appearances', they are 'appearings'; rather than 'events', they are 'eventings'; rather than describing our experiences 'in language', we express them by 'languaging' them, by in fact 'verbing' them[102] — we are always trying to make sense of what to do next, from within the midst of a set of intra-mingling streams of still-emerging activities happening *now*, all with their own particular "feelings of tendency" (James) directing us into the future.

Perceiving a situation, at first sight, seems like a remarkably simple operation; we just look around us, and 'see' what there is to see — don't

---

[102] We can get a sense of what is needed from Whorf's account of a style of language based in *activities* and *events*, and not *objects*, very different from our own: "In Hopi," says Whorf (1956), "all such phase terms, like 'morning, winter', etc., are not nouns at all but, says Whorf, a kind of adverb. Nor are these 'temporals' ever used as nouns, neither as subjects nor as objects. Thus they would not say, as we do, 'in the morning', but 'while morning-ing'. Indeed, as Whorf says, Hopi is a timeless language in the sense that, what we feel must be explicitly recognized as features of the passage of time, are not recognized as such in Hopi. Neither is there any 'thingifying' of time as a region, extent, or quantity; nothing is suggested about it in Hopi, says Whorf, other than the 'getting later' or 'latering' of it" (Shotter, 1993, p.106).

we? But the operation that seems most simple is actually the most complicated. It is just, as we have seen, that most of the action occurs within us, spontaneously, below the level of our awareness; looking at and perceiving the world is an active process of meaning-making that shapes and biases as it unfolds, step-by-step, the rest of our *supposed* decision-making processes.

In other words, to repeat what has been said many times above, we now need to accept that the physical reality is, in itself, *indeterminate*, and that what we observe as *objective* in our particular inquiries is a matter of the particular *subjective expectations* we were entertaining in beginning our inquiries in the first place. Thus, as Simons & Resnick (2005), for instance, are now making very clear (what many have suspected for a long time), what we 'see' is a matter of what we *expect* to see, and what we expect to see is *in relation* to our task in hand, to our end in view[103] — what we 'see' *is 'in' the relations* between our outgoing, explorative activities towards aspects of our surroundings and their incoming results. The distinction, the cut or split, between what we count as *subjective* and what as *objective*, thus is up to us; it is not 'given' to us ahead of time (Barad, 2007).

Being immersed in the happening of humanifying

But even with this degree of flexibility and open possibility, we are still limiting ourselves, *developmentally*, by entertaining particular *subjective expectations* of our own formulation right from the beginning our inquiries. Whereas, as we have seen above, if our task is to understand *what* we experience and perceive only in terms of what it *means* to us in the moment of our experiencing and perceiving *it*, then we must talk and act *from within the living* of our lives, rather than from an *illusory* place outside them. This is because the unfolding of its unique time-course in the world cannot at all be likened to the performance of a pre-existing script, but is much more like the way, say, an awareness of what one has just said or done works to differentiate ones circumstances further, thus to increase the possibilities available as to what one might go on to say or to do next.

Crucial here, then, is our allowing ourselves to be immersed in the 'happening' of those 'in-the-moment' meanings — in those dialogically-structured, hermeneutical *moments*[104] from out of which, eventually, another, uniquely new, particular holistic unity, that will enlarge the array of human possibilities available to us, will emerge — which, to repeat, 'just happen' to us, and it is in their just happening nature that

---

[103]".... object perception is highly dynamic — the properties consciously perceived at any moment are just those needed for the task at hand" (Simons & Resnick, 2005, p.17).

[104] See section below on: *Beginnings, noticings, and moments* ...

such moments can take us *beyond* possibilities already implicitly available to us.

This is why Ingold (2015) suggests that we need a verb here to designate the existence of new kind of activity that we have not before recognized: to *humanify*. "For humans to humanify, ... is not to *humanise* the world," he says, "That is to say, it is not — as an ontology more conventional to the western tradition would have it — to superimpose a preconceived order of their own on a given substrate of nature. *It is rather to forge their existence within the crucible of a common lifeworld.* Their humanness is not given from the start, as an *a priori* condition, but emerges as a productive achievement — one, moreover, that they have continually to work at for as long as life goes on, without ever reaching a final conclusion" (p.117, my italics) — where what is involved in creating and sustaining the unfragmented nature of that *crucible* is the point and purpose of this book.

Doing more together than we can do apart

Our worry was, and is, fragmentation. In our modernist forms of inquiry, as exemplified in all our Cartesianism forms of inquiry, we tend to move forward from particularity to universality, we hardly ever look back. In our urge to discover the precise functional techniques that will enable us to adjust 'reality' to our own, imposed specifications, we leave behind, ignored, the just happening binding contingencies at work in the *humanifying* activities (Ingold, 2015) that link us to each other, along with the structures of time and place within which, in our *meetings*, we enact what I am calling our 'relational becomings'.

Speaking, actually

In claiming that our words in their speaking matter, actually, I want to draw attention to the fact, once we have 'grown up into' a particular languaged social group, and begin to make *use of* the ordinary, everyday ways of speaking already at work within our surroundings, we find ourselves saying and doing various 'things' spontaneously, in an effortless way, with the others around us *responding* to us as we *expect* them to respond. Thus *speaking, actually* — speaking in all its variations — in speaking a language in common with all the others around me, I am assuming in the context of this book that this is the primal *human* activity, and that in our speakings we can *shape* both our world and ourselves.

Yet, it is very difficult for us to turn what we usually leave in the 'background', into something we can focus on as topic in itself. As Cassirer (2000) puts it, "the cultural object requires a different [kind of] observation [from natural objects]; for it lies, so to speak, behind us" (p.85). This is where the tendency to *fragment* our holistic grasp on what Cassirer (2000) calls our "cosmos" — the just happening binding contingencies that link us all to each other — begins. For again, under the Cartesian influence of *I think therefore I am*, instead of moving around in an exploratory fashion within the *particular* circumstance that is, initially, bewildering us, thus to arrive at a *distinctively felt sense* of its 'thisness' (and not 'thatness'), we find it all too easy to formulate for ourselves, ahead of time, a rational schematism, an unambiguous theoretical single order of connectedness, that seems to us to *correspond with* crucial, objective features out in the world before us.

What is so special about this move, is that enables us to avoid stepping out into the still 'wild', 'open', and 'fluid' world, full of unforeseeable, unclassifiable happenings, unfolding in time — a world that is not yet an aspect of our cosmos, a world of *dynamic stabilities* that we do not yet feel 'at home' in. But in doing this, in being content to focus only on events that *we can make happen*, and ignoring what *just happens* to us — *spontaneously* occurring events — we are ignoring the occurrence of *unique* events, 'striking', 'touching', or 'moving' events that can change us in our very way-of-being-in the-world.

Spontaneous responsivity

It is because as living beings we are *spontaneously responsive* to events occurring around us that we can be struck, touched, or moved. This is crucial. It means, clearly, that we need to distinguish what is involved in coming to a grasp of the nature of dead forms, in contrast to our ways of relating ourselves to living forms. Each requires understanding in its own way. While we can come to an understanding of a dead form in terms of objective, explanatory theories representing the sequence of events supposed to have caused it, *a quite different form of engaged, responsive understanding becomes available to us with a living form*. It can call out spontaneous reactions from us in way that is quite impossible for a dead form. It is this that makes these two kinds of understanding so very different from each other. While we can study already completed, dead forms at a distance, seeking to understand the pattern of *past* events that caused them to come into existence, we can enter into a relationship with a living form and, in making ourselves open to its movements, find ourselves spontaneously responding to it.

In noting that we can adopt two ways of orienting, or of relating ourselves to what Cassirer (2000) called "cultural objects or works:" (1) Observing them as if *from the outside* as dead things, and (2) that of coming to an understanding of them *from within* the involvements we enter-into with them, we can relate to them as *inert objects*, or as *expressive entities*, or better, as 'relational becomings' that can 'call out' responses from us, spontaneously.

I have assumed in this book that our *spontaneous responsiveness* to the activities of the others and othernessess around us, as *expressive beings*, is primary; in other words, the world of *I-thou* relations — within which our 'works' are fashioned — is more primordial than the world of what we take to be physical objects, the world of *I-it* relations. Further, as I see it, we have for too long been in awe of the remarkable success of the physical sciences, and this has misled us into taking as central to all our attempts at thinking and speaking rationally, what I will call a retrospective, *after-the-fact*, achieved version of an itemized objectivity. Indeed, it is an objectivity that needs to be established in a particular local circumstance *as required* for a particular purpose.

What is already at work within our shared, background common-sense

Thus yet again, we need to examine *the importance of our disregard of what is already at work within our shared, background common-sense*, and the consequences of our ignoring it, and thinking that we can simply start afresh in formulating a 'framework' within which to 'think about' *the problems* we face. For what we have also failed to notice, is that many of our difficulties in life *do not have the character of problems*, but are to do with *our way or ways of relating ourselves* to occurrences in our surroundings. My purpose in doing this, in trying to highlight the existence of what I have called an already instituted, thick, prospective, *before-the-fact*, holistic common-sense, is it provides us as participants within it, not only with a shared *sense of the circumstances* we are currently occupying, but also, prior to all our more deliberate undertakings within it, with a *sense* of what certain particular words we use *mean*.

This means that — when, in our Cartesian *I think* moments, we assume that the theories we formulate reach down and anchor themselves in a fundamentally neutral, already existing physical reality to which symbols in the theory correspond in a one-to-one fashion — we are mistaken. For the fact is, whenever we speak of such 'things' as atoms and molecules, or of the laws of nature, we are speaking of what we mean, by the expressions 'atoms', 'molecules' and 'laws of nature' (Winch, 1958); they are all expressions associated with a particular way of 'seeing' the world and of manipulating it by the means it provides.

In science, as Kuhn (1970) makes clear, theories are grounded in the activities which give research practices their reproducibility, in the activities which give research practices their reproducibility, namely, their *accountability* (Shotter, 1984) amongst those conducting them. But notice how this accountability is achieved. Participants begin by appreciating how, given the practical phenomena confronting them, theoretical categories can be used to constitute them as events of a recognizable kind — the research practice provides practitioners with an *account* (Mills, 1940; Shotter, 1984) as to how a theory should be used and applied. Such categories are used as an unquestioned (and unquestionable) resource in organizing one's perception of events within a research paradigm (Hanson, 1958) — they represent how things *are*, naturally.

The otherness that enters us and makes us other

Consider, by comparison, the process of listening to an *account*: if the facts so far are unsatisfactory, incomplete or even bewildering, one waits for later facts and uses them in an attempt to decide the sense of the earlier ones; what sense there is to be found is not decided beforehand, but is discovered in the course of the exchange within which the account is offered. But clearly, this is what makes the nature of our efforts and struggles to describe what goes on, *before-the-fact* of our actually saying or doing something so difficult: we can only say what their 'fluid', dynamical, still-in-process nature *is like*, while accepting that each metaphor we use both *reveals* and *conceals* — which means that we have to explore a circumstance in terms of a number of different metaphors, while assuming, as Gadamer (2000) puts it, that its different aspects will "not simply cancel one another out as research proceeds, but ... [will] combine [into a particular hermeneutical unity] only in us" (p.284). In other words, *just happening, striking events* can work in us to enlarge our shared, everyday, thick common-sense, enabling us now to do deliberately what in the past we have only done spontaneously, all unawares.

Amartya Sen (2009) provides us with an important example here. Rather than seeking *ideal* notions of what justice actually *is*: "What moves us, reasonably enough," he remarks, "is not the realization that the world falls short of being completely just — which few of us expect — but that there are clearly remediable injustices around us which we want to eliminate" (p.vii). Thus, by situating ourselves within a particular practical situation within which we can gain a shared sense — along with all the others around us — of a particular *injustice* at work, there is a real chance of us all, working together, of arriving at a way of remedying it. For we can all find in such a situation both, a guiding motivation, and, as we mentally move about within it, *ways to bring to light* the resources we need to move on from that injustice — where the *ways* we need will involve our *theories*.... to be used, not as explanatory devices, but as *objects of comparison* to help us in coming to a *felt sense* of what the *particular injustice in question is like*, a detailed 'touching', 'moving' account is required.

Writing — details and particularities

> "The ethnographer "inscribes" social discourse; *he writes it down*. In so doing, he turns it from a passing event, which exists only to its own moment of occurrence, into an account, which exists in its inscriptions and can be reconsulted".
>
> (Geertz, 1973, p.19)

This is why my writing takes on, sometimes, a rather unusual nature. I emphasize the need for attention to *details* and *particularities* because I am not concerned with the *results* of any inquiries into the *properties* of our acts and utterances *in general*; nor with any *causal explanations*. Instead, in trying to craft short *vignettes* or *dramatic portrayals* or *synoptic condensations*, my point or purpose is not to *explain* or *define* any 'thing', but to arouse in readers a distinctive *from-to movement of feeling*, a *pointing* towards a next place to go in one's current activities. In other words, my concern is not to provide *other people* with the *completed ends* of *my* investigations, but with *possible beginnings* for *their* own inquiries (Shotter, 2007, 2012) — beginnings that in our everyday activities are always 'in transition', but which can always be 'gestured toward', 'pointed out', or 'attended to' in our writing.

Once we accept that we do not live in a ready-made world, but in an indeterminate world that we can make determinate in countless different ways, then it becomes clear that prior to any *thought* about the difficulty or difficulties we face, we need to formulate the *subject matter* of our inquiry, initially at least, in the common-sense terms available to us in our ordinary, everyday language — for initially at least, we need to find it intelligible, open to our explorations of its meanings for us. For us to be able to make such investigations, we must be able to draw on *the ways of making sense* shared with those around us, that is, on the anonymous, agential ways of thinking that *come to happen within us* as a result, as we saw above, of our growing up as a member of a *particular languaged social group*. And we exhibit our ability to do this in the way or ways we *word* our sense-making expressions, where, in making use of such shared ways, we are making use of, to repeat Vico's (1968) way of putting it, a "judgment without reflection" (para 142, p.63), i.e., we are *in deed* judging, in a way the others around us share, that what is before us is an X and not a Y.

The dynamics of the giving of meaning — Love, actually

Having begun with Cassirer's (2000) concern with the fragmentation of our knowledge and understanding of ourselves and our world, I now want to turn to what he had to say in a later (his last) work, concerned with how we might go about overcoming it. What was central to how he put it there, was that it is oriented toward "the dynamics of the giving of meaning, in and through which the growth and delimitation of specific spheres of being and meaning occur in the first place. It seeks to understand and illuminate the riddle of the becoming of form as such— not so much as a finished determination but rather with determination as a process. This process does not follow a single, predefined course leading from a specific beginning to an equally fixed end, which has been determined in advance. Thought does not flow here in a finished riverbed which has been made for it; rather, it must find its own way —

it must first dig its own bed for itself. This movement of thought searching for itself is not limited at the outset to a single, particular direction. Instead, distinctly different approaches emerge in it, different centres of power and different tendencies"(pp.4-5) — for the fact is, we are never not immersed within a continuous flow of intra-mingling activities which, here at this moment, and there at that moment, create *particular*, unfolding, *dynamic stabilities* that can change us in our very way-of-being-in-the- world.

Above, I pointed out that in adopting the Cartesian *I think* approach, we leave behind, ignored, the *humanifying* activities (Ingold, 2015) that link us to each other, along with the structures of time and place within which, in our *meetings*, we enact what I am calling our 'relational becomings' — the most important of these, I think, we call "love:" Lovers can *notice* in loved ones, tendencies that outsiders ignore; lovers can 'set a scene' that 'invites' a loved one to 'realize' such tendencies more fully. This is what is so special about the nature of *dialogically-structured*, developmental processes. As Bakhtin (1986) puts it, such a process, "always creates something that never existed before, something absolutely new and unrepeatable, and, moreover, it always has some relation to value ... What is given is completely transformed in what is created" (pp.119-120).

Relinquishing our craving for generalities

It is at this point that I would like to return to Ingold and Palsson (2013), and their account of "bio-social becomings." As they see it, and I agree, the *intellectualist* paradigm that has for some long time (and still in many spheres of inquiry still) dictates *how we should make sense* of our circumstances, is undermined "by the manifest circularity of its explanations" (p.1) — its accounts need turning back-to-front, and inside-out, so that we come to focus not, yet again, on nameable *forms*, but, as they say, "to give primacy to the processes of ontogenesis — to the fluxes and flows of materials entailed in making and growing — over the forms that arise within them" (p.7). In other words, what they recommend is the overcoming of a fallacy by simply *reversing* the order in which we consider the 'steps' in an unfolding step-by-step process to be taking place — a solution that "may be simple," but as they say, "the implications are profound" (p.7).

Not least, is its effect on the tendency towards fragmentation produced by our use of methods of inquiry structured in *after-the-fact* terms, which, as they say, "relentlessly drives us apart, in our capacity for self-knowledge, from the continuum of organic life within which our existence is encompassed" (p.8).

Overcoming the fragmentation by *reversing* the process in which we use of methods of inquiry structured in, what I have called above, a thin, retrospective, *after-the-fact*, achieved version of an itemized objectivity, and turning instead to the already existing *common-sense* enacted in our spontaneous uses of our everyday ways of talking — the pre-existing source from which, in fact, we *select* what we take for practical purposes to be the facts of the matter. In other words, prior to all our *after-the-fact* forms of itemized objectivity, we in fact live immersed within one or another version of a thick, prospective, *before-the-fact*, already instituted, intra-woven form of objectivity, a holistic common-sense that provides to all the participants within it, a shared *sense of the circumstances* they are currently occupying.

In setting out the possibility of this new, *before-the-fact orientation* for our inquiries into the nature of our social activities (and especially communication) in this fashion — as a matter of trying to bring to light their *genesis*, their *coming into being* as the activities they are — I am reminded of how Thomas Kuhn (1970) ended his account of *The Structure of Scientific Revolutions*; he said: "We are all deeply accustomed to seeing science as the one enterprise that draws constantly nearer to some goal set by nature in advance. But need there be any such goal? If we can learn to substitute evolution-from-what-we-do-know for evolution-toward-what-we-wish-to-know, a number of vexing problems may vanish in the process" (p.170). And this, of course, is what I am proposing here: that we relinquish the still unfulfilled — and, as I see it, *forever unfulfillable* — dream of gaining the very *general* results we desire in our inquiries, and to be content with the limited, partial, and situated results that we *can in fact obtain* — which, in the end, will, I believe, perhaps surprisingly, turn out to be of far greater practical use and value to us. Especially if it can contribute, as I have been suggesting that it can in this book, to an ending of the fragmentation of our relations to each other, and the discovery of how much more we can do together than we can do apart.

Just one more thing...

The Primacy of the Improbable,
the Unique, the Singular

"But if, as metaphysicians, we are more curious about the inner nature of reality or about what really makes it go, we must turn our backs upon our winged concepts altogether, and bury ourselves in the thickness of those passing moments over the surface of which they fly, and on particular points of which they occasionally rest and perch."

(James, 1996, pp.251-252)

"My present field of consciousness is a centre surrounded by a fringe that shades insensibly into a subconscious more. I use three separate terms here to describe, this fact; but I might as well use three hundred, for the fact is all shades and no boundaries."

(James, 1996, p.288)

Above, I have been emphasizing the importance of *singular events*, of things happening for "another first time" (Garfinkel, 1967, p.9), and how we can, and do, make sense of them. I have also been emphasizing the importance of what I have called our 'disquiets'[105] — the fact that many of us, no matter how expert and knowledgeable we might have become within a particular field of study, always feel that there is a 'something more' that we have not yet 'grasped', not simply a *known-unknown,* but an *unknown-unknown.* Something unlocatable that places a restriction on our freedom of action. Hence Hamlet's counter to Horatio's fulsome trust of him: "There are more things in heaven and earth, Horatio,/Than are dreamt of in your philosophy" (Hamlet, 1.5.167-8) — but more than this, sometimes *startling*, or *shocking* events occur, and although *rare*, such events can lead us into re-orienting ourselves in relation to our surroundings in quite astonishing ways.

---

[105] Wittgenstein (1953) describes the motivation for his investigations thus: "The problems arising through a misinterpretation of our forms of language have the character of *depth*. They are deep disquietudes ... A simile that has been absorbed into the forms of our language produces a false appearance, and this disquiets us. 'But this isn't how it is!' — we say. 'Yet this is how it has to be!'" (nos.111, 112). In other words, if he is (and we are) to get in touch with the array of details available to us in 'big B' Being in his investigations, then: "When I talk about language (words, sentences, etc.) I must speak the language of every day ... In giving explanations I already have to use language full-blown (not some sort of preparatory, provisional one)" (no.120).

From relying on one's own experiences to using other sources of information— the drastic underestimation of the effect of rare events

This book was almost finished before I happened to read Nassim Taleb's (2007) book, *The Black Swan*. I hadn't read it because I thought it was wholly about statistics and economic reasoning and thus had very little to say to me; I was wrong: As I read his book, his concerns began to seem very similar to mine. For instance, born in Lebanon in 1960 — which from 1975 to 1990/1992 was stricken by a civil war between Muslims and Christians — he found himself mediating on what people said in *their* attempts to *forecast* what was going to be its outcome. When young: "I was constantly told by adults the war, which ended up lasting close to seventeen years, was going to end in 'only a matter of days'" (p.9); and then later, in mediating on people's *inability to accept unpredictability*, and their *compulsion* to create *explanatory accounts* of how, in fact, inexplicable events would unfold. But, just as I concluded above — that our intellectually arrived at accounts are *after-the-fact* of the activities already having been performed, so Taleb (2000) came to the same conclusion: "These events were unexplainable, but intelligent people thought they were capable of providing convincing explanations for them — after the fact ... What's more worrisome is that all these beliefs and accounts appeared to be logically coherent and devoid of inconsistencies" (p.10).

They appear to be logically coherent and devoid of inconsistencies because, as we have seen above (Chapter Five), once we *impose* concepts and definitions of our own devising, we block our awareness of *the array of details* from which we *select* the 'boundaried samenesses' making up a concept. Clearly, to repeat, it is the *intellectualism* implicit in the power of 'the I think' as a starting point for all our inquiries, that has stood, and still now, stands in the way of our recognizing the extent and the power of the anonymous, agential influences at work in our bodies, aroused in us in the course of our, spontaneous, unconsidered, everyday involvements with all the others and othernesses around us.

What is of special interest to Nassim Taleb (2007), is the extent to which we can, in some circumstances, drastically *underestimate* the *effect* that the occurrence of rare events can have on our subsequent activities — for instance, as an *unknown-unknown*, each unforeseen 'terrorist' activity raises a *particular* kind of difficulty to which there is no *general* response. Thus, we continually see *proposed solutions*, only to notice a few days later, their revision, and the implementation of an alternative that also needs revising later, and so on. As Taleb sees it, people severely underestimate the risks involved in an action when they make a judgement from their own experience — this is because we far too easily assume that when we turn to our experience, we are already in touch with the totality of 'big B' Being, and in drawing on that, we can come to a *best* conclusion. But this is clearly not the case, due to our *intellectualist* stance, we only ever experience a world of 'little b' beings. It is only when people are provided with other, outside sources of information that they come to *overestimate* the risk involved[106].

Regarding terrorism, Taleb (2007) notes: "Terrorism kills, but the biggest killer remains the environment, responsible for close to 13 million deaths annually. But terrorism causes outrage, which makes us overestimate the likelihood of a potential terrorist attack — and react more violently to one when it happens. We feel the sting of man-made damage far more than that caused by nature" (p.80). Clearly, as a cool 'calculational' person, Taleb thinks that *in cost-benefit terms* we should channel our resources towards dealing with climate change, and put terrorism on a back-burner. We are too *emotionally* influenced by the occurrence of some rare events, to make a *best* judgment. As he puts it: "I said earlier that our perceptual system may not react to what does not lie in front of our eyes, or what does not arouse our emotional attention … Out of sight, out of mind: we harbor a natural, even physical, scorn of the abstract" (p.121).

I have mentioned Taleb here for two main reasons: (1) his recognition of the pervasiveness of *after-the-fact* thinking, but also, most importantly, (2) for his bringing into rational visibility the all-to-easily ignored excessive influence that *rare events* can exert in our everyday activities, often leading us into all kinds of misdirected activities. The fact is, in relation to such events, we know not what to do, nor what our doings will do, as we try to act for the best in relation to such events. We have a sense of unease, that there is something missing from what we are doing, but we often feel that it is best to let catastrophes happen — because then we can deal with something concrete and particular — rather than searching around for much more diffuse reasons for our unease. Taleb suggests simply that it is our scorn for the abstract, and our being swayed by our emotions that lands us in trouble. But is it? Let me now turn away from Taleb's rationalistic way of dealing with our responses to *rare* events, to what might be a more productive alternative — Giambattista Vico's (1968) poetic alternative.

Making sense of rare events — the power of the extraordinary

> "From Jove that the muse began".
>
> (Vico, 1968, para.391)

---

[106] See Taleb (2007, pp.77-78).

"This division between invention and judgment arose first among the Greeks just because they did not pay attention to the proper faculty of knowing. This faculty is mother wit, the creative power through which man is capable of recognizing likenesses and making them himself. We see it in children, whom nature is more integral and less corrupted by convictions and prejudices, that the first faculty to emerge is that of seeing similarities. For example, they call all men fathers and all women mothers and they make likeness: "They build huts, hitch mice to little wagons, play odds and evens, and ride on a great hobby horse of a stick."

(Vico, 1988, pp.101-102)

"So that, as rational metaphysics teaches that man becomes all things by understanding them, this imaginative metaphysics shows that man becomes all things by *not* understanding them; and perhaps the latter proposition is truer than the former, for when man understands, he extends his mind and takes in the things, but when he does not understand, he makes the things out of himself and becomes them by transforming himself into them."

(1968, para.405)

As both Frankfurt (1998) and Nussbaum (2001a) make clear above, some of our emotional reactions and attitudes *matter to us personally* because: "They are *my* emotions, and they relate to issues that *matter* to me..." (Nussbaum, 2001a, p.27). In other words, there are often *good reasons* for our seemingly excessive reactions to particular rare events: It is because of their *personal mattering* to us that we focus on the part they can play (or are playing) in our lives, currently; I do not go about fearing any and every catastrophic event occurring out in the world at large. Thus, rather than trying to *explain* such events (after-the-fact of their occurrence), we can by *dwelling within them* and *moving around within them*, come to a sense of them as a *'thing' of a particular sort*, a 'something' that is related to my own freedom of action.

Rather than as an unlocatable abstraction, my emotional attitudes, rather than being a diffuse influence at work in the world at large, can become to be localized and particular; they take their stand in my life and exert their influence within the quite specific transitions occurring within my living of it. So what I want to try to show here, is that, if we take the trouble 'to dwell within' and 'to move around within' the many different practical spheres of our lives, *we can to an extent live forward* in terms of our sense of those *'somethings more'* that emerge within us; we can receive *intimations* of where next we might go in our efforts to relate ourselves to the others and othernesses around us in a more intelligible manner.

The fear of thunder — a first 'sensory topic' that can be 'found again'

Descartes began by taking 'the mind' as already containing 'something(s)' and by seeking to discover what, basically, they are, his answer was: "innate ideas" — Descartes's world here is, of course, the mechanistic world. Vico, however, begins in a very different way: by asking how it is that the mind comes to have anything present to it at all — where Vico's world is at first a world of undifferentiated flowing activities.

For Vico, then, this question really is of the utmost importance, for it concerns people's abilities to create and establish within the flow of experience between them "stopping places," to establish an "is" within the flux of sensation which can be found again — a *fixed* meaning or feeling in relation to one's otherwise continuously changing circumstances. Without the possibility of referring to such *stabilized* feelings or sensings, Vico (1968) notes: "the minds of the first gentile world took things one at a time, being in this respect little better than the minds of beasts, for which each new sensation cancels the preceding (which is the cause of their being unable to compare and reason discursively), therefore their sentences must all have been taken as singulars by those who heard them" (para.703).

Thus for Vico, the first anchor point — the roots of a "civil society" — are to be found in the formation of "sensory topics", i.e. the fashioning of a shared *sense* within an *already shared* circumstance or state of affairs, in terms of a shared linguistic significance.

As an example, Vico analyses (in para 391) what he calls the "civil history" of the saying that it is "From Jove that the muse began." Taking it seriously, he suggests that fear of thunder is indeed the paradigm for the first "sensory topic," the first fixed reference point which people can "find again" within themselves and know that others "feel in the same way." For, as they all flee to the caves to shelter from the thunder, all in a state of fear, an opportunity exists for them to realize that it is the *same 'thing'* that they all fear; and a look or a gesture will communicate this: a *moment of common reference* exists between them.

What the 'inner mechanisms' might be which make such a realization possible is not Vico's concern here; his concern is with the 'outer' social conditions making it possible for us to be *in a community* with each other. "Thus," says Vico (para 382), "it was fear which created gods in the world; not fear awakened in men by other men, but fear awakened in men by themselves" — a fear expressed in the character of people's bodily activities together in shared circumstances. But this kind of fear is not an ordinary fear of an immediately present dangerous event whose character is obvious to them all; there is no immediate practical response available to them all in response to thunder. Their fear seems to point *beyond* the thunder. When people hear it, they become confused and disoriented, they move furtively and with concern for one another — the thunder's presence is the *unspoken* explanation of their actions. And often, "when men are ignorant of the natural causes producing things, "says Vico (para 180), " ... they attribute their own nature to them;" they assimilate them to what is familiar to them. Thus, they attribute their fear, in this instance, *to the anger of a being like themselves* but more powerful.

What we have here, then, Vico suggests, following the emergence of a shared feeling in a shared circumstance — a "sensory topic" — is the creation of an "imaginative universal," the image of a *particular something*, a *real presence* (Shotter, 2003), that is first expressed by everyone acting, bodily, in the same way in the same circumstance, but which is expressed later, *metaphorically*, in the fable of *Jove*. As an "imaginary universal," the image of *Jove* both gives articulate form to, but is rooted in, the sensuous totality in which thunder is linked with the recognition of fears at the limits of one's being shared with others because of shared bodily activities.

That sensuous totality, however, is not simply a disorderly amalgam of events, but a hermeneutically created *unity*, emerging from within a developed and still developing sequence of relations occurring within a social group. In other words, the image of *Jove* is a *particular* imaginative universal in which a whole array of sequentially occurring events — all in responsive connection with each other — are brought together into a distinctive unity without, in fact, the particularities involved being blended into a undifferentiated whole. He thus arrives at his *master key*: "We find that the principle of these origins both of languages and of letters," he says, "lies in the fact that the early gentile peoples, *by a demonstrated necessity of nature*[107], were poets who spoke in poetic characters. This discovery, which is the master key of this Science, has cost us the persistent research of almost all our literary life, because with our civilized natures we cannot at all imagine and can

---

[107]By this phrase, Vico wants to highlight a tendency, a movement *necessarily* occurring within human communities in which, with the passage of time, they increasingly tend towards realizing new potentials emerging within them, with each realization creating further new possibilities: As Vico (1968) puts it: "Men mean to gratify their bestial lust and abandon their offspring, and they inaugurate the chastity of marriage from which the families arise... The reigning orders of nobles mean to abuse their lordly freedom over the plebeians, and they are obliged to submit to the laws which establish popular liberty" (para.1108); in other words, the sense always of there being a 'something more' pervades all our social activities.

only understand by great toil the poetic nature of these first men" (Vico, 1968, para.34, my italics).

The sensory topic from which the image of Jove originated, is thus a 'topos', a 'place' in which it is possible to 're-feel' *everything* which is present at those times when 'Jove' is active. And, as such feelings are slowly transformed into more external symbolic forms, the inarticulate *feelings* remain as the 'standards' against which the more explicit forms may be judged as to whether they are adequate characterizations or not. Sensory topics are thus the primordial places, the *loci*, constituting the background basis of the mentality of a people. They make up its common-sense, its *sensus communis*, the basic *certainties* which, as C.W.Mills (1940) put it above, actors give as "unquestioned answer[s] to questions concerning social and lingual conduct... [and use as] ultimate[s] in justificatory conversation" (p.907).

Divine Providence — the sensing of new beginnings

> "Truly, if you were to apply the geometric method to practical life, 'you would no more than spend your labour on going mad rationally', and you would drive a straight furrow through the vicissitudes of life as if whim, rashness, opportunity, and luck did not dominate the human condition".
>
> (Vico, 1988, pp.98-99)

> "All this is set forth in these Notes, to show how uncertain, unseemly, defective, or vain are the beginnings of the nations".
>
> (Vico, 1968, para.43)

> "Doctrines must take their beginnings from that of the matters of which they treat".
>
> (Vico, 1968, para.314)

Vico's *new science*, in accord with what we have encountered so far, is very much a science of beginnings and beginnings. Central to it, is something very special, *sui generis*, at work in the 'making' of social institutions: he calls it "divine providence." But by that, he does not mean the working of any supernatural agency or agencies coming in from the outside to impose an order upon our own intelligent human activities; nor does he mean by divine providence the workings of chance, or fate, or any blind cause and effect processes. For, he says: "That which did all this was mind, for men did it with intelligence; it was not fate, for they did it by choice; not chance, for the results of their always so acting are perpetually the same" (para. 1108) — that is, they always, everywhere, produce a social world with a moral order to it.

So although the 'making' of a moral order is not an 'accountable' or 'visibly-rational-and-reportable' activity (Garfinkel) within the social reality of a particular society — for such activities are a precondition of people being able to give accounts and reports to one another — there are in fact, nonetheless, *natural provisions* for the coming into being of such an order within the very nature of our social activities themselves. It is precisely this, Vico maintains, which all the social philosophers before him have missed. They have missed it because it is 'hidden' — not as already something full-blown inside people's minds — but *in the incipient beginnings of it still coming into being*:

"The philosophers have been altogether ignorant of it," Vico (1968) says, "as the Stoics and Epicureans were, the latter asserting that human affairs are agitated by a blind concourse of atoms, the former that they are drawn by a deaf [inexorable] chain of cause and effect.... But they ought to have studied it in the economy of civil institutions, in keeping with the full meaning of applying to providence the term 'divinity' [i.e. the power of divining], from *divinari,* to divine, which is to understand what is hidden *from* men — the future — or what is hidden *in* them — their consciousness' (para. 342).

In other words, what can further unfold or be made more explicit in our social activities is, in some sense, already present and 'at work' implicitly in our daily social activities. Prior to our being able to 'say what it is', it 'shows up' in our activities. Our coming to say *what* it is, is clarified by our 'constructing' a larger whole into which it can be fitted — a process of essentially a hermeneutical nature. For involved is a step-by-step specificatory process in which 'something', which is already partly specified, is specified further, thus rendering what was at first strange, alien or unfamiliar, *as* something familiar, as something with a comprehensible part to play in the whole in which it has its being. Thus: "Our new science must therefore be a demonstration, so to speak, of what providence has wrought in history, for it must be a history of the forms of order which, without human discernment or intent, and often against the designs of men, providence has given to this great city of the human race. *For though this world has been created in time and particular*, the orders established therein by providence are universal and eternal" (Vico, 1968, para.342, my italics). This world has been created *in time and particular* by the historical fact of *providence*, by the provision of new beginnings occasioned within us by the occurrence of *rare* and *striking* events.

This is why I have focussed in this book on *words in their speaking*, rather than on *patterns of already spoken words*. For, as we have seen over and over again, our *ways of speaking* are very basic, in that they 'work' in terms arousing in our listeners (and in ourselves) shaping and directive tendencies or anticipations as to *where* next and *what* next we will do in our languaged or linguistically-structured activities.

If we try to start our inquiries as thinkers, by trying to posit formal, theoretical schematisms, principles, rules, or laws prior to our inquiries (as we will see in more detail below), we will find, not only that we *immobilize* what was in movement, but also in *selecting* certain features as essential to our schematisms, we *exclude* others, crucially the *specific tendencies* to change and development present in almost all human activities. Vico, in his day, was aware of this as we are now; hence his concern with finding a new starting point for his inquiries in the *beginnings* of our social institutions, in the beginnings of our relations to the others and othernesses around us that make everything else that we can do and say possible — including the art of writing.

Hence my hope in all of this, is that *you*, my readers, can find yourselves *guided* by these letterings on the page to such an extent, that you can find them arousing in you, distinctive *movements of feeling* that work to connect your seeing of the letters with my speakings. For, to repeat, my overall aim, is not that of fitting what we experience into an already existing theoretical-scheme, framework, or perspective scheme in order to *explain* it, but that of grasping how, in our everyday contexts of *the use of language*, we can negotiate or navigate between us the collaborative construction of extremely subtle outcomes, particular outcomes which, once achieved, remain 'on hand', so to speak, as a resource for use in general by us all.

Overcoming separation and fragmentation — beginnings in 'striking' events

"The 'otherness' which enters us makes us other".
(George Steiner, 1989, p.188)

"Hate between men comes from our cutting ourselves off from each other".
(Wittgenstein, 1980a, p.46)

To end where we began: We cannot continue with the intellectualist *ways of thinking* we currently take for granted — ways of thinking based in *theoretical* and *conceptual* formulations that we take as *corresponding* in an *ideal* fashion with reality. For such science-like, scientistic ways of thinking work *to separate their focal topics from each other*, so that we then need to seek ways of trying to re-relate them back into a *holistic* reality again — but this time, one in our own interests. In beginning our inquiries in this way, in our *individualistic thinking*, we currently take it for granted that we can *conceptualize* or *define* the situation we are in, in relation to our current ends-in-view (Dewey, Wittgenstein). In so doing, we give primacy to the Cartesian, mechanistic world view: In that view, not only do we take it that proper decision-making is a matter of *calculation*, but also, that language is simply a *representational* servant of mind, working in terms of *symbols* standing for 'things' in such a way, that we can see reasoning as a matter of executing a sequence of geometry-like deductions from 'axioms' and 'principles' in order to arrive at a 'result', which one can then try to implement in practice. But as we can see from the account above, in Vico the matter is entirely reversed. As we move from an already existing world consisting in a great assemblage of particles in motion, to a still-to-be-differentiated world of intra-mingling, flowing activities, we meet the most fundamental novelty of all in his work: Mind does not precede our expressive activities (language), but arises within them, and both in turn, Mind and Language, are the results of a spontaneous attempt, gradually made conscious, to grasp a startling or striking experience[108] through images that are familiar, the results of a social urgency, a *need* (Todes), a *necessity of nature* to regain one's *orientation* within one's surroundings.

Thus, in a process that begins spontaneously in terms of mere gestures, in reactions, or in actions taken in common, the organizing images (the "imaginative universals") become in time articulate and complex, often along with the establishment of professional institutions within which they can become powerful influences in *structuring* all our relations to the others and othernesses around us. This elaborate universe of meaning, always restless and changing, remains intact so long as those who inhabit it continue to have *a common-sense of things* — and this, precisely, is the danger that I have been trying to highlight in this book. For in the professionalization of our disciplines, while whole areas of experience may, in the process achieve the status of refined, seemingly-independent 'arts' and 'sciences' (Shotter, 2015), this does nothing to overcome the current worrisome fragmentation and separation. If this *fragmentation* and *separation* does occur, if we allow that founding sense of things we continually find *in our collective efforts at trying to realize the yet-more potentials that become available to us* — as the human *bio-social becomings* (Ingold & Palsson, 2013) we are — to be overturned by events, or let the struggle for a *before-the-fact*, thick common-sense give way to a thin, *before-the-fact*, rationalistic tyranny exerted by an authoritarian professional group, then the dialogically-structured activities needed to sustain that common-sense will fail to occur, and the much needed common ground will become an un-navigable quagmire.

---

[108] "The origin and primitive form of the language game is a reaction; only from this can more complicated forms develop. Language – I want to say – is a refinement, 'in the beginning was the deed'[Goethe]" (Wittgenstein, 1980a, p.31).

References

Andersen, Tom (1992). Reflections on reflecting with families. In McNamee, Sheila & Gergen, Kenneth J. (Eds.) (1992) *Therapy as Social Construction*. London: Sage Publications.

Andersen, Tom (2008). Reflecting Talks: My Version. In Karin Jordan (Ed.) *The Quick Theory Reference Guide: A Resource for Expert and Novice Mental Health Professionals*. New York: Nova Publishers, pp.427-443.

Austin, John L. (1962). *How to do Things with Words*. London: Oxford.

Austin, John L. (1970). *Philosophical Papers*. London: Oxford University Press.

Bakhtin, Mikhail Mikhailovich (1993). *Toward a Philosophy of the Act*, with translation and notes by Vadim Lianpov, edited by Michael. Holquist. Austin, TX: University of Texas Press.

Barad, Karen (2007). *Meeting the Universe Halfway: Quantum Physics and the Entanglement of Matter and Meaning*. Durham & London: Duke University Press.

Barfield, Owen (1999). *A Felt Change of Consciousness*, in a Barfield Reader: Selections from the Writings of Owen Barfield / edited and with an introduction by G.B. Tennyson. Hanover and London: University Press of New England, pp.78-79.

Bartlett, Frederick C. (1923). *Psychology and Primitive Culture*. Cambridge: Cambridge Univ. Press.

Bergson, Henri (1955). *An Introduction to Metaphysics*, trans. T. E. Hulme. New York: Bobbs-Merrill, first pub.1912.

Berlin, Isaiah (1996). *A Sense of Reality*. New York: Farrar, Straus & Giroux.

Billig, Michael (1987). *Arguing and Thinking: a Rhetorical Approach to Social Psychology*. Cambridge: Cambridge University Press.

Billig, Michael (2013). *Learn to Write Badly: How to Succeed in the Social Sciences*. Cambridge: Cambridge University Press.

Bohm, David (1965). Appendix, in *The Special Theory of Relativity*. New York: Benjamin, pp.185-230.

Bohm, David (1980). *Wholeness and the Implicate Order*. London: Routledge and Kegan Paul.

Borthoft, Henri (2012). *Taking Appearance Seriously: the Dynamic Way of Seeing in Goethe and European Thought*. Edinburgh: Floris Books.

Cassirer, E. (1957). *The Philosophy of Symbolic Forms: vol.3: The Phenomenology of Knowledge*. New Haven: Univ. of Yale Press.

Cassirer, Ernst (1996). *The Philosophy of Symbolic Forms: vol.4: The Metaphysics of Symbolic Forms*. Edited by J.M. Krois & D.P. Verene. New Haven: Univ. of Yale Press.

Cassirer, Ernst (2000). *The Logic of the Cultural Sciences*. New Haven & London: Yale University Press (German ed. 1942).

Dewey, John (1896). The concept of the reflex arc in psychology.

Psychol. Rev., 3, 13-32. Reprinted in W. Dennis (Ed.) *Readings in the History of Psychology.* New York: Appleton-Century-Crofts, 1944.

Dewey, John (1910). "What is thought?" Chapter 1 in *How we think.* Lexington, Mass: D.C. Heath, pp.1-13.

Dreyfus, Hubert L. and Rabinow, Paul (1982). *Michel Foucault: Beyond Structuralism and Hermeneutics.* Sussex: Harvester Press.

Eldridge, Richard (2010). Wittgenstein on aspect-seeing, the nature of discursive consciousness, and the experience of agency. In Day, W. & Krebs, V. J. (2010). *Seeing Wittgenstein Anew.* Cambridge & New York: Cambridge University Press, pp.162-179.

Foucault, Michel (1972). *The Archaeology of Knowledge.* trans. A.M. Sheridan, London: Tavistock.

Foucault, Michel (1972). Appendix: The Discourse on Language. In Michael Foucault *Archaeology of Knowledge* (American Edition), trans A.M Sheridan. New York: Pantheon Books, pp.215-237.

Frankfurt, Harry (1998). *The Importance of What We Care About.* New York, NY: Cambridge University Press.

Frankfurt, Harry (2005). *On Bullshit.* Princeton, NJ: Princeton University Press.

Gallie, Walter B. (1955-56). Essentially contested concepts. *Proc. of the Aristotelian Soc.,* 56. 167-198.

Geertz, Clifford (1973). *The Interpretation of Cultures.* New York: Basic Books.

Geertz, Clifford (1983). *Local Knowledge: Further Essays in Interpretative Anthropology.* New York: Basic Books.

Gergen, Kenneth J. (2009). *Relational Being: Beyond Self and Community.* Oxford: Oxford University Press.

Gibson, James J. (1979). *The Ecological Approach to Visual Perception.* London: Houghton Mifflin.

Giddens, Anthony (1984). *The Constitution of Society.* Cambridge: Polity Press.

Goldstein, Kurt (1995). *The Organism: a Holistic Approach to Biology derived from Pathological Data in Man.* New York: Zone Books, first pub. 1933.

Goodwin, Charles (1995). Co-constructing meaning in conversation with an aphasic man. *Research on Language and Social Interaction, 28(3),* pp.233-260.

Habermas, Jürgen (1972). *Knowledge and Human Interests.* London: Heinemann.

Heraclitus (2001) *Heraclitus — Fragments.* Trans. Brooks Hatton, foreword by James Hillman. London: Penguin Books.

Heidegger, Martin (1962). *Being and Time.* Oxford: Blackwell.

Heidegger, Martin (1977). Letter on humanism. In M. Heidegger *Basic Writings,* edited and with a general introduction by D.F. Krell. San Francisco: Harper Collins, pp.190-282.

Ingold, Tim. (2008). Bindings against boundaries: entanglements of life in an open world. *Environment and Planning*, 40, pp.1796-1810.

Ingold, Tim (2011). *Being Alive: Essays on Movement, Knowledge and Description*. London & New York: Routledge.

Ingold, Tim (2015). *The Life of Lines*. London & New York: Routledge.

Ingold, Tim & Palsson, Gisli (2013). *Biosocial Becomings: Integrating Social and Biological Anthropology*. Cambridge: Cambridge University Press.

James, William (1897/1956). *The Will to Believe*. New York, Dover.

James, William (1996). *A Pluralistic Universe: Hibbert Lectures at Manchester College on the Present Situation in Philosophy*. Lincoln and London: University of Nebraska Press, first pub. 1909.

James, William (2003). A World of Pure Experience, Chapter 2 in *Essays in Radical Empiricism*. New York: Dover, pp.21-47, first pub.1912.

Jakobson, Roman, Fant, Gunnar and Halle, Morris (1952). *Preliminaries to Speech Analysis. The distinctive features and their correlates*. Acoustics Laboratory, Massachusetts Inst. of Technology, Technical Report No. 13 (58 pages). (Re-published by MIT press, seventh edition, 1967).

Kant, Immanuel (1786/2004). *The Metaphysical Foundations of Natural Science*, trans & edited by Michael Freidman. Cambridge & London; Cambridge University Press.

Katz, Arlene M., & Shotter, John (1996). Hearing the patient's "voice": Toward a social poetics in diagnostic interviews. Social Science and Medicine, 43(6), pp.919-931.

Keller, Helen (1990). *The Story of My Life*. New York: Bantam Books.

Koch, Sigmund (1964). Psychology and emerging conceptions of knowledge and unitary. T.W. Wann (Ed.) *Behaviourism and Phenomenology*. Chicago: University of Chicago Press.

Kuhn, Thomas S. (1970). *The Structure of Scientific Revolutions, 2nd Edition, Enlarged*. Chicago, Il: University of Chicago Press.

Kuhn, Thomas S. (1977). *The Essential Tension: Selected Essays in Scientific Tradition and Change*. Chicago: University Of Chicago Press.

Kuhn, Thomas S. (2000). *The Road Since Structure: Philosophical Essays, 1970-1993, with an Autobiographical Interview*. Edited by James Conant & John Haugeland. Chicago: University of Chicago Press.

Kundera, Milan (1993). *Á la Recherche du Présent Perdu*, in *Testaments Betrayed: an Essay in Nine Parts*. New York, NY: Harper Perennial, pp.121-146.

Levy-Bruhl, Lucien (1926). *How Natives Think (Les Fonctions Mentales dans les Sociétés Inférieurs)*, trans. by L.A. Clare. London: George Allen and Unwin, first pub.1926.

McDowell, John (1998). *Mind, Value, Reality. Cambridge*. MA: Harvard University Press.

Merleau-Ponty, Maurice (1964). *Signs,* translated by Richard M.

McCleary. Evanston, Il: Northwestern University Press.

Merleau-Ponty, Maurice (1968). *The Visible and the Invisible*, Edited by Claude Lefort, translated by Alphonso Lingis. Evanston, Il: Northwestern University Press.

Merleau-Ponty, Maurice (1970). *Themes from the Lectures at the College de France* (trans. John O'Neill). Evanston: North-Western University Press.

Malloch, Stephen & Trevarthen, Colwyn (Eds.) (2009). *Communicative Musicality. Exploring the Basis of Human Companionship*. Oxford: Oxford University Press.

Nussbaum, Martha (2001a). Emotions as judgments of value: a philosophical dialogue. In *Upheavals of Thought: the Intelligence of Emotions*. Cambridge, UK & New York, USA: Cambridge University Press, pp.19-88.

Nussbaum, Martha (2001b). *Upheavals of Thought: the Intelligence of Emotions*. Cambridge, UK & New York, USA: Cambridge University Press.

Plato (1987). *Thaetetus*, trans. with and essay by R.A.H. Waterfield. Harmondsworth: Penguin Books.

Schear, Joseph K. (ed.) *Mind, Reason, and Being-in-the-World: The McDowell-Dreyfus Debate*. London and New York: Routledge.

Scheler, Max (2009/1923). *The Nature of Sympathy*. New Brunswick, NJ & London: Transaction Publishers.

Shotter, John (1974). The development of personal powers. In M.P.M. Richards (Ed.) *The Integration of a Child into a Social World*. Cambridge: Cambridge University Press, pp.215-244.

Shotter, John (1981). Telling and reporting: prospective and retrospective uses of self-ascriptions. C. Antaki (Ed.) *The Psychology of Ordinary Explanations of Social Behaviour*. London: Academic Press, pp.157-181.

Shotter, John (1984). *Social Accountability and Selfhood*. Oxford: Blackwell.

Shotter, John (1993). *Conversational Realities: Constructing Life through Language*. London: Sage.

Shotter, John (2003). Real presences: meaning as living movement in a participatory world. *Theory & Psychology, 13(4)*. pp.435-468.

Shotter, John (2005a). Vygotsky and consciousness as *con-scientia*, as witnessable knowing along with others. *Theory and Psychology*, 16(1), pp.16-36.

Shotter, John (2005b). Inside processes: transitory understandings, action guiding anticipations, and witness thinking. *International Journal of Action Research*, 1(1), pp.157-189.

Shotter, John (2005c). Goethe and the refiguring of intellectual inquiry: from 'aboutness'-thinking to 'withness'-thinking in everyday life. *Janus Head: Journal of Interdisciplinary Studies in Literature, Continental Philosophy, Phenomenological Psychology and the Arts*, 8(1), pp.132-158.

Shotter, John (2008). Dialogism and polyphony in organizational theorizing: action guiding anticipations and the continuous creation of novelty. *Organization Studies*, 29(4), pp.501-524.

Shotter, John (1993). *Conversational Realities: Constructing Life through Language*. London: Sage.

Shotter, John (2004). The manufacture of personhood, and the institutionalization of mutual humiliation. *Concepts and Transformation, 9(1)*, pp.1-38.

Shotter, John (2007). Wittgenstein and his philosophy of first-time events. *History & Philosophy of Psychology*, 9(1), pp.1-11.

Shotter, John (2010). *Social Constructionism on the Edge: 'Withness'-Thinking and Embodiment*. Chagrin Falls, OH: Taos Institute Press.

Shotter, John (2011). *Getting It: Withness Thinking and the Dialogical... in Practice.*. Creskill, NJ: Hampton Press.

Shotter, John (2012). *Wittgenstein in Practice: His Philosophy of Beginnings, and Beginnings, and Beginnings*. Chagrin Falls, OH: Taos Institute Press. Copyright 2012, ISBN: 978-0-9848656-3-5

Shotter, John (2015a). Undisciplining Social Science: Wittgenstein and the Art of Creating *Situated* Practices of Social Inquiry. *Journal for the Theory of Social Behaviour*, Article first published online: 22 Jan 2015 DOI: 10.1111/jtsb.12080.

Shotter, John (2015b). On "Relational Things": A New Realm of Inquiry — Pre-Understandings and Performative Understandings of People's Meanings. In *The Emergence of Novelty in Organizations*. Edited by R. Garud, B. Simpson, A. Langley, and H. Tsoukas. Oxford: Oxford University Press.

Shotter, John & Tsoukas, Haridimos (2014). Performing *phronesis*: On the way to engaged judgment. *Management Learning*, 45(4), pp.377–396.

Simons, Daniel J. & Resnick, Ronald A. (2005) Change blindness: Past, present, and future. *Trends in Cognitive Sciences*, 9, pp.16-20.

Steiner, George (1989). *Real Presences*. Chicago, Ill: University of Chicago Press.

Stern, Daniel N. (2004). *The Present Moment: in Psychotherapy and Everyday Life*. New York: W.W. Norton.

Stolzenberg, Gabriel (1978). Can an inquiry into the foundations of mathematics tell us anything interesting about mind?. G.A. Miller and E. Lenneberg (Eds.) *Psychology and Biology of Language and Thought: Essays in Honour of Eric Lenneberg*. New York: Academic Press, pp..221-267.

Saussure, Ferdinand de (1959). Course in General Linguistics, trans. W. Baskin, New York and Toronto: McGraw-Hill, first pub.1911.

Taleb, Nassim (2007). The Black Swan: The Impact of the Highly Improbable. London: Random House.

Sheets-Johnstone, Maxine (2011). *The Primacy of Movement*, expanded second edition. Amsterdam & Philadelphia: John Benjamins.

Vico, Giambattista (1944). *The Autobiography of Giambattista Vico,* trans. by M.H. Fisch and T.G. Bergin. Ithaca: Cornell University Press.

Vico, Giambattista (1965). *On the Study Methods of Our Time*, trans Elio Gianturco. New York: Bobbs-Merrill.

Vico, Giambattista (1968). *The New Science of Giambattista Vico.* Ed. and trans. by T.G. Bergin and M.H. Fisch. Ithaca, N.Y.: Cornell University Press.

Vico, Giambattista (1988). *On the Most Ancient Wisdom of the Italians,* trans. Lucina Palmer. Ithaca: Cornell University Press.

Vygotsky, Lev S. (1962). *Thought and Language.* Edited and translated by E. Hanfmann and G. Vakar. Cambridge, MA: MIT Press.

Vygotsky, Lev S. (1978). *Mind in Society: the Development of Higher Psychological Processes.* Edited by M. Cole, V. John-Steiner, S. Scribner, and E. Souberman (Eds.) Cambridge, MA: Harvard University Press.

Vygotsky, Lev S. (1986). *Thought and Language.* Translation newly revised by Alex Kozulin. Cambridge, MA: MIT Press.

Watterson, Bill (2005/2012). *The Complete Calvin and Hobbes.* London: Andrews MacMeel Publishing LLC.

Whitehead, Alfred North (1967/1925). *Science and the Modern World.* London: Collins/Fontana; New York: Free Press, first pub. 1925.

Whorf, Benjamin L. (1956). *Language, Thought and Reality: Selected Writings of Benjamin Lee Whorf. Ed. J.B. Carroll.* Cambridge, Mass: M.I.T. Press.

Winnicott, Donald (1988). *Babies and their Mothers.* London: Free Association Books.

Wittgenstein, Ludwig (1965). *The Blue and the Brown Books.* New: York Harper Torch Books.

Wittgenstein, Ludwig (1966). *Lectures and Conversations on Aesthetics, Psychology, and Religious Belief.* Edited by Cyril Barrett. Oxford: Blackwell.

Wittgenstein, Ludwig (1980a). *Culture and Value,* introduction by G. Von Wright, and translated by P. Winch. Oxford: Blackwell.

Wittgenstein, Ludwig (1980b). *Remarks on the Philosophy of Psychology*, vols. 1 and 2. Oxford: Blackwell.

Wittgenstein, Ludwig (1980c). *Wittgenstein's Lectures: Cambridge 1930-1932.* D. Lee (ed.) Oxford: Blackwell.

Wittgenstein, Ludwig (1981). *Zettel,* (2nd. Ed.), G.E.M. Anscombe and G.H.V. Wright (Eds.). Oxford: Blackwell.

Wittgenstein, Ludwig (1990). *Last Writings on the Philosophy of Psychology*, vol.1, ed. by G. H. von Wright & H. Nyman, trans. by C.G. Luckhardt & M.A.E. Aue. Oxford: Blackwell.

Wittgenstein, Ludwig (1993a). Remarks of Frazer's 'Golden Bough'. In J. Klagge and A. Nordman (Eds.) *Ludwig Wittgenstein: Philosophical Occasions.* Indianapolis and Cambridge: Hackett Publishing Company, pp.118-159.

Wittgenstein, Ludwig (1993b). Philosophy. In J. Klagge & A. Nordman
   (Eds.) *Ludwig Wittgenstein: Philosophical Occasions*. Indianapolis
   and Cambridge: Hackett Publishing Company, pp.160-199.
Woolf, Virginia (2008). *The Waves*, edited with an introduction by
   Gillian Beer. Oxford: Oxford University Press.

Further Everything is Connected Press Publications

Systemic Inquiry.
Innovations in Reflexive Practice Research
Editors: Gail Simon & Alex Chard
ISBN 978-0-9930723-0-7

Systemic Therapy and Transformative Practice
Editors: Imelda McCarthy & Gail Simon
ISBN 978-0-9930723-2-1

www.eicpress.com

19337394R00121

Printed in Great Britain
by Amazon